Marriage, Kidneys, and Other Dark Organs

A Memoir

by

Venera Di Bella Barles

1stBooks - rev. 2/6/02

we must tell the children
tell them the stories of the land we left behind
tell them what we have had to endure and overcome and triumphed
we must tell them so they can really know who they are

ACKNOWLEDGMENTS

To my loving husband, Edward, for seeing me through my dark moments, being patient, a good sport and not taking my humor to heart.

And to Gina Cee and Carisa, my daughters, and to my grandchildren, Alexia, Julian, and Isabella for giving me the reason to leave my thoughts.

A special thanks to my fellow writers, Harriet Davis, Nancy Fraÿchineaud, Noni Kott, Dave Kragen, Margaret Nevinski, Barbara Winther, who encouraged, helped, taught, stood by me through hours of ups and downs in the preparation of this book, and to my other friends who had confidence in me.

Venera DiBella Barles

PREFACE

What could I leave my children and grandchildren besides chairs, linens and tombstones? What could they remember about their mother? They may have thought they knew how I evolved, but I needed to speak and tell the stories as I felt and saw them. I wouldn't be able to have them taste the tears or hear the laughter. I could only describe the sounds from my heart.

What did it all mean and what did it teach me? Those early years were tattooed on my brain and laid the groundwork for years to follow. I learned it all in the first ten years. I became more acquainted with its lessons the next ten.

My father, with the greatest force and loudest voice, received the most attention. I could not save my mother from herself, but I understood her better through these memories.

As difficult as it was at times, I do know how precious my parents and family are and were. With time, I came to understand the complicated love that was generated in our familial relationship. Sometimes, I believe I wanted the same things my father fought so hard for—a zest for life and the struggle to feel its depths.

I give you my stories.

Bainbridge Island, Washington
August 2001

V.D.B.

WORKS CONSULTED

Inscription:
Public Television Series 1999.
We Must Tell The Children: Italian-Americans II: A Beautiful Song

Inscription:
Comes the Dawn" attributed to Veronica A. Schoffstall.

Kogos, Fred. A Dictionary of Yiddish Slang & Idioms. Kogos Publications Co. Citadel Press, Inc. This edition published by Castle Books, a division of Book Sales Inc. of Secaucus, N.J. 1967.

Mawson, C.O. Sylvester. Dictionary of Foreign Terms. Second Edition. Revised and Updated by Charles Berlitz. Copyright 1975 by Thomas Y. Crowell Company, Inc.

Partnow, Elaine. The New Quotable Woman. Revised and Updated 1992. Facts On File. New York-Oxford.

SONGS

"O paese d' 'o sole", an old Neapolitan song. Author Unknown.

"Swinging On A Star" Bing Crosby. 1940's.

"Don't Fence Me In" Cole Porter" 1940's

"Daniel" Elton John & Bernie Taupin. Album; Love Songs. 1972.

"Angels Flying To Close To The Ground" Willie Nelson

PART I

THE NEAPOLITANS AND SICILIANS

Venera Di Bella Barles

2

The Big Mix: Olive Oil and Fire

3

Venera Di Bella Barles

Never Is A Long Day (1947)

La Vita Dolce Piccante: The Bittersweet Life (1940's)

Hollywood Expose' (1949)

Make Believe (1949)

Anatomy Of A Peacemaker

To Love Or Not To Love (1946-1951)

SOGGIORNO: SOJOURN

"Ancora imparo>" (It.)
"I still learn."
Motto of Michaelangelo

Wooden saw horses cleverly hold my bed, next to the stark, brick chimney and unfinished windowless attic walls. From my pillow I can see lined on the studs, by my bed sack, an orderly display of treasures along with my tin tea set and crayons. At night the blackness is smothering when Dad turns out the hanging bulb. My eyes search the dark for any glimmer of light. Fear has become my companion.

Momma says, "You'd better be good or the bogey-man will get you." Grandpa says that too!

I dare not leave my bed. The frightening dream will start soon, bringing with it the specter of the heavy, black lead ball that lies on my chest, waiting to suffocate me. Somewhere in this frigid house, my parents, Antonietta and Salvatore, also bed down near skeletal, wooden two by fours. I am nearly five years old.

It is miserably cold that morning in Albany, New York. It is March of 1937. Father shakes me awake with words I'll never forget.

"Venere! Get up, honey! We gotta get ready. We go to Italy!"

"Are we going in the car, Daddy? Can I take my coloring book? Is Momma going?"

But there never are enough answers to all my questions.

We live in that unfinished and isolated house for some time; first in the cellar then as work is completed, we make our way to the top floors. Father moves a beat-up, upright piano into the basement; then builds the second story on, never giving a thought as to how it will be removed in the future.

Daddy says, It's too damn hard to work and finish our house in this freezing weather, so we might as well go to see his brothers and sisters in Sicily. I wish Momma would be glad to see where she was born near Naples. She's always upset. We're going on a big ship. Momma doesn't look too happy. Momma says it could sink and we could all die.

Father hasn't seen his people since he was in his early twenties. He regularly mentions how bad he feels leaving them when they were so poor. Mother had no memory of her relatives from Italy, since she was still an infant when she left for America.

Momma says that Daddy just wants to show-off. She's too nervous about going to Italy. Momma is afraid of water, because she almost drowned when she was a little girl. She's nervous a lot, especially when Daddy yells. He yells at her a lot. It scares me.

When I am young, I never understand the many discrepancies in our lives. Why is there always plenty of money for show, but I never have the feeling of means? Those hidden areas reveal it all; our worn out underclothes, holes in shoes, thin blankets, torn sheets, empty refrigerators. These fill my senses with the feeling of poor.

We buy the most fashionable clothes for this voyage and a professional photograph is published in the *Albany Times* newspaper. The whole world must know that the Di Bellas are doing something significant.

SOJOURN—Mr. and Mrs. Salvatore Di Bella of 179 Fairlawn Avenue who are sailing to Italy for a six months vacation. With them is their daughter, Venera.

I can see the clothes we're wearing in the faded and yellowed photo: hats, fur coats, muffs, gloves and my father's cigar gives us instant status; verified happiness, importance, perfection and dignity. Who could want more?

Father, Mother and I leave Albany, and as we near the port in New York City, the exquisite ocean liner, The *Conte di Savoia*, looms large in the distance waiting to hold us. I have only seen such majestic vessels in movies. I can't tell if the throngs of people on the dock, who hug and cry, are sad or happy.

I hold my father's hand tightly as we start up the wooden gangway aware that my red patent leather shoes tap out my arrival. Momma moans as she teeters up the steep boarding ramp in her high heels.

"Oh Sal, I'm so scared. I'm gonna fall."

My heart also skips a beat at the sight of the water far below. Consciously, I avoid the gaps between the boards.

"We're going to see movies and all kinds of things here, aren't we, Daddy? Will there be other kids? We're not going to drown like Momma says, are we?"

My eyes take in everything. So much happens. Sailors hang to the ships sides to finish last minute painting. Trunks and luggage are hauled up the ramp, the decks are mopped and brass rails are given another shine. Entire families with children such as ours, board the waiting *Conte*, along with the elegant and ostentatious rich with their servants.

This Italian luxury liner, city on water, far surpasses present day cruise ships. The Atlantic Ocean can be among the worst of passages. Our crossing time is to be eight days, and since we are leaving in March, the rough seas have the upper hand. Despite the fact the *Conte* is touted as "the smoothest sail on the Atlantic", the first major liner to have a gyro-stabilizer system, mainly the adults, still experience the worst of the *mal de mer.*

Under the personal guidance and strict instructions of Mussolini himself; a pair of ocean greats, the *Rex* and the *Conte di Savoia*, are built in 1932. The Italian Blue Ribbon winners have the first of several outdoor pools.

I watch the Captain greet everyone as they step aboard, while the sailors stand at attention in white gloves and uniforms. It is time to sail. The smoke stacks discharge a thunderous ear-splitting belch and smoke reaches for the heavens. I wonder why everyone cries as they wave their handkerchiefs with their good-byes. Another blast of a horn announces our departure. My stomach feels the sudden drop as *The Conte di Savoia,* leaves her stationary holding blocks and slides into the sea of the cold Atlantic.

Mother cries, "I just know this boat is gonna sink, and we're all gonna drown. Venera, don't play too close to the railing with those kids; you'll fall in the water! Oh God! I'm so nervous."

I see her body sway. Her face is pale even with her rouged cheeks and softly painted lips. Her blue eyes have faded. Every little thing makes my mother apprehensive and troubled. She always takes her superstitions of life with her. Now, she's left the shelter of her family's town to go with her dynamic and forceful husband. It does not take much to convince her we are all going to die.

The large vessel smashes the waves reminding her guests who is in charge. Luckily children are typically spared the affects of the ship's movement. My newfound friends and I continue to play our child deck games, despite our seasick parents grasping the rails of the giant vessel.

The next day Father takes us for a tour. Surrounding one of the several pools, is sand scattered about the deck, recreating the resorts of the beautiful Mediterranean and Italian Riviera. Stewards in striped shirts serve coffee and drinks to heartily bundled passengers in reclining deck chairs. The colorful sun umbrellas are folded down. Even with the chattering temperatures and wind gales, there are rubber-capped men swimming.

I am a mere inch standing in the many lavish lounges and dance halls with their vaulted ceilings.

It looks like Cinderella's ballroom. Daddy says, that probably Momma and he are going to dance the tango here tonight.

A couple of nights later, we see Ginger Rogers and Fred Astaire, speaking Italian in the movie, Top Hat. Each minute brings new wonders. We have breakfast in one room and lunch and dinner in another.

Daddy always makes Momma put this big bow in my hair. She calls it taffeta. I have to sleep with my hair in rags every night. It hurts my head. She makes it too tight. When she's mad at Daddy, she pulls my hair. I have to be dressed-up all day and night. We eat all the time. I have to be real good. A lot of people talk Italian. Daddy wants Momma to talk to me in Italian. When she doesn't, he gets mad and yells. I know what he's saying but I don't know how to answer him. Momma doesn't talk Italian as good as Daddy. I didn't know there were so many people that could talk Italian. There are a lot of fancy people here.

There are special rooms for varied leisures and events; movies, gambling lounges, bars, smoking drawing rooms a hospital and a church. Father is in heaven playing cards and meeting new people. Each evening he dresses in his finest, carries his walking cane, lights his cigar, and maneuvers about with his new friends. Mother and I, are usually left to fend for our selves. My unlearned eyes observe carefully as attractive, potent men in tuxedos and self-assured women in jeweled gowns and furs, are drawn to my charismatic father, a quality so seductive and disarming that its uniqueness filters through my life and separates him from most people.

Three days into the voyage I sit wide-eyed, captivated with a conversation my mother is having with some ladies.

"Poor little thing, she wasn't even a year old," says the elegant woman with the veiled hat. "It was so quick. She just got sick and died."

"I understand they can't even wait until we reach Italy," voices another lady with a fox fur about her neck. "They're going to have to bury her in the ocean!"

"You know she's their only child!" the veiled hat says "*Madonna Mia!* What a tragedy!"

"The burial is early tomorrow," Mother timidly whispers.

So many words without meanings, they frighten me.

The next morning, we stand on the wet, icy deck; the wind sprays us with a curtain of salty seawater.

Daddy says we are going to say good-bye to the little girl. They call it a funeral. He's crying! He's holding my hand so tight. Momma is crying too!

Swept with fears, Mother sways as she holds her face in her hands. I have seen her like this before. It always gives me uncertainties.

"What's the matter, Momma?"

"The dead baby is in the box."

"The dead baby is in the box?"

No questions answered. The priest prays and sprinkles holy water over the 'box'. My father picks me up to watch the small container they call a casket about to be swallowed by the sea. The sailors drop the coffin overboard. I watch it plunge and disappear into the choppy waters. The surrounding ladies comfort Mother, who now is quite unstable.

I wish someone could make me feel good with all these scary thoughts. Maybe I will be next? If they put me in a box, it'll be dark! I won't be able to breathe! And then I'll drown!

A couple of nights later, I am quickly reminded of this scene when a fish bone lodges in my throat and suddenly a whole shipload of animated Italians are on me forcing me to swallow bread and mush. Momma scurries about wringing her hands.

"She'll probably die. Oh my God, what are we going to do?" Mother wails.

"She's not breathing, *Signora.*"

"*Mangia!* Eat the bread, sweetheart!" Dad says as I sit on his lap. "You no gonna die!"

Die? Die? What is this thing called die? What does it feel like? Grandma Valente has pictures of two kids who died, Momma says they're in caskets, but they look like they're just sleeping. Are they going to stick me in a casket and throw me in the water like that other kid? Momma and Daddy are sure upset. Yes, and nervous too. I wish I could see houses again.

11

Our arrival in Naples is as dramatic as our departure from America with the brass bands, noisy horns, and again the shouting and crying as the sky fills with streamers and confetti. All moves quickly. All is so strange. Now, no one speaks English except us.

We rent a grand, flashy, black car called a Citroen. Momma sits in the back seat, just as she always does back in Albany. Dad gives boys and men rides from the villages, and when they stand on the running boards, holding the window frames and handles, I can't see out. Not many villagers have ridden in a car before.

A ferry from the mainland takes us through the Straits of Messina on to Sicily, and the Citroen motors on the road towards Mt. Etna. The land is dry, not green as the hills in the Adirondacks. Lemon and olive trees line our curving upward drive. Dad speaks of Mussolini with reverence for the many improvements made throughout Italy, one of which is the splendid highways. It is not hard to understand the loyalties Mr. Mussolini has gathered.

I remember Dad telling me how the sea is always blue here. He is right. We come to the bustling city of Catania, with its showy gardens and fountains. The scenes are from picture books, not a bit like Albany. Our first major and important stop is to a pastry shop. Dad and I go in to buy some of the mouth-watering choices while Momma sits quietly in the back seat of the car.

"Momma, why don't you want to come into the store? Are you mad at Daddy?"

She turns her head away from me and silently looks out the window.

Why is she always mad at me? She says I'm spoiled.

We continue our drive and he points to a mountain in the distance and I hear my name.

"You see, sweetheart, *monte Venere*, the Italian Venus," Dad says. "Justa like my mother's name and you name."

My father's parents are long gone. He tells me that one time his mother died, and as they walked to the graveyard and were getting ready to bury her, she awoke to live a few more years.

Maybe the baby girl in the water is still alive. Who's gonna help her?

As we motor up the winding mountain road toward his village of Linguaglossa, he begins to tell me more tales of his boyhood. Stories of the exploding mountain, of climbing into a wine vat with a friend, and drinking themselves silly until forever he can't even stand the smell of wine. Once again, he stops the car to look at the still lava that has rolled down into the fields. He explains how hard the land is to farm because of the problems with lava.

"Why don't they just move away like we do, Daddy?"

My simplistic mind can't grasp, as yet, the complexity of people's lives and motives. I am to learn much of these matters in the next couple of years. It is as if each mile to his village reminds him of the years he has been away. Tears stream down his face, and even as a little girl, I begin to feel and see the impact of this trip. My daddy is home.

When we arrive in Linguaglossa, Mother and I, meet Dad's many relatives: two sisters, two brothers, cousins and friends, with much talent amongst them. *Zio* Pepino and *Zia* Carmelina run the tailor shop. Uncle Emilio, a journalist, will become a war correspondent. A few years before, Uncle Antonio, the eldest brother, had moved to Buenos Aires. Other than knowing he is a prolific sculptor-artist, I know little else about him or why he left. The family never sees him again.

13

Venera Di Bella Barles

As I look back on it all, I can't help but think how difficult this trip must have been for my timid twenty-eight year old mother, the Americanized, Italian bride. To complicate matters, she is a Neapolitan in Sicily. It is like a Yank in Southern Georgia. Her poor Italian-speaking skills must have compounded her shyness and many fears. She would have had quite an adjustment to the inquisitive and judgmental nature of my father's people. She holds my hand tightly when we walk in the village. Her high heel shoes clicking on the tricky cobble stone streets, her eyes cast down as she goes past the appreciative eyes and subtle remarks of the village males. I can feel her uneasiness.

But there is trouble for Salvatore with this visit. His family does not appear to comprehend his spirit and his thinking. Because they believe he is rich, their expectations of what he can and will do for them, grants them only disappointments. I hear the assumptions that anyone who gets to the United States and finds work, must surely be well off. Father suffers the disease of many of us; the compulsion to impress family with overstated successes. Their poverty doesn't care for vain airs. These proud people have overcome great demands on their lives, and although they respect Salvatore, I often wonder if they also hate him. When he encounters friends and relatives, characteristically, he is generous with them. What is unusual is his sudden generosity with material gifts for Mother and me. I do not remember receiving these showers of clothes and accessories again. He is determined that we look our best to his public. I'm convinced all our savings are used for this display of ego. I quickly realize that we are his showpieces, and I will carry resentment for this into adulthood.

We live upstairs over the tailor shop with Dad's unmarried sister and brother, *Zia* Carmelina, and, *Zio* Pepino. My aunt, territorial and dominating, distinctly lets Mother know where the line is drawn.

"Sal, she doesn't like me because I'm an American. I try to help her but she pushes me away. She's so jealous. She doesn't think I know how to do anything!"

As for me, I escape the daily disagreements by being sent to a convent day school to learn Italian. This thing called class is another new adjustment. I am lumped with other kids from the village into one building. We all dress alike in long-sleeve smocks with big white collars, except the girls have floppy bows in their hair. At lunch, with cloth napkins wrapped about our necks, we sit on tiny stools at long, short, wooden tables as well prepared dishes of pasta are served. This is the best part of school. I excel here.

The strict nuns at the abbey are related in one way or another to Dad's family. Often they pile into the Citroen and travel with us to other cities. How strange it is to sit amidst the sea of black habits and starched wimples. I had only seen these mystical women from afar back in Albany. All is so different. My life changes quickly.

The narrow cobblestone streets of Linguaglossa are dwarfed by Father's car as he maneuvers the mechanical monster about. The townspeople observe us with curious reverence.

Who is this native son who can travel so far from the land of golden roads, and who gives such an imposing view of his self?

In April, one month after we arrive, Dad plans an enormous party for my fifth birthday. Everyone in the village is invited.

Momma says he's always showing off. She's always mad at Daddy. It's just a party. She says I'm spoiled and I get too much attention. It makes me feel bad when she says that. She doesn't like me. I wish she would try to be happy. She doesn't talk much to people.

The community gathers. Special delicacies are made. Musicians and magicians bring their talents.

Dad insists that my pretty eighteen-year-old, unmarried cousin, a talented lace-maker, be at my party. But there is sadness in her household. Her father is terminally ill. Our cousin, nursing a bad cold, pleads with my dad to let her stay at home. His persistence wins, when he tells her she will be all right. To satisfy Dad's wish she comes to the festive gathering. A week after the party, she becomes gravely ill, and develops pneumonia. In two weeks she is dead.

Things turn incredibly bad. Salvatore is broken. He cries and pounds the floor from pangs of guilt.

I don't like to see my daddy so upset and crying. I hear him say it's his fault that she died. There they are, those words again; died, death, funeral. What will happen? I hear people say they are going to bury her in the ground. Not in the water? Everybody is crying all the time.

He assumes responsibility for her death and funeral. Since embalming is not used, the wake for my cousin takes place in the coolness of an antiquated cellar. My father keeps a continuous vigil until her burial.

One evening, after everyone leaves, Dad and I come the short distance from, *Zia's* home, to the dead house. We are to stay until morning. From out of the warm night air, we enter a narrow stone staircase into the dark, cool basement.

It's cold down here. It feels like the catacombs, like we saw in Rome.

Straight wooden chairs are aligned in rows. The only lights are from assorted shapes and sizes of flickering candles. I am instantly struck with the

16

aroma of lemon blossoms that fill the room, trying to smother the musty, ancient odors. Ahead of us, in a wine alcove, is my cousin's last resting bed, a glass covered casket, lined in satin and lace. I am stunned to see her in a lacy dress and matching scull cap, lying so still. She looks asleep.

She's got a pretty bed like the kids in the pictures in Grandma's house.

As we near the glass case, my father cries and heaves his body. I have not seen him in such profound torment. He holds me tightly by his side. We are alone; Dad, me and the dead girl in the suffocating, windowless room.

I have so many questions. I wish I could ask Daddy some questions. But I don't think I can. Why doesn't she move? Is she sleeping? How can she breathe? She can't sit up with that glass. Why are we here? It's so quiet here. I'm a little scared. Daddy is crying too much. Everything is so different. I wish I could see Grandma.

I sit quietly and remember my party. Only a short time before, she is laughing and singing. I watch her. Her hair is flowing as she twirls about the room dancing with my father.

When I get older, I'm going to dance around the room with my hair flying like hers.

We take our seats in front of the casket and remain there for hours. I have a child's inability to get a comfortable position on the hard, straight chairs. I am afraid and worried about my father. His sobs, throughout the silent night, alarm me. Eventually I fall asleep across his lap.

Venera Di Bella Barles

Sometime during the early morning hours, I awake to a shattering blast, and Father's agonizing wail. He grabs me and we run towards the darkened steps, out of the building into the pre-dawn morning.

Daddy says the glass cover on the coffin blew off, because of the gases. Is she awake? What does it all mean?

I will never forget that sound or that long night. Dad suffers tremendous guilt, the remainder of his life...one I also feel. After all, it was my party. In just a short time, I've come to know death twice, in extraordinary ways.

The news devastates many families. Salvatore's visit is blamed for her untimely end. Superstitions abound. Everyone attempts to prevent our young cousin's elderly father from discovering the tragic news of his much-loved daughter's demise. But the awful truth is revealed to him one morning, as he walks out onto the balcony and sees the black shroud hanging over the railing, the customary sign of death.

In America, I see parades only on special occasions, like the Fourth of July, but here I see military happenings or some commemoration of a saint, on a daily basis. Men and children march in black military dress, while fathers, sons, and husbands ride their handsome horses in proud processions. Like their fathers, my friends wear the Fascist party uniform. This is a world of male displays, opinions and influences. Women only wave them on.

We visit Rome and the Vatican often to hear and see Pope Pius XII. At Christmas Mass in the Basilica of St. Peters, I am a speck and almost crushed, as I stand next to the enormous colonnades near the altar. In spring we return to Rome for Easter services.

Momma looks pretty wearing her hat and gloves. She doesn't talk much. I like wearing the hat and cape Aunt Philly made. I'm going to tell Grandma when I go back to Albany that I saw the Pope talk from the high window and he blessed us. Now, we're waiting to see him in his car. It's so crowded. Daddy says we have to stand near the curb. I can see him! I can see him! He's waving!

We also listen to Mussolini in Rome expound his virtues from his lofty balcony. But the topper is the day we see the Nazi leader, Hitler, and Mussolini, in a massive review. They stand in a convertible saluting us with their arms straight and high. At the edge of the street, where we stand, it would take only three steps to touch the powerful figures. Once again, there are crowds and the deafening cheers. People's tears flow as they wave white linen handkerchiefs to *Il Duce* and *der Fuhrer.*

Who knew then, that my clear brown innocent eyes were seeing terrible history?

Salvatore, who enjoys pushing the limits, knows he should not have a camera. It is no surprise when he is hastily arrested for snapping photos. The police confiscate his film and return the camera, but he doesn't reveal to them about the roll previously taken and hidden in his pocket.

I'm scared. Momma's afraid too. Grown-ups act so crazy sometimes. The policemen are mad at Daddy.

After a few months, I develop a serious bronchial pneumonia. Both lungs are affected along with dramatic nosebleeds.

Am I sick just like my cousin? Why is everyone crying? Momma is praying and acting afraid too. Daddy is crying. I'm feeling very nervous like Momma.

Venera Di Bella Barles

They place me in *Zia* Carmelina's, immense high back, beautifully carved bed. It is covered with starched, handmade, lace-edge, pillowcases and sheets. On a wood stand, watching me, in one corner of the room, is the chiseled marble bust of one of my relatives. Each day the people from the village come to visit and whisper their concerns.

Momma is scaring me. She doesn't talk to me. Why are all these people here? Why are they whispering?

"It looks like she will die, *Signora* Di Bella, you'd better get the priest."
"Oh my God!" Momma cries, "I knew we shouldn't have come here."

Will they put me in a glass box and take me home on the big ship to my grandpa and grandma in New York? Maybe they'll drop me in the ocean! Or maybe I'll blow up!

Even though knowing folks are brought in to see what can be done, I am given Last Rites.

The priest is praying. He says he's putting holy oil on my forehead. Everybody is crying. I feel funny. Daddy and Momma are crying. They say I'm going to die.

I feel no connection to them. The large room suddenly appears smaller. It closes in on me.

I can't breathe! I can't breathe! Everybody is too close!

Several men, I've never seen before, take me from my bed and put me on a chair near the light from the balcony windows. They lift my nightshirt, stick a small knife into my right side and put leeches on my skin.

Why are they putting worms on me? Are they going to chew me up? Here comes Zia with that soup again. She says, "Mangia la minestra di verdura, figa mia". Every day she makes me eat it.

Soon I begin to regain my health and strength. Aunt's green soup, their medicine, and the sucking worms have saved my life. I have escaped my day in a box.

Political problems heat up considerably, and the possibility is great that Italy will soon be involved in a war. My parents are told to hurry and leave the country. Questions. Always so many questions.

What is this thing called war? They're always talking about that man I saw, Hitler. Why is everyone so afraid of him?

By this time, our six-month vacation has lasted for over a year and a half, and I speak Italian fairly well. I have added many new friends to my young life and have been included in their social circles. Father's younger brother, Emilio, the journalist, voices strong concerns for us and insists that we should return to the United States. There is fear if we wait too long we might not be able to leave.

Something is wrong. Everybody is crying again. Oh no, did someone die again? Why won't anybody tell me what's wrong? We're going home to Grandma and Grandpa's grocery store.

My thoughts are haywire. Everyone is worried.

We set sail for home on the famous, *Rex,* the last Italian luxury liner to leave Europe, an even greater and incomparable one than the, *Conte di Savoia.*

Years later, as a young adult, I feel intense sadness and anxiety when I see newsreels of sinking ships. It is as if an entire city is swallowed with its many dreams and promises. Like the baby in the box. I learn that these two great vessels are used in the Second World War. The *Rex,* is bombed south of Trieste, in September 1944; and the *Conte di Savoia,* ends her days a year earlier, not far from Venice. Both the big Italians eventually fall to their water graves, adding to my list of personal and memorable deaths. I also learn about the barbaric madness of a killer...Adolph Hitler.

I arrive home and enter the first grade of a public school and then onto Catholic school for the remainder of my grades up until the ninth. This voyage gave my young years much wisdom to proceed with my life. Except for an incident at the age of three, when I fall down a set of stairs holding a bottle of milk that breaks and cuts my chin, not much registered in my memory before that cold day in 1937. From this day forward I begin to gather thoughts and information, and begin to witness all people. These humans made it possible to have memories.

Memories, more indelible than ink.

#2 Salvatore, Antonietta and Venera departing for Italy in 1937

VALENTE'S HEART

"Vedi Napoli, e poi mori." (It.)
"See Naples and then die."

In the evening, as I walk towards the room, in back of the store, I hear the Victrola play *Celeste Aida* and the melodious tenor, Caruso, fills the tired walls with his sound. Sometimes Uncle Joe changes the record to Bing Crosby or Rudy Vallee, but always the world's top performers have an opportunity to be with us in this heartbeat of a room.

Grandpa Valente purchased the fatigued building, sandwiched between others, in Albany, New York, around the 1920's. There are two stores on the ground floor, one of which is Valente's Grocery. At one point Grandpa even has a tavern in the other. Above the shops are two more stories, each level with two apartments. In all my years only Grandfather's progeny live here. They are the starter homes for my mother, aunt, uncles and their children. My mother's parents, Carmela and Anthony Valente, came to America from the picturesque village of Muro Lucano, near Naples. Their hopes, I presume, were to fashion a life and improve on their severe beginnings.

The two stores and the four high ceiling apartments are mirror images with windows only at the back and front of the building. On each floor, in the hallway, is one toilet with a pull chain and a water box. I remember that room of

24

solitude. As a young child I sit, a little scared, aware of the long black, sooty shaft above, and at the very top daylight strives to brighten the three-by-four-foot cave. No bathtub, sink or shower. When needed, galvanized tubs are placed by the woodburning stove in the kitchen. Often, I wonder whether the bogeyman can climb through the transoms over the doors from the dark, dingy hallway with its' single light bulb and pull string. Everywhere patterned linoleum flows from the entry halls into the kitchens, even in the living room, but fancier. Then there are the breath-absorbing sets of steep stairs, which the older citizens soon learn to avoid. Grandma and Grandpa devise a system of communication between the store and the apartment's kitchen, a series of knocks on the water pipes to signal their needs. Tap, tap, tap. Bring up onions. We all learn the talk and deliver without complaints.

From the kitchen I walk through Aunt Felicia's windowless, sleeping alcove, into the parlor. The many photos there, tell the stories of the faces that walk through our lives. On either side of the living-room doorway are two eerie large-sized, tinted pictures of their two dead children lying in satin-lined caskets, as if asleep. No one ever discusses them. I occasionally lie quiet and still on the daybed beneath one of the photographs, close my eyes, cross my hands and imagine my final repose. As a little girl I am already well acquainted with death.

Sometimes I pretend I can play the player piano in the living room. I can't believe I can produce such dulcet sounds by moving a lever, even though my feet barely reach the pumping pedals. And when I discover I can engage the family by putting on rolls of Italian songs, it is pure magic. My short, rotund grandma rushes from the kitchen, turning crimson with the exertion, to sing the Neapolitan songs. I'm filled with such joy and fixed with power at being able to bring happiness to this melancholy lady. The family works hard and long, probably wondering when their fortune will change and convince them that they had sound reasons for leaving their sunny land. But they will live out their lifetime in this tenement, with nothing to show for their efforts except debts and troubles, some laughs, but mostly sadness.

Over a viaduct, The New York Central Railroad sweeps close to the building, spewing soot and noise, invasively becoming part of our lives. We feel the roar of the steam engine inside our bodies and engineers claim rights to our friendship as they wave to us from their metal houses. They are as confined in their quarters, as we are in ours. The area of homes and businesses is entirely blanketed by the black, coal ash. Grandma's starched; crisp, white lace curtains need to be washed at least twice a month. Her handmade clean crochet-bordered linens reflect an insistence that normality is expected and will prevail, despite the backbreaking efforts to present this picture. In winter the snow is dirty. On the other hand, the soot adds to grandfathers' summer garden; the black earth contributes to the bonanza crops of basil, tomatoes and vegetables. What the family does not use will be sold in the grocery store.

In Fall, the family women do the canning and I am given specific jobs, which might be just to put the basil leaves into each jar of tomatoes, but the wholesome sense that all is right with my family, permeates the air. Winter comes bringing the wonderful smells of sauces cooking and Grandma rolling out homemade pastas for a big family dinner. A large meat roll, *Bracciole*, stuffed with hard boiled egg, garlic, bread crumbs, cheeses and parsley, is cooked in the tomato sauce, then sliced into delicious pinwheels. All I need do is shut my eyes to retaste these meals.

Laundry day in Grandma's kitchen is a particularly intriguing experience. The multi-purpose room changes into a steam bath. It can reach below zero outdoors, but anyone who stands near the large boiling pots soon exhibits beads of sweat and understands the magnitude of this operation. Grandma Carmela Valente, first boils the clothes in a large galvanized pan on top of the wood stove, and then lifts the heavy load out with a shortened broomstick

26

placing them into the washing machine's hot water, that has also been previously heated on the stove. She then pushes the heavy machine on wheels over to the two foot wide sink, where a hose empties its contents, after two rinses, then all the clean fabric is put through a ringer several times. Now she is ready to hang the clean laundry, but Grandma must wipe the soot each time from the lines at the back porch. She reaches high to pin each piece separately with wooden clothespins; long-johns, bloomers, grocery aprons and jackets, sheets, slips, nothing is spared a bath. It takes all day. When she removes them from the line, the laundry is frozen solid and appears as extra-terrestrial beings without heads. Grandma props them in the kitchen until thawed and dried, then promptly mends, irons and piles the fresh smelling wash high until next week's ceremony. There is very little time for much else.

Grandpa, Grandma and Uncle Joe usually run the grocery store, except when World War II comes and all my uncles are service bound. Each morning Grandpa puts out the American flag and lets down the awning. The store is open from early morning until after midnight, only closing for short periods of time on special holidays or for funerals. A vacation is never even thought of or taken.

It is as if I am watching theater when Grandpa prepares his grooming for the business day. As he stands in his trousers and undershirt, suspenders down, I stare at him as he sharpens the straight razor on the leather strop that hangs by the mirror in the kitchen. It seems it is the only looking glass in the house. He carefully shaves, but leaves his large black mustache. There is not a hair out of place. Each day he wears a clean uniform: white shirt with black tie, a white butcher's apron, topped with a heavily starched, white cotton jacket. His dedication to this store and his patrons gives way to arguments with Grandma Valente. It is an on-going battle. The store is located in an economically depressed area of the city and customers can hardly afford the bare necessities of life. Grandpa extends credit, even though paying his own creditors should be primary. His mainly black clients, who are stingingly poor, come in, hand him a small book and he marks down the price, not always naming the item. When they are able, they pay, most times not.

At five cents a cone, the ice cream counter is the big draw on hot July evenings. It is the social station of young and old in the neighborhood. In the evenings the family sits outdoors in front of the store, to cool off, on wooden milk crates. There is always an attempt to solve all the political woes of the nation; aware their own problems cannot easily be dealt with.

One day, I see Grandpa purposely drop pennies on the sidewalk and three little boys come towards the coins, pick them up and leap for joy. They make a quick entrance to the shop and promptly buy some peanuts and Tootsie rolls.

Located inside the store is a public phone booth with a privacy door. Since most homes in the neighborhood have no phones, children hang around to deliver messages and receive treats. The grocery store is in many ways part of their families, serving as a supportive conduit. I often hear questions asked of Grandpa. Advice is freely given.

He fills his day with quips with nonsensical sayings. "Do you walk to work or carry your lunch?" or "Gotta a nickel? Buy a pickle." Or the equally silly, "You like fish? Go fish!"

There are a variety of things that can be accomplished in this market. There is a telegraph service and no one seems to want those yellow Western Union messages. Utility bills are paid, paychecks cashed, and one can even purchase articles of clothing, such as socks and underwear or a few household utensils. Grandpa brought his talents as a butcher from Italy and although he is not set up as a deli, that does not stop him from making delicious sandwiches for anyone who might ask. As the word spreads, workmen soon drop in for the special lunches. The Italian sausage never lasts very long when they know Mr. Valente is making a fresh batch. A kerosene pump sits in one corner of the store, the fuel most people use for their heaters and cooking. His customers bring their bottles to be filled and as they get to the cash register, Mr. Valente asks.

"Do you wanna to drink it here or taka with you?"

"Oh my, Mr. Valente, that's silly."

I am amazed that the place does not go up in flames. Which brings to mind, I was told, that Grandpa was at one time the County Sheriff, while his secret love was inventing. I hear tell that he invented a sprinkler system for buildings. He tried various inventions, but his dreams were never realized. He remained a poor storekeeper.

Now, the room behind the store is the 'real' parlor of all the apartments. The large pot bellied stove dominates. In the back corner is a toilet with a much friendlier atmosphere than the one in the upstairs hallway. A variety of worn chairs, including a black leather lounge, surround a rustic, rectangular table. The walls are laced with metal advertisement signs, important newspaper articles and photos. This is where we children learn it all. Here is where we see the interplay of adults. Here is where we are taught manners, how to negotiate and who is in charge. There is no doubt in this room my grandpa is lead man. This is his room.

Occasionally, in the evening for supper, he goes to the large glass, walk-in, refrigerator, and takes out an immense slab of beef, slicing off steaks. Grandpa then splashes salt in a cast iron skillet, places it directly on the fire of the old stove and when the frying pan reaches the desired temp, he quickly sears the steaks to the right juiciness.

The smell peaks our senses, while the phonograph sets the mood.

Grandma crochets quietly in a stiff chair as she listens to the thoughts of her daughters, while my father, grandpa and the other men pour their hearts into the politics of the day. There are no winners or losers, just amiable understandings of differences. During the early forties only the older men gather, while my uncles are at war. Grandma, Grandpa and my father have all left relatives in Europe.

Around the warmth of the stove, you can nearly always find an assortment of animals of every shape and size; cats, kittens, small dogs lying on top of some of the large older ones for added comfort; a St. Bernard, German Shepherds, and mixed breeds all take refuge for the winter in Grandpa's sanctuary. In spring, some of the animals seem to have made other arrangements. But back they come again in late Fall, with relatives.

Years later, Grandpa buys a television set, which he places high in the corner of the shop. Everyone comes to see Mr. Valente's new TV and to view the popular show, Howdy Doody.

Things change quickly. I am older, a teenager with other things to think about. The war is over and my father is building a trailer to move us to California. My uncles return from service and Uncle Jimmy, the youngest, and his wife, Aunt Joan, opens an ice cream parlor next to the grocery store.

I return to see my grandparents and the shops for the last time in 1949. I am seventeen. I have grown and left this wonderful beating heart. I can hear the sounds and smells still come back to me: the cash register, the sound of the wood floor creaking beneath Grandfather's shortened left leg, the odor and pumping of kerosene, the smell of the sizzling steak, sweet bunches of basil, fresh laundry and Grandma's sauce and roasted chickens cooking while the phonograph plays the Neapolitan song...

O paese d' 'o sole... The land of the sun.

This day I could weep for joy!
Can it be true I've returned to Naples?
The train arrived in the station and I heard mandolins playing!
This is the land of sun. This is the land of sea.
This is the land where every word, sweet and bitter, is of love.
Why go to foreign lands seeking fortune when I want to be in Naples?
I can drink wine, get drunk and in my own four walls be happy.
Mamma is nearby singing.
This is the land of sun. This is the land of sea.
This is the land where every word, sweet and bitter, is of love.

Old Neapolitan song; Author Unknown

#3 Grandma Carmela and Grandpa Antonio Valente
In Albany, New York. (1940's)

If YOU GET to HEAVEN BEFORE I Do, JUST CUT a HOLE and PULL ME THROUGH

"What is it, Venera?

"Well, Sister Domenica, how can there be three people in one God? You know, The Father, The Son and The Holy Ghost? Aren't there any women? Why are there only men? What does it mean?"

Questions. For eternity so many unanswered questions.

"Miss DI BELLA, just study your Catechism and cease tormenting me with all your inquiries."

This is how most of my religious queries are answered. They aren't.

Slowly I begin to understand blind faith and why we are called flock. Just accept and just follow the person in front of you. For most of my first nineteen years I am an ardent follower with very few answers, always shadowing, head bowed, never seeing where I am going, always fearful I will do it wrong.

I learn most moral things this way. Is this a sin or is that a sin? If it feels good it's usually a sin. Then I'm supposed to confess to the priest my private thoughts so he can inform me how much I have sinned. In my life, in church, or at home, only men seemed to have the right to tell me if I am doing it right. I can only get to heaven on their say so, with the help of their handmaidens, the nuns.

In Italy, at the age of five, I visit more churches than homes. A Christmas Mass at the Vatican nearly swallows me in a crush of human devotees. My father points out the Pope at his raised altar, the head religious man on earth surrounded by men in ancient, colorful, vestments, speaking and singing the dead language of Latin. As the Holy Father speaks, the populace responds as robots with holy phrases. They've learned their lessons well.

In villages and cities, statues of saints are hauled on the backs of sinners and marched through streets in mass processions. Even food is named after the saint of the day. Every occasion seems to involve the church. It is the Great Pentagon of Permission for everything between birth and death. No one makes a decision without the Holy Father giving his say so. Now that's power!

My return to America gives me an undeniable understanding that I had better try to duplicate the religious fervor of my ancestors' homeland. The first time, at the age of seven, I kneel in a confessional box in preparation for my first Holy Communion, I am already fearful of the priest sitting behind the wooden screen and not sure what I am to confess.

This feels just like the boogey man.

My knees are numb. My hands, clasped together in prayer formation, are damp with perspiration. I bow my head. I am afraid I will do it wrong.

As instructed I declare.

"Bless me Father for I have sinned."

"Yes Father, I told a lie."

"Yes Father, I told a lie to a man on the phone."

"Because my daddy told me to."

"No Father I don't think I have other sins. I'm not sure."

"Hail Mary, full of grace..."

We are all dressed in white. We walk down the church aisle towards the altar, boys in one row and munchkin girl brides, in veils, in another. This is to be the third Sacrament I receive; the first, Baptism at birth, second Extreme Unction or last rites, given when I was five and ill, and now Holy Communion.

At seven, I am told I have reached the use of reason. I am ready to take on the world.

What does that mean? I've been thinking and deciding since I was very small. I can tell when I hurt someone and I sure can tell when others are not nice or putting pain on each other. I know when my parents are wrong. But I better not say anything.

I squirrel away the information for later life.

I am told I must go to church or burn in hell. Mother takes me on Sundays. I stand beside her as she prays.

What does she pray about? I know she won't tell me if I ask. She'll just say, "Be quiet, Venera. You always ask too many questions.

Why do only women mostly go to church? Are they the biggest sinners? My father only goes when there is a wedding, a funeral or something special like Easter and Christmas. He thinks as long as one of us from the family goes to church that's good enough. Besides he's a man. He makes his own rules.

My parents guarantee me a baby brother if I deposit money in the basket on Sundays. I place all my spare change, nickels, pennies and dimes in the church envelope to be given towards my sibling's arrival. Every week I tally my contribution on a piece of paper. After a few years, and a donation of $264.23, my brother Nick arrives. These figures come in handy when he gets out of line.

"Listen Nicky, you'd better be quiet and quit bugging me. You cost me plenty—$264.23 to be exact."

I soon find comfort in going to church daily, on my own. It's easy with the school right next door and besides it becomes a safe sanctuary to get away from the madness of my home. I sit in the enormous church quietly, not praying, but listening to the sounds and echoes as ladies change the altar linens, replace spent candles and freshen flowers. I welcome the feeling of orderliness and sanity. The smell of burnt wax and incense still wafts in the air from early Mass. Sometimes, there are only a few people kneeling in prayer, and then usually someone walks to the front, near the tabernacle, drops coins in the slot and lights votive candles. It's all so mysterious. It is another world.

The larger than life statues representing all those who have left their holy mark on earth, spellbind me.

How did they get that good? They probably never told a lie or stole a Tootsie Roll. It seems like most holy people lived a very long time ago. I don't see any saint statues with short skirts and big hoop earrings or any wearing a suit, hat and tie. Who decides when you're holy and when you can become a saint? Probably all those men in the Vatican. I know a lot of good people. Mrs. Feinstein, is awfully nice and always helps people. She brings food to the sick and listens to their sad stories. She's a very nice lady. I don't understand why she doesn't get picked. How can the Pope and all his men helpers know about this kind lady? See what I mean? No one ever asks me! All these questions. My head is not restful.

I keep the thoughts to myself, but they remain always questions on my mind. But I learn one thing well. In order to be a good person, you must have guilt. It's an important ingredient in my religious growth. There are all those sins I have to get straight or I'd end up in hell or purgatory.

I've never talked to anyone who's been to any of these places so how can I be sure if they are as bad as they tell me?

My goal is supposed to be heaven.

What kind of place is heaven? I see pictures and it looks like it's in the clouds. Lot's of angels. Everyone is in white, barefoot and all alike. No colors. No hats. No jewelry. No neat shoes. No roller skates. Why would I want to go there? I like trees, flowers and colored dresses. Why can't we have heaven in the Catskills or in my Grandma's kitchen?

I'm not allowed to enter my girlfriend's churches.

I'm not sure what happens to you when you go into them. I think they have a different set of rules. Maybe even different sins. So maybe when they go to heaven, they have their own cloud. My, oh my, all these questions.

"Sister Mary Domenica, can I be an altar boy? Well, not a boy, you know what I mean, like an altar girl?"

"Don't be silly, Di Bella. Girls don't serve at Mass only boys and men."

See? What did I tell you? What is it about women and girls? Why do we want to be part of a man's club where we can't make any of the rules?

Anyway, in those early years I am so pure I can hardly stand it. I know how to use my rosary with great dexterity and piousness. All the time I accept that I am a Catholic, but not sure why.

Around the age of thirteen I receive the Holy Sacrament of Confirmation. As usual, I am caught up in the ritual and pomp and once again I don't really understand why I am being confirmed. All I know is, by this time, I begin contemplating becoming a nun. Why? I'm convinced, next to the priests and my father, they wield the greatest power over my life. I need some of that strong stuff. Besides, their house is quiet and peaceful.

If I become a nun, I won't have to worry about someone hitting us or about what to wear when I wake-up. I like their uniforms better than mine. I bet they even have their own cook. But they still have a Father to check up on them. So now I understand. We girls really need a lot of supervision and instructions in order to make it to heaven.

In my teens, I begin to see things differently. I work hard as a devoted parishioner, but I'm not sure if my prayers are ever heard. I'm not allowed to date, or talk to my parents about my fears or go anywhere with friends. I now know the family is crazy. The more I pray the crazier they get. The nunnery definitely looks good.

In my later travels, the inequities of organized religion become further recognizable. I have trouble accepting the power, wealth and some of the unfair laws they exhibit. As I stand in a famous church in Mexico, where precious stones and gold lace the artifacts, I assume it takes a great deal of money to build such a grand, beautiful edifice. My eyes are drawn to poor people, mostly women scooting on their knees, approaching the church from great distances. Some must be helped with their raw legs, and when they reach the church they deposit their few pesos into the coffer. Coins they can hardly afford. I am filled with sadness and anger to watch women and children beg outside of the regal building only to see them give over their food money. I wonder what it is about religion that leaves many people stripped of logic? And if the church really cares and understands their parishioner's needs, why do they not conquer some of these problems?

There is hypocrisy surrounding religion in my own home. I recall the blatant lies, sins and prejudices and how much they embarrass me. The justification used to explain them, confounds my understanding further.

And then it all comes to an end. The shutdown. I fall in love. I never stop to check my new friend's credentials. He isn't Catholic. He isn't Italian. I know things will not go well with my father, but I never consider that the Church will not accept me unless I insist my Jewish fiancée relinquishes his faith to become a Catholic. I am not allowed to marry in the church, even though I have been a good and loyal servant most of my life. Now when I need their understanding more than ever, I feel abandoned. Somewhere along the way I miss the lesson that says I can't fall in love except with another Catholic. I walk away from the church without a fight, never to return.

Years later, after a horrendous struggle with guilt and confusion, my head suddenly clears and I retrieve my "use of reason". It serves me well as a youngster and I welcome it back. I release an internal scream of judgment concerning it all and determine I can live without formal cult crutches.

Within me, I realize, is the greatest spiritualism. I begin to look at the world with clarity. I do not need to rely on outside tools or forces to know I am a whole and decent person. I do not need man's regimented religion to answer my needs.

My use of reason brought me to the never-ending search for truth and a need to help others in their quest for the same, and to help with the welfare of others, and not destroy or hurt. The hardest lesson is to teach myself tolerance of religions and human choices. Always having to remind myself that no philosophy should be superior to human life. How can I feel I am without sin, if everyone does not have an equal claim to life, liberty and the pursuit of happiness? To be frightened into a belief is to imprison our minds.

Oh Saint Mrs. Feinstein, wherever you may be, don't forget to pull me through I want to be where you are.

GIRDLE of LOVE

In summer the apartment door is kept open to allow the hallway breeze to enter. I stand in the doorway watching as she readies to comb her long hair. It is her daily ritual. She is still in her corset and petticoat. I see her bright red, hypertensive face in the mirrored wood medicine cabinet. There are no words between us only the return of a gentle smile. First the pins are removed along with three tortoise-shell side combs, and then the long thin pigtail falls down her back. As she loosens the braid, the familial gray streak stemming from her forehead takes its place in the waves cascading past her girdled waist. Grandma Valente leans her head forward and with slow steady strokes brushes the long pepper and silver hair. When she is through, she re-combs the last two-thirds into a braid, then places it atop her head into her usual pompadour Gibson girl fashion. It is the style she wore since a young woman.

I am the first of her eight grandchildren and as I think of my Neapolitan, maternal grandmother, Carmela, I can't remember ever seeing her 4' 11" frame without the big, many boned corset. It can be seen and felt through her dresses and slips. The bodice support starts from just beneath her ample breasts to her lap. She has one measurement from top to bottom. Perfectly square. No indentation for a waist. I usually get a good look at this foundation garment, when its pale peach, freshly washed twin hangs out on the clothesline, its laces bobbing in the wind. There is a feeling she can encircle

41

you at any moment, since her arms cannot hang close to her body. Bending at the hips never happens.

I wonder how she gets up if she falls over? How does she get her corset on? And why? But it must be important. Grandma only does important things.

In winter she wears laced, black, leather shoes with Cuban heels; in summer they are white. At home and while at work in the grocery store she wears cotton stockings and when she dresses-up they are sheer with a seam, rolled in garters below her knees. Because the bellyband encircling her middle is stiff, she has to sit perfectly straight in a chair with her legs spread apart and her ankles crossed for balance. The long crisply starched dress is below her calf for modesty. Her lap is gone.

When there aren't customers to tend to, she crochets. It is her lifelong friend long after her vision leaves. You can usually see her sitting on a Bentwood chair, near the candy counter, with her handwork, I imagine by design. The family has a difficult task to restrain Grandma from feeding her sweet tooth, which destabilizes her diabetes, it keeps her weight high and plays havoc with her blood pressure. Aunt Felicia gives her a daily shot of insulin. When I visit my grandmother, she lets me pick out whatever candies I desire. I notice a few Tootsie Rolls find their way into her apron pockets.

But the best time I share with her is when, on special rare occasions, she takes me to town.

One day she announces that because Easter is coming, she would like me to have a new pair of shoes, maybe like Shirley Temple's.

I am in dreamland with the news.

After she powders her face she pins the cameo on her best lace-collar dress, dons a black, veiled straw hat, and sticks it with the large pearl hat pin. I

42

know we are ready when she slips the multi-pocketed leather purse on her arm. She has the recognizable sweet, clean grandma fragrance.

We catch the bus across from the grocery store, beneath the train viaduct, and sit ourselves in back of the driver. Typically Grandma has few words to say. I sit at the edge of my seat looking intensely at her face for the signal to pull the bell cord. The streets are filled with shoppers.

I wonder if they know I'm with my grandma? Maybe there are other kids with grandmas.

She holds my hand as we walk from one shop to another, squeezing my fingers when she wants me to take note of something. I acknowledge by a look at her twinkling eyes. We travel until we arrive at a children's shoe store. We look into the window. She spots a pair of Mary Janes, with a strap and button. My heart goes thump. We enter the shop and I sit next to her, my feet unable to reach the floor. I can smell the new shoes.

The salesman measures my foot with his metal ruler. He leaves and brings back a white pair of leather beauties. I can scarcely contain my joy at the fit. I am actually going to have a fancier pair. Grandma makes one more inquiry to the salesman. I can't hear her question, but I hear the answer.

"Yes, ma'am I believe we do. I'll be right back."

He returns with another box. As he opens the lid, I strain to see the shoes hidden under the tissue. Off come my good fitting white shoes.

Oh no, I'm not going to get them!

I glance at Grandma and there is a vague look on her face. The man removes the other pair from the box.

43

Oh, oh, oh! They're red! They're shiny red! How did Grandma know I always wanted red shoes?

He slips the magical shoes on my feet and the fit is even better than the white pair.

I will never take these shoes off. I can dance in these.

A deal is struck. Grandma squeezes my fingers and I am allowed to wear them for the rest of our journey, secure in the knowledge that all little girls who lay eyes upon my shiny patent leather red shoes, will suffer pangs of jealousy and longing.

Nothing but nothing can compare to this excursion. But before our return home we stop at the dime store for three more purchases.

"Oh Grandma! My own handkerchief and comb to put into my purse?"

Grandma Valente, opens her double-sided coin purse and pays the clerk for the last purchase of the day. It is a small, cameo locket, on a chain, that opens with space for two pictures.

Now I feel properly dressed just like my grandma.

And maybe when I grow up I will probably need to wear a pale peach corset.

INDEPENDENCE

Seven years old is when the Catholic Church says we reach the use of reason. I am now supposedly able to understand concepts beyond my immediate self and question people's motives with reasonable intelligence.

I think I am ready for independence. At four I became an international traveler with my parents, and yet at seven my world is restricted to only half a block on Buchanan Street. I am allowed to walk beyond a mile to parochial school, but not to wander or explore beyond my path. On my block I can go to the corner, cross the street and come up the other side, as far as Betty Ann Nelson's house—the one with the screened porch. Betty Ann is my closest friend and lives with her grandparents, Mr. and Mrs. Stroble. Every week in summer Mr. Stroble calls all the kids on the block over to his back porch and we wait and wait as he churns the machine that makes peach ice cream.

I wonder why Betty Ann doesn't live with her momma and daddy? They visit her sometimes and bring her presents. I wonder why they don't like to stay near her? Mrs. Stroble has a crippled leg with a metal cage that clicks when she walks. I love to visit their home. Betty Ann's grandma decorates the house inside and out at Christmas. She says her decorations come all the way from Germany. My mom doesn't like to decorate our house too much. Our Christmas tree is usually a skinny one. Their home is always friendly.

The houses, clapboard white, two story bungalows of the 1920's, have wide porches, screened and replaced with storm windows in winter. Garages in some cases, an after thought, are set to the back of the homes. Buchanan Street, arched by enormous ancient chestnut trees, is a quiet, pleasant residential area of Albany, N.Y. Lawns and shrubs are immaculately manicured, bordered by sidewalks of uneven slate that resound hollow when we skate over them like lightening.

Rocking chairs can frequently be heard creaking in the summer's night, some fast, some slow, depending on the occupants' attitude. Very seldom do you hear conversation. It is as if speaking violates the evening, cutting into the intercourse of crickets. At times you hear the wiss, wiss, wiss of lawn sprinklers, bathing the blades of grass and cooling the overheated earth. Porch lights are not turned on, to restrict the neighborhood mosquitoes from getting their nightly plasma. After dinner, until even after sundown, we children play Hide and Seek, Red Light-Green Light or Simon Says. Usually my mother has the Philco radio tuned to the Kate Smith Hour. Miss Smith sings our country's song, God Bless America, Land That I Love...

Our summer days are filled playing with baby dolls and paper dolls, dress-ups, and giving neighborhood stage plays for the untiring few adults and children who willingly sit and listen. Sometimes we gather horse chestnuts with Ronnie, who lives on the corner with his older brother, who didn't have a name. Betty Ann and the redheaded Fitzgerald twins are never far behind. The unofficial contest is to see who can collect the most bags of nuts by the end of fall. This is a serious endeavor and we often take foolish chances by climbing high into the trees for these treasures. After we choose our winner, the squirrels reap the benefits.

Daily, I watch the lady next door with fascination, as she leaves for her place of employment, carefully dressed, like Joan Crawford, in seamed stockings, heels, hat, gloves and purse. She looks important and walks confidently to her Pontiac coupe with her set of keys in her hands. *Her* keys. *Her* car. *Her* job. No other woman I know, except Dad's real estate lady, drives an automobile or is independent enough to do this kind of thing. As I play, I imitate the lady.

When I grow up I'm gonna drive my own car and be all dressed up and go to work. I will have my own keys.

The humidity and temperature soar this Fourth of July, 1939, and I have the wildest case of chicken pox ever given to a kid. There is not a spot on my body untouched by the miserable stuff and I am not allowed to leave my bed. I am sure I'm being punished. I can hear my family and the neighbors in their gardens, heartily enjoying the traditional picnic. This is the one of two times a year that Grandpa leaves and closes his grocery store. He brings the fireworks to be fired off in the evening after dinner. Momma, Aunt Felicia and Grandma Valente, are in charge of the kitchen.

Why won't they let me out of bed? It smells so good downstairs. I'm so itchy and I'm sick of coloring, reading and playing with paper dolls. I have to grow up faster. This is not fun.

One day my father announces.
"Venere, I think you biga girl now. I gonna let you go to grocer store for your mother."
My heart stops beating.

Did I hear Daddy right? Around the corner? I'm going to go to the end of our block, turn, go down that whole street and then cross at the red light? Holy Moses. By myself?

I do well. My first trip is uneventful, even though I've been warned about the two tough little German boys who like to pester and torment kids as they pass their home. I bring back the can of tomatoes from Franklin's Grocery store and I watch the boys with caution as they eye me. Who is this new woman, who dares walk on their block? I stroll by them exhibiting my independence, revealing no fear. In all probability they are being held captive on their property. I am ready for my next assignment. It comes. Off I go. Two cans of tomatoes and an onion.

The boys are watching me. I'll bet they can't go to the grocery store for their daddy.

"Hey vinegar puss!" They yell, as they stand at the edge of their lawn. "Com'ere guinea-wop! Hey you hatchet face!"

What did they call me? They're throwing stones! I'll walk fast in front of their house. Maybe I'd better cross the street at that other corner. Whooo, that house is sure dark under all those big Chestnut trees. Whooo! I think that's the one they call the ghost house. Boy it's creepy! I see a light moving in the windows. Holy Mackerel! I'm getting out of here. Wait 'til I tell Betty Ann and the kids.

Later that evening as I sit on the porch steps with my friends, Ronnie's older kid brother, the one without a name, confirms my worst fears. He tells us that the house *is* haunted and that it doesn't have electricity. And then he reports that an old man lives there by himself, except for his dead wife who sits at the table with him for dinner. That night my dreams turn to nightmares, more than usual. All I can think about is the scene of a skeleton with a dress on, propped in a chair. The story builds new fears.

O.K. Now what do I do? If I cross the street, the two mean kids are going to pelt me with stones and if I walk past the spooky house, something is liable to grab me for sure. Wow! This seven year old may never see her eighth birthday.

And there is another dilemma. I discover the best chestnut trees are around the haunted house and the other kids haven't discovered the cache as yet.

If I could just be braver. Maybe the skeleton can't see that well. But what if the old man catches me stealing the valuable nuts? I don't want to eat pasta with the dead lady. Will Daddy know where to look for me if I don't come home with the groceries?

Life certainly becomes more complicated since the start of my new freedom. The week before, my Mother took me to see the new movie, "Snow White and the Seven Dwarfs". The witch scares the wind out of me. I barely make it through the talking trees and magic mirror.

Who knows maybe the witch lives in the haunted house, across from the mean little boys. I sure had a bad dream last night.

I continue to go to the market but as I approach both houses, there is a decidedly faster pace. Then the day arrives for a true challenge. I come from the store carrying a sack of potatoes, and as I walk past the boys they begin to ridicule me, tossing pebbles with each taunt. My rage mounts. I reach into the grocery bag for a tuber. One by one I aim them at my target until all are gone. Many of them reach their mark. I have just learned to do battle in a foreign land. The two-legged terrors retreat. I triumphantly march ahead. As I near my home I know I will be in a big trouble with my dad. The potatoes are gone. I have nothing to show my father. But in spite of a good loud tongue-lashing I think he understands.

I am pleased with my accomplishment. I can now walk with my head high. The feisty little buggers, continue their barrage of insults but stop throwing stones.

I begin to feel daring, so one day when mother sends me to the store, I carry an extra paper sack. I am determined to get those wonderful chestnuts from the gardens of the haunted house. As I near the dark brown house, shaded by the largest chestnut trees in the world, I see a cellar door near the side where I need to walk.

Maybe this is where he keeps other bodies. Maybe he catches kids every year as they steal his chestnuts and drags them to his secret hiding place in the basement. But I'll be fast. He won't catch me.

Quickly I fill my bag to capacity, my head and eyes down, looking for any and all stray nuts. Suddenly I hear a noise. I look up to see the unshaven, wild-haired, old man from the house staring at me. My seven years flash before me.

"What do you think you are doing? You don't belong here! Go on, go on, go away! I better not catch you."

No kidding!

I have no idea what I said or did, but I do know I dropped the bag filled with the priceless chestnuts. I run as fast as my scared, stone legs will carry me. The next few days I remain indoors, contented to play alone.

I have decided chestnuts aren't that important to my life. Actually leaving my half block isn't that terrific either. Maybe I'm just not ready for all this independence.

What's that, Daddy? You're going to let me walk to my piano lessons? Isn't that where you walk through the woods? Near that pond? Near that funny shack?

CRY UNCLE

"La speranza e' il pan de' miseri." (It.)
"Hope is the bread of the wretched."

"For cryin' out loud!" My uncle angrily shouts when he sees me eyeing him primp. "How long have you been standing there, Venera?"

"Just a little while, Uncle Joe. I was only watching you shave and comb your hair."

"Well, you ought to say something!"

"Gee, I'm sorry." I guiltily maintain.

I can see my intrusion into his privacy has embarrassed and upset him. But I'm transfixed by his ablution and tonsorial ceremony. There is a secret pleasure in peeking at my narcissistic, handsome uncle as he preens for his dates in front of the small, wooden mirrored medicine cabinet, mounted on a sidewall of my grandparent's large kitchen. Whenever I come for a visit, I study and watch my relatives in this mirror as they groom themselves. Daily, Grandpa and Uncle Joe, use the leather-shaving strop to sharpen their straightedge razors. Sometimes we grandkids are threatened with the strop when our behavior doesn't quite come up to snuff.

Uncle Joe applies pomade to his thick, straight and silken, dark brown hair. Not a strand out of place. His after-shave lotion leaves him glowing. His grooming is impeccable.

All the Valente boys, including Joe, graduated from Christian Brothers Academy. In later years, he is the major helper in his parent's grocery store. Smooth and jaunty Joe, the second oldest son, is the family comic. His warm and fun-loving demeanor leaves people that know him in stitches. He is a serious fan of boxing and can, at times, generate a few of his own bouts, usually after a full night of drinking with buddies. His progressive heavy imbibing contributes to his early death. Alcoholism, unfortunately, is an often seen culprit disease in my mother's family.

Young Joe, a good barber, owns a successful shop located in the diverse neighborhood near my school, Blessed Sacrament. On my way to class, I usually drop in for a visit. Down the steps, past the red and white turning barber pole, I hurry to the basement hair palace located beneath the corner diner. The two window fronts on either side of the door lead to the black and white, diamond-patterned linoleum tile. Opposite the mirrored walls, is a row of black leather and chrome, curved waiting seats. Three barber chairs.

"Uncle Joe, why do you need three chairs? You're the only one working here."

Questions. So many questions.

The occasional tables have a general scattering of girlie and sport magazines. The waiting male customers usually smoke, drink coffee, and confer as to who will win the next prizefight. The price of hair cutting includes a 'Joe' floorshow, whether they want it or not. It is a parlor of satisfaction and comfort.

Despite his strictness, I genuinely sense he likes me. I relish being introduced to his friends as he tells Mr. So an So of my small abilities.

"I want you to meet my sister's girl, Venera." He points with his comb. "She's a nice kid. In fourth grade. Right?" He doesn't wait for my answer. "Skates up a storm too. Goes to Mass everyday before school. Right? She says she's going to be a doctor when she grows up. Right?" The men have an approving smile on their faces. I feel a warm glow as I shake my head in agreement. "Likes to stop in on her way to school. Here's a quarter, Venera, maybe you'd like to go upstairs to the diner and order something for yourself."

I bid a hasty good-bye and fly out of the shop, anticipating my usual fare. I run up the stairs to the restaurant and sit on a red leather-covered, chrome stool. Doris, the lady with the big fan-shaped, starched, lace handkerchief stuck in her pink uniform pocket, with matching nurses cap, recognizes me. She loves make-up.

"Well, good morning, Venera. Been to see your uncle all ready, I see. Are you still going to church and putting all your extra money in the basket?"

"Yes Doris, my dad said if I put my money in the basket, I'll get a baby brother. But, he sure takes a long time to get here."

"One of these days. Just be patient. I guess you'd like your regular treat?"

She knows exactly what my taste buds desire. I respond in my most adult sounding voice.

"Yes. I would like a cup of cocoa with whipped cream, and a Parker house roll, please."

The fresh, warm, bread slathered in butter and the hot chocolate is pure ecstasy after the piercing cold walk from home. I garner a feeling of respect from the grown-up transaction.

Now and then I stop for lunch at Aunt Kate's, Uncle Joe's wife, and she gives me a steaming bowl of Campbell's tomato soup or clam chowder with oyster crackers, listens to my woes, and I hear hers. It is good tenderness. But the marriage to Aunt Kate does not last, much to my sadness. I sense a great loss when she doesn't remain part of the family. Uncle is quite exhausting when he drinks. I'm sure this takes a toll on their lives.

The barbershop closes in the 1940's when Joe enters military service in World War II. And when he returns one of his fingers is permanently maimed from the war. Unfortunately, it hampers his ability to continue barbering. The reality is hard for him to accept.

After the war, Dad buys a nightclub and offers a partnership to Uncle Joe. For a while it works, but Joe's drinking results in disputes with contentious customers. One night Uncle leaves Club Paradise, and has a brawl in a back alley with a black man. His handsome face is sliced open and scarred for life. After this episode he maintains a high prejudice for a while against blacks, replacing a long-time good relationship with them.

The disfigurement plunges him into an on-going depression. His alcoholism intensifies. Years later I understand how this must have shattered his ego. He is no longer confident of his physical prowess. His marriage is lifeless; a tremendous sense of loss, his adeptness and dexterity to barber and earn a living diminishes. All add to his broken spirit.

After I reach my teens, I never see him again. My family locates on the West coast and communication with my mother's relatives is minimal. Occasional letters are exchanged. I hear that Joe likes to spend time fishing on the Hudson River. His love of boxing continues. My parents receive a photograph of him with Argentine Rocco, a boxer of some repute. I am sad when I see his alcohol swollen scarred face, with his eternal cigarette dangling to the side of his mouth. In the photo he holds up his hero's arm in a winner's salute. He continues to work in the family grocery and settles into a life of oneness. When he doesn't drink, his kind-heartedness always shines through. He offers much to those that need.

As an adult, I so wished I could have known more about him, but I let my own selfish world replace sensible pursuits. I'm not sure what his life was like after I left. I didn't know where his interests went. Did he want to do big things with his education? I wondered if he got together with any of his boxing buddies or his old barber customers to hash over what might have been. I do know he never remarried and stayed to care for my aging grandparents in the dingy, tired, deteriorated tenement. His body caved much too early. His years of drink canceled out old age.

He is still special in my eyes. I often think of my handsome uncle and how he searched for love. I think of his jovial young spirit and how fate gave him a difficult path. For me he left a legacy of his sad heart.

The ANNIVERSARY

July is a good month for a garden party in the Hudson Valley. Summer parties always remind me of one so many years ago when I was eight. This is cousin Lucia and Joseph's twenty-fifth wedding anniversary, and the grand celebration is to be held on the coming Saturday. When first married they couldn't afford to give each other much in the way of recognition of their love. With year after year of hard work, they put off any glorification of the day. Consequently, Joe Jr. and his sister Francis decide to give the commemoration to their parents with a grand party.

They plan for weeks. Francis writes the invitations, making sure all her mother's and father's friends and relatives will not be slighted. Her brother Joe hires the orchestra. Not just any orchestra, but the city's top of the line Italian musicians. There will be mandolins, guitars, clarinets, all the necessary mosaic sounds to make a *Mazurka* or *Tarantella* come alive and in turn redeem old tired feet and restore libido.

The Italian delicatessen helps cater the food. There is a never ending assortment of much desired and longed-for Italian soul delicacies; *Ravioli di San Giuseppe, Arancini di Riso, Cannoli alla Siciliana, Cassata Gelata,* and these are only the desserts. Inside the tasteful large Craftsman style, Eastern home, tables are set indoors and throughout the garden. The long buffets are brimming with dishes of the fanciful native fare. There is every imaginable antipasti; stuffed fishes, meat-rolls, roast chickens, relishes of every kind, so much one cannot possibly sample all. The dining room holds the main courses; *Salsicce Arroste, Maccheroni alla Calabrese, Cannelloni alla. Napoletana, Saltimbocca* and the ever craved, stuffed meat rolls *Involtini alla Milanese.* Every room has its own gourmand spread.

Lucia and Joseph place much hope and anticipation in their children's education and future. The bright and promising students are first in this family of immigrants to go on to higher learning. Joe, twenty-four, a little older than his sister, knows many young people from the University and town. The prosperous Luccas are highly respected and well known in the community. Their humanitarian efforts leave their home always open for whoever is in need.

Sarafina, the youngest, who wants to be a nurse, takes me, when we visit, on adventures in her neighborhood, like the new hamburger stand down by the soda shop. It is exciting to be eight. We are allowed to get one small hamburger with ketchup and pickles, and later we return for an ice cream soda.

Sarafina's mother, Lucia, my father's first cousin, introduce my parents, and well, we all know what a great match this was. But our families are close and when the invitation arrives, Dad is ecstatic. Joe Jr., asks him if he will sing and help with the entertainment for the special evening. My father, Salvatore, never shy, is always ready for a celebration and welcomes the opportunity to perform. They decide they should also add some Americanized musicians, since there will be many young people at the gala affair. Many friends from college. I listen with great anticipation of the evenings' plans. I know all my Italian friends will probably be there including Delia, Fumi, and maybe Laura and of course Sarafina.

Everything is set. The doors open for the party in the family's home. The American band unloads their instruments and set up in the garden and the Italian orchestra is in the solarium, next to the living room. The terrace and parlor, with its terrazzo floor, are perfect for dancing. The furniture is moved to the side and chairs are placed for all those who wish to eat, sit, and talk.

The grand house is in an affluent attractive residential area on a wide boulevard in our hometown. Many of the guests must park blocks away. Surely the whole city is here this evening. As many times as I have been in the house, I have never seen it so festive. The music can be heard from the street. Men bring their homemade wines and everyone salutes Mr. and Mrs. Lucca with *Asti Spumanti.*

My friends and I grab a front line view in the parlor to watch the elder, well corseted, Italians do their fancy footwork. Occasionally, we children dance with each other, our fathers, or who ever will take us on. Women dance with women, no problem. No partners? Dance alone.

I can hear my father strumming his guitar, while he sings *Stornelli,* the haunting Italian ballads and songs of their childhood and native country. The guests cheer Cousins Lucia and Joseph as they freely dance alone the intricate steps of the *Mazurka* and *Tango.* They beam. Even as a little girl, I can see how much they bask in the special honor of this evening. They will absolutely remember it always.

I hear the popular 1939-1940's music playing in the garden. Someone imitates Bing Crosby and Rudy Vallee on the microphone, while the young people dance the fashionable new dances of the day. Sarafina, my friend, passes trays of pastries to seated guests. Dark eyed, wavy-haired, handsome young Joe, although shy and quiet, plays a solo on his clarinet, and his sister, Francis, sings an Italian love song to her father and mother. They surprise everyone. Bravos are sent to the proud brother and sister. The party is a success. They have done very nicely for their parents.

Sometime after midnight, still warm and humid, guests begin to leave and most are gone by three o'clock, except for the few that stay to cleanup and assist the musicians to load instruments into their cars. My father and mother stay.

I hear a spine tingling, frantic announcement. Someone is hurt in the driveway. From that point forward, everything and everyone moves at lightening speed.

"Who is it, Momma?" I ask. "What's happened? What's the matter?"

She doesn't answer. Never many answers to my questions.

I hear sentences spoken in mixtures of Italian and English. Mr. d'Angelo shouts to call for an ambulance. Another yells to get the police. I see my father run outdoors with others. I hear screams. Then more shouts, blood-curdling cries from the depths of despair. I have heard this kind of terrible outcry before in my young life. My heart moves from its safe place.

My father cries, "*No, no, no, no, no, non e vero (it's not true!)."*

I want to run outside with everyone, but I am stopped along with the other children. Sarafina and Fumi stand close beside me. We hold each other and listen by the window, straining to get a view.

"*Madona Mia*, don't let her see him," a woman shouts in Italian.

"Where is the ambulance?"

"Its no use, I think he's dead! Oh God! Oh God! How could this happen?"

Another voice. "He was loading the bass fiddle in the trunk."

"That car, over there, came out of nowhere and smashed right into him. How can it be? Is he dead? I think he's dead."

"Where is the guy who hit him?"

"Over there, still sitting in his car. Drunk as a skunk! He doesn't even know what he's done, that's how drunk he is!"

"Let's cover him before they see him."

"*Dio, Dio mio*, the blood...there's so much!"

We children helplessly cry as the screams and cries terrorize us. Then we hear the awful news.

"It's Joe!"

Lucia and Joseph's beloved son, Joe, has been killed.

Monday night, we are back at our cousins' home. All the guests from the party, now in mourning clothes, have returned to the somber house to pay respects to Joe Jr. and the family. My father with many kind friends stay with the grief struck parents. Many attempt to scrub the blood and death from the front of the house. But much remains. A terrible reminder, of the incredible ending to a magnificent evening.

I can only imagine what is about to happen. The last time I had been to a wake, I was five years old in Italy and another young cousin dies as a result of pneumonia complications after attending my birthday party. Her death has left a very fresh and ineffaceable picture in my mind.

As I enter the house with my parents, everything is dark except for candles in the hallway, dining room and parlor. Many friends have gathered in the dimly lit kitchen. The women are in black and men wear the traditional black armbands and ties. They speak in hushed tones. Their handkerchiefs soak up the tears as they weep. I glance over to the kitchen nook and see women fanning, ashen and nearly unconscious, Cousin Lucia. Cousin Joseph, pats her hand, as tears stream down his sorrowful face. His two daughters cling to him tightly.

In the hallway a lamenter's refrain, "How could this happen to these dear souls? Lucia says it wouldn't have happened if she hadn't been celebrating. Who could know?"

My dad tells me that he will take me to see Joe.

Oh, oh, oh. I remember the last time we did this. Am I going to be afraid again? Where? In the living room? Why is it always so dark?

As we walk into the parlor I hold my father's hand. When I look into the dimly lit room, my eyes suddenly become adjusted to the light and the scene before me. We slowly walk down the middle of the room; many people sit in chairs that are set up in rows on both sides of our pathway. The same chairs that were rented for the party. The drapes are drawn. The room is so different from Saturday night. We are in the very spot that Joe's parents' danced on, surrounded with lively music and singing. I remember the smell. The heavy odor of candles and flowers, the room's sauna temperature intensifies the overwhelming floral perfume. The large candelabras that outline the mourning room, flicker strangely as we pass them, as if to announce our arrival. I look ahead and see the steps that lead up to the casket mounted on a pedestal. Dad takes me up the two steps. Tearfully, he tells me to kiss Joe good-bye. I look at my father with a questioned look. But I still trust my parent's instructions.

I stare at Joe. I overhear a comment—someone says he looks like an angel. To me he looks like one of the sleeping marble statues of Rome. Everything inside the satin lined coffin is pure white; shoes, suit and shirt. His once handsome face is rouged, painted to appear as if asleep.

My father picks me up to reach Joe's cheek. I press my warm, child lips to the cold, hard skin and wait for him to respond. But there will never, ever be any more responses. Now I understand death. The reality of it becomes clear. I will never see Joe again. The dark wavy hair can never be tousled again. No more Saturdays of laughter. I have to remind myself that it will be the last time I will ever see him. Will I remember him? I want to think of him as the laughing Joe who always takes us kids for rides on his back on that very floor. The cheerful boy who nuzzled his mother in the kitchen, who pulled and untied her apron and stole meatballs. His sisters' protector and confidant. His father's pride. Always respectful to his parents' needs, fixing the motors of his father's and friend's cars. Anyone who needed called on Joe. Truly an angel.

After they bury Joe Jr., the family is never more the same. His mother sheds her bright colors and forever after wears only black, and in her laments, punishes herself with *if only*. Joseph Sr. pines for his son, unable to get back his jovial spirit. Their two daughters are lost in the languished roteness of their parents' daily lives. Their house loses the zest of life.

Friends always make it a point to be with them on their anniversary.

Venera Di Bella Barles

WISDOM TEETH

Sister Mary Agnes, my fourth grade teacher, has very little patience lately. As a matter of fact she's downright cranky. We all know the trouble she's been having with her teeth. Weekly, she keeps us informed of her visits to the dentist. Her bad days are often reflected in the delivery of lessons.

Her mouth is poorly formed. The teeth are bucked, protruding outside her lips with large spaces between, and when she smiles her gleaming cream-colored pearlies fill her face like a singing horse. We're fascinated with her appearance. Although we like her, we're also careful not to get caught snickering. The price tag is high.

In this parish we're mostly Irish and Italian and the priests, for the most part, are Irish. Everything about the church is mystical to me. To my nine-year-old eyes Blessed Sacrament Church and School appear to be the largest buildings on the boulevard. The stone facade and imposing heavy metal doors of the church, add to the overall mystique. The Sisters of Mercy have been in charge of me since I became an inmate of this convent school in second grade. Their power constantly compels. There is no doubt who runs the show.

They are recognizable by their black sweeping habits, framed by the heavily starched, tightly bound, white wimple and topped by a coal black flowing veil. The weighty, wooden, metal cross that dangles at their sides does much to tweak our conscience. When they stand they tower over us.

Their arms disappear within the folds of the garment like an imposing Army of Cossacks.

The girls' uniforms are navy pleated skirts, nautical collared, white middy blouses, and red satin ties. The boys wear white shirts and black ties. You invariably know when the boys are nearby; their gray corduroy pants give off a distinctive sound as legs chafe against each other. Each morning we arrive clean and tidy, but by lunchtime our hems are hanging, half our bobby socks are in our shoes with only bare heels showing, the bows in our hair are untied and our blouses have food and ink stains. The boys' shoelaces are straggling and the once white shirts, at the beginning of the year, have turned grayish and lost their ability to stay inside the unzipped trousers.

After school, girls get together, to play and fantasize about our favorite personalities, the nuns. We dress-up in long skirts, don makeshift veils and carry big sticks. Let's talk about the big stick. I'm sure the wooden rod, with its magical powers, is issued with each nun the day she takes her vows. This attitude changer, an extension of Sister's arm, has the ability to reach and do all things unimaginable. It can remove hats, separate lancing foes, extricate secret notes from pockets, make lines straight and wipe smiles from faces. The talk is strong that we will all become nuns.

Easter vacation is coming and everyone has plans, even Sister Agnes. Her announcement comes that she is to get new teeth while we are away.

"Yes class, the old ones are to be pulled and I will have new ones. Then I won't have any more troubles with them. Isn't that just grand?"

We anticipate a striking change in our revered teacher. The school is abuzz with the coming event. Nothing like this has happened since Sister Monica had a bunion operation.

Wonderful Spring is finally here and even though our vacation is over we are eager for Sister's new chompers. We enter our class, take our seats, and ready ourselves for our customary and required greeting to stand and acknowledge any adult as they enter a room.

"Good Morning, Sister Mary Agnes" we all cry out as the door opens.

We stand at attention everyone straining to see the transformation. Not a sound is heard. She greets us with her usual big smile.

"Welcome back class. Good to see you all. I trust you all had a good vacation. You may sit down."

Wait a minute. There's no change! Can it be? Her teeth are still hanging out! What happened? Didn't she go to the dentist for her new ones?

"Sister Agnes, how are your teeth feeling?" A brave student asks. "Didn't you go to the dentist?"

"Yes, Patricia, and everything is just fine. I am just so happy with my new dentures."

Heads swivel to heads in unison. To our utter amazement there is no change. The new false plates are identical to her old teeth, spaces, protrusion and all!

Now, it's difficult to keep our minds on lessons this morning. The room vibrates with whispers and giggles. Sister, unaware of the reason her disloyal class is unruly, loses her grip and swings into action. Many of us, whom are the usual known offenders, are immediately transported to the front desks. I am placed in the first seat of the second row. For a change, I am obediently quiet, still stunned at the results of Sister Mary Agnes' mouth.

"Patrick Mooney! Move." We hear the annoyance in her voice. "I want you up here! Right now!"

Those awful boys in the back seats just will not behave.

66

But I'm on my best behavior, sensing it will not be wise to test her. She leans against my desk and delivers the morning assignment. But the steady buzz of talking and tittering continues along with note passing, I notice her face has changed to the color of my tie matching the fiery glaze in her eyes. As if possessed of the devil, Sister Mary Agnes, begins to sputter and spit in anger. Her arms extend high above me.

"I will have immediate silence! You are going to have extra homework tonight every last one of you!"

By now I have my hands up to my face as in a protective shield.

"Who threw that wad of paper? I want all who are responsible for this disruption to stand at the chalkboard. This minute!"

I lean back to avoid her spittle. She is transforming before my eyes. Her arms are railing, the wing-like fabric of her black habit appears vampiric. Sister Agnes looms large as she names the evil offenders. She catches me wincing. I meekly smile back. But suddenly, Sister Mary Agnes reaches the pinnacle of her vocal pitch, pounds the well-used pointer on the top of my desk and screams her commandments. Without warning, her upper false plate flies out of her mouth like a Fourth of July roman rocket. The airborne teeth seem to hang in the air, as it searches for its target—my desk. I stop breathing. I look at the wide uneven dentures staring back at me and wonder how am I to survive this. My muscles are glued. Sister glares, as she waits for me to make my usual unwise decision. Quickly her hand and arm come towards me.

"Don't you budge, Di Bella!" she gums.

My life will be over if I stir an inch. Who's the best Saint to save me? I'll do anything just spare me this time.

The room is stunned into deathly silence.

Sister Mary Agnes grabs her teeth and stomps out of the room. We can hear a gnat praying in the quiet. We are dead meat.

How will we ever get out of this? We probably will have to do penance and Hail Marys until we die!

Mother Superior, who has, I'm sure, been trained in Gestapo camps, takes over our class the next two days and gives us each hearty lessons in conduct and decorum. We have just used up three of our lives. There is no greater enforcer than fear and guilt.

I have decided to go to Mass daily.

#4 Venera and Nicky's Godmother (1942)

Venera Di Bella Barles

WAR on the HOMEFRONT

The radio plays as usual this Sunday. I am lying on the oriental carpet, in the warm stream of sunlight, reading the funnies, Maggie and Jiggs, and practicing my new love, whistling. Out of our living room picture window I see branches of the leafless chestnut trees hanging heavy with snow and icicles. It always looks as if there is too much snow to melt in time for spring. Dad has just come in from shoveling a path to the curb and Mom is in the kitchen making her delicious specialty, homemade ravioli with spinach, meat, and cheese. Our friends are visiting this evening to share our meal. All is right for my nine-year-old mind.

"Venere, *zitti*. Don talk. I gotta hear."

A special bulletin interrupts the radio program and Daddy looks nervous.

"Well, zats zat. Here we go! We gonna go to war. They bomb Pearl Harbor."

I look as he paces the floor and wonder where Pearl Harbor is and what it can possibly mean to us. I flash back to when we lived in Italy, three years earlier, and everyone talked about the coming war. How fearful all my relatives were. I still don't understand what it means or how it will affect us.

Gosh, it's almost Christmas, we're supposed to get our Christmas tree tomorrow. I wonder if this news is going to upset Daddy? Oh, oh, Mom is starting to get worried.

70

Dad tells Mom not to be troubled, they won't take him, he's too old, and besides we're going to have another baby soon. My brother Nick is born three months after World War II is declared.

When we can get them, ordinary everyday items now are luxuries. Our new Buick has a sticker on its window, in order to buy gas. We're issued red coin disks and ration books. Food is limited, but we adjust to the scarcity. Flags hang from front porches and stars begin to appear in windows of many homes, marking where service men and women have left to fight our battles. The next few years will give us many lessons, and I am growing up faster.

Nicky, my new baby brother has pneumonia. Everyone is frightened. As I peer into his crib, I am fearful for him as the memory of my own dramatic illness with the same ailment looms fiercely. I wonder if he will get well. I watch the concern on my parents' faces. Mom layers the little guy with shirts and piles on the blankets. Even as he gets older she continues this practice, and we kid Nicky how husky he looks with all the extra padding. Our house always feels cold. We have little heat and no hot water. Dad's idea of economy.

We are living in one of the three homes Dad purchases on Buchanan Street. He remodels the single-family house into a duplex, and we live in the lower unit. Between 1941 and the end of the war in 1945, he buys and restores two more homes. Usually he finds the most decrepit houses, moves us into them as the repairs are being done, and when they are clean and beautiful, sells them, and we move again.

The neighbors and children say the house next door is haunted. It's pretty creepy walking past the dried lawn and the tall weeds that climb to the chipped rail of the porch. The peeled paint shows a color from another era. The side windows of the house, covered with papers, are visible from our upstairs bedrooms. It's been a couple of years since my last dealings with another *haunted* house around the corner, so I'm not eager to revive fearful memories again.

Daddy says there are three old people living there, two sisters and a brother. They keep one of the women indoors, because she's crazy. Momma says she's afraid of crazy people. She says they put you in the crazy house and you never can get out.

I hear stories that the family had been accomplished violinists and musicians. In the short time we live next-door, two of the unmarried siblings die leaving the remaining unstable woman to fend for herself. Dad says they may have died of malnutrition. Eventually, the house is put up for sale. In the evening, the neighborhood kids sit on the porches telling wild ghost stories and wondering who will be the new people to move into such a scary house.

Dad announces we are to move.

I hope I don't lose all my friends again? I wonder where my next home will be. Did he say next door? Not in the haunted house!

That's the end of my restful sleep.

I remember the day Dad and I walk into the dilapidated Victorian house. Our flashlights point to the rubble in the darkened rooms. I see the windows covered in yellowed sheet music. Every room is completely jammed with stacks of papers, music and boxes of books and souvenirs. The large house, with basement and attic, is filled with their family history. Most of the bedrooms are upstairs. I follow my father closely up the litter-strewn steps. My light casts large ghostly shadows. The dark wood paneling, floors, and heavy, ornate, creaking staircase adds to the ominous feeling. The unopened windows seal in the smells of the past occupants' lives.

How did this happen? Why did they live like this? Didn't they have a Mom and Dad?

We walk into the three upstairs bedrooms. The front one looks out towards the street. Dad removes some of the sheet music from one of the bay windows and the light immediately streams in taking its rightful position of warmth. I wonder which lady stayed here? It must have been a pretty room at one time but now the flowered wallpaper has lost its color and hangs in loose strips. My father opens the attic door to a set of narrow stairs, and my knees turn gelatinous.

This is just too darn scary. Wait until I tell my friend Betty Ann and the other kids. I don't think I want to sleep here.

I recall other tense occasions where my father led me by the hand. I think my dad assumes I will always be brave. I can't let him down.

Up the stairs we climb. The light flashes on some ancient, musty trunks and hundreds of tiny old, colored prescription bottles, half filled with liquids and powders. I glance around and suddenly my breath catches in my throat. In the corner is a dressmaker's form, with large pins poking out of the chest area. The dutiful model wears a long skirt with lace inserted in the pleats. It casts a shadow of a giant headless woman moving beyond. Cobwebs join everything together. A military uniform is folded neatly in one of the trunks. I wonder if all people have had military costumes to mark their time on earth?

Stacked hatboxes and containers hold treasures of their lives. Again the windows are covered to seal out the light. What were they afraid of?

We descend the stairs and move to the kitchen. Filth and debris beyond belief greet us. Nothing has been discarded or cleaned for years.

"How are we going to get this house cleaned, Daddy, or fixed so we can live in it?"

I can't tell Dad I'm scared. I hope I never have to sleep in the attic.

We open the back kitchen door to let in light, but the doorway is completely blocked with a choking creeper. It is another world. It feels like the grounds in Beauty and the Beast. We discover treasures under the brier, wonderful rose and lilac bushes, some old benches, birdbaths under hidden arbors. It must have been an elegant family home at one time. The neighbors have always praised my father's ability to perform magic on these old dwellings. I wonder if he can give this tired one new life and dignity?

After working for weeks getting the trash out of the house, Dad and I end up with a serious dermatitis. Eventually the home is reasonably clean for us to inhabit, but then the remodeling takes place. We never seem to live in finished homes like my friends. Everything is always a mess. Always impermanent. Every time we make it attractive; it's time to move on. No one wants to visit my home. I'm embarrassed.

The war is getting ugly. Our previous house next door, has been rented to two sets of tenants. For the first time I am promised my own bedroom and I choose the front one with the large bay windows, next to the attic door. All the years of sleeping between my parents are finally over. I choke with the memory of the claustrophobic feeling it left me with. To this day, I struggle with this awful feeling. Even though I have no furniture, except a bed, I make little tables with boxes and cover them with fabric. I bring in lilacs from the garden and put them into my grandmother's canning jars. The room smells delicious. It takes me awhile to get comfortable with the idea of sleeping alone, especially near the entrance to the top floor. My fantasies overwork and I imagine sounds and movements I can't distinguish. But after some time, I make peace with the attic, and find solace in that formerly fearful place. I make a soft seat by the window. From my sky parlor I can look out over my small world. I can see Betty Ann's and the Fitzgerald twins houses from here. In my quiet retreat, away from the harsh sounds of Mom and Dad's bickering, I read the dictionary, play with paper dolls, or just daydream and listen to the rain as it pelts the slate roof.

Construction work is scarce for Dad during the war, so while we live in this home, Mom takes an outside job at a dry soup factory, to help supplement our income. She has never been away from us. It's an unusual sight to watch her say good-bye each day. She catches a bus that takes her to work the night shift packaging rations for soldiers. When I get home from school, Mom gives me specific instructions before she leaves for work, on how to tend to my brother. I am to bathe, change, and feed him. Dad cooks the evening meal, concocting all combinations of foods into one pot or skillet; his specialty, "weel (veal) and peppers." He takes fine care of us and saves Mom's meal to be reheated later. Momma comes home, late each evening, covered in pea-green powdered soup. I'm fascinated at the sight of my working mother being taken care of by my father. These feel like good times. Nicky glows when Antonietta, the Working Lady, comes through the door.

One day, while my folks are away for the day, Nicky decides to have one whopper of a crying tantrum. I'm scared stiff as he turns blue holding his breath. How will I explain to my parents that I failed baby-sitting? In my panic, I haul the big chunker in my arms, run out the front door, and cross the street to Betty Ann's grandmother.

"He's blue. He's crying so hard, he's blue. I changed him and I know he's not hungry! What am I going to do, Mrs. Stroble?"

"Now, Venera, don't worry. Calm down he's all right. He's just trying to tell you whose boss. He's just fine. Here let's tickle his feet. See, he's pulling his foot away and starting to smile."

The little twerp frightens the pasta out of me. I am so grateful to this kind lady. If anything ever happened to him I wouldn't be writing this sentence.

Venera Di Bella Barles

On weekend nights, our family seldom fails to visit the Colonial or Palace Theater, where Rita Hayworth, Errol Flynn or any number of the famous stars become part of our lives. Even my brother, as small as he is, jumping like a puppy, understands. Even bitter, cold nights do not stop our desire to see films. Occasionally we take our dear, elderly, bachelor friend with the thick glasses, Don Felice, who I'm surprised can even see the pictures. Many movies are dramas or musicals of soldiers and their loves. There're so many sailors and service men dancing in threes on tables and stairs it must be part of their training. The newsreels highlight the war, and when I see the bombing and devastation in Europe, I understand some of the misery of these times. I watch ships sink to the bottom of the sea and remember our trip on an ocean liner not too long ago. Salvatore worries for his family in Italy.

Many times, in summer, Mom tells me to go to the large grocers on Central Avenue. I take our war ration book and skate to the market, gliding swiftly over the slate sidewalks. I love this sport, but I'm nearly always in trouble for demolishing my shoes. The skates pull the bottoms from the tops, and I forever walk with flapping soles.

In time, we move from the quiet little neighborhood Buchanan Street, the haunted house and all the addresses I had lived in since six years of age. But this time the move is to a character-lacking duplex, on a busy boulevard. While Dad rebuilds the lower unit, we live in the upstairs apartment. The war has made times difficult to buy building materials, or for that matter, any sort of products. But my father, in his resourceful way, finds recycled doors, cabinets, and windows and even rebends used nails. I spend every free moment, when not in school, helping him strip old houses that are waiting to be torn down. We salvage as many parts and pieces as we can get our hands on. Around March of that year I break my ankle while walking home in a harsh blizzard and I'm not much help.

Also, in summer, now that Nicky is at a manageable age, I enjoy taking him places. Often, we explore the city together by bus. We even take a day excursion on a steamship down the Hudson River to West Point. Sundays he joins me in church, and although he sits quietly for a short while, his attention span soon diverts quickly. During one the priest's delivery of a sleeper sermon, my little brother lies down in the pew, kicks his feet in the air, and loudly and innocently sings the popular tune of the day.

"Oh give me land, lots of land under starry skies above. Don't fence me in."

The good Father acknowledges the commentary as profound.

I no longer take piano lessons but enjoy my small accomplishment with music. I will carry this treasure forever. Lately I've begun to play by ear, making up melodies that sound a great deal the way my father plays.

I have become old enough to understand some of the harsh arguments and terrible physical fights between my father and mother, but I can do little to prevent them. Usually if I intervene, I get whacked soundly. I want to hide so desperately from it all.

Why can't they be like Betty Ann's family? Kind and happy. I get so afraid he will kill Momma or me.

Around the time the war ends, we move to our last home in Albany, and Dad buys Club Paradise, a nightclub. Nicky, three and a half, happily finds his first playmate, Donny. Everyday I see them in their play uniforms with cowboy hats, guns, and holsters. Their greeting usually consists of one or the other being shot in whatever imaginary scene they devise. So his joy is no surprise when Dad announces that we will be moving to Cowboy land, the West.

I have graduated from eighth grade in Blessed Sacrament and begin as a freshman in a new Catholic school. I haven't any friends close by. Everything is so different and new. I encounter difficulties with algebra, nuns, general growing pains and an embarrassing disaster with my period. Girls sure have a tough time, sometimes. First we're babies wetting our diapers, then we get potty trained and just when you think everything is under control, here comes your menstrual and we're back in diapers again, and everything is out of control once again.

Our popular president, Franklin Delano Roosevelt, dies just before my thirteenth birthday. The war in Europe ends soon after. I see many homes that have the representative stars in their windows for sons, daughters, and loved ones who will never come back to their neighborhoods or friends.

We survive the war years. Our lives are still intact. Our scars on the home front are from personal battles. We sell Club Paradise and Dad builds a trailer to take us to California.

5 Last photo taken in Albany with family; Momma, Dad, Nicky, and
Venera (1945-46)

Venera Di Bella Barles

The WINTER of ACHILLES

Albany's blizzards are usually a doozie. It snows without a pause that week. Ice formations cling to roofs and windowpanes. Everything is frozen solid. It is 1945 and I am twelve. I'm beginning to understand life's reason and rhythm. As I sit in class at Blessed Sacrament, I refine daydreaming to an accomplished art form. I find it hard to concentrate on the lesson as I watch the white lace mantilla fall from the sky.

Gads, it's really snowing hard. Super! I hope Sister will let us out early. Maybe if I wish hard enough.

The ice-rain continues its journey to the ground. My reverie is suddenly interrupted with an announcement over the loud speaker from Mother Superior.

"Class, because of the heavy snowfall, I am excusing you for the rest of the week."

Finally the payoff! Somebody is listening. It's good to be in the right place.

She continues, "You will take home whatever extra assignment Sister decides and when you return you will be making up the lost days."

A groan mixed with pleasure emanates from my classmates. Motivation takes on new meaning as the movement in class comes alive. The ordinarily *sotto voce*, creaking wooden floor now vibrates with the pulse of a hundred piece marching band.

"Not so fast, folks," Sister Mary Aloysious commands. "You are to give me a report when you return, on the products these countries produce." She chalks our assignment on the blackboard. "And you are to read chapters eight through nineteen in your Geography book. There will be a written test when you return."

Ohhh shoot. There goes all my time for fun in the snow. It's not enough that Dad keeps me busy helping him all the time. I wonder if she ever was a kid?

The clamor in the cloakroom continues, as everyone prepares frantically to leave, as if they were to march on to Valley Forge. The convent school protégées don their articles of clothing in mixed order; on go galoshes, sweaters under the teddy bear coats, ear muffs on top of hand-knitted caps, and well wrapped scarves surround our necks and faces. I waste no time packing my books into my plump leather satchel, but I have difficulty cinching up the two buckles.

"Remember you are to go directly to your homes."

Sister puts on her black sweater over her habit, under her veil. "This snowstorm is coming down hard and quick. I don't want your parents worrying. When everyone is ready I'll walk you to the front doors. Jack you have your boots on the wrong foot."

Everyone groans. Patience is already out the door.

"Now you may go. Walk, thank you!"

Finally cries of pleasant relief.

"Goodbye Sister. Goodbye!"

We scatter in all directions down the concrete steps to freedom and familiar paths. A few misdirected snowballs wiz by my head.

"Call me when you get home, Jennie."

"O.K. Loretta. I will."

I envy my two classmates closeness. I am friendless, since my family's last move. By the time I am a block into my walk, I can no longer see beyond five feet. The heavy blowing wind and swirling snowfall pulls at my limbs. My school pouch is hardly able to stay closed, overloaded with too much stuff.

I can't even see how far I've gone. Is this Mrs. Porter's stoop? No, it looks like Patsy Ann's house. Jiminy Crickets, my nose is running and I'm getting icicles in the drips. I can't get to my handkerchief and my eyelids are getting stuck together, too! Boy, what a mess.

The normal three miles has lengthened to six.

Finally. It looks like the intersection near the house. But I can't see if traffic is coming or not. I'll just run for it across the street. Gads, my hands and feet are numb. I can hardly hold my school bag. O.K., I'm going as soon as the trolley passes.

As I approach the center of the street, I see the headlights of an on-coming car in the distance, but I do not see the ice-encased streetcar tracks. My foot catches the slippery mound and suddenly my whole body comes smack down on top of my foot. Book bag and all. The car gets closer as I stumble to rise.

"Hey, hey, hey, here I am down here," I scream, as I wave wildly.

And just as it comes within a few feet he swerves around me and continues on his way.

Why can't I get up? I can't believe this. Oh, oh, oh, it hurts so much.

I hobble to the curb. It takes an eternity to cross the street. The blizzard continues with greater intensity. The pain is dramatic, but through my tears I can see my house. Crawling is more tolerable. As I near my home I see my father shoveling our walk paths. I call to him. He helps me climb the unforgiving fifteen steps to our upstairs duplex.

My father debates that I need medical care. He thinks it is just a badly sprained ankle, so for two days I sit with a foot about the size of a football. He isn't hot on the idea of springing for doctors.

Easy for him. It's not his hoof.

After a couple of agonizing days he finally takes me for help to our "El cheapo" lecherous, horse doctor.

"Well, well, Miss Cutie," Dr. Lech says. "I haven't seen you for awhile. I see you've managed to break your heel."

I am not happy to see him again. After an hour of much pushing and pulling, he finally sets my ankle with a cast to my knee.

"You're going to have to keep it propped up as much as possible. It's probably, also a good idea to stay indoors. Too risky in this weather on crutches."

Crutches? Oh no. I'll have to be indoors for a couple of months? Which means I won't be able to continue school. Hey that's not so bad. But I won't be able to see any of the kids. I can't believe what's happening. I'm going to be stuck in the house with my parents and baby brother FOR THE ENTIRE WINTER? *Aw, beans!*

It is a long hard, boring and lonely season, except when my school chums come to bring me homework. Once, two of my teachers, Sister Mary Loyola and Sister Mary Aloysius, visit me with a truckload of assignments. I wish they weren't so kind. The crutches burn a hole in my armpits as I wander from room to room for variety. Everything is new when you only have one foot to work with. Most of my days are spent gazing out the window, thinking about the raw deal I've been given. Around February I return to the doctor.

I remember last year when I had my first physical with this carnal pumpkin head. I am lying on the examining table stark naked with just a sheet to cover me, when unannounced, he appears and leans into my arm. I can see some of his breakfast still in his mustache and his breath reeks from last nights dinner, when suddenly he yanks back the sheet and with a wink says, "My, aren't you getting to be a big girl!"

I'm ready for that old coot, now. One more crack out of him and I'll aim this cast at parts of his body that he has never seen.

He removes the plaster cast and tells me to stand on my foot. My heel doesn't touch the floor! It has mended improperly. He must re-break, reset and cast it once again. And this time it will be over my knee. Thanks to Dr. Mengele the process is painful and grueling.

No, no, no. What is going on? What's happening to my life? All my friends get to ice skate and sled and I'm living with an itchy leg propped on a chair. Maybe if Dad would have been willing to find and pay for a full-time doctor instead of a part-time lecherous plasterer, I might have been through with this stinking mess.

Storms of all magnitudes come and go, external and internal. Mother's passivity usually triggers Dad's short fuse. I read everything I can get my hands on. Can labels, cereal boxes, chair labels, and dictionary. Everything. Except, of course, my schoolbooks. My mangy stuccoed leg is heavy and driving me nuts. I seldom leave the living room. Mother, as usual, has very little to say to me and for the most part ignores me. I haven't seen my grandparents since Christmas. The only adult guest who comes to visit is Don Felice, our 75 year-old bachelor friend, whose eyesight is in about as good shape as my foot. His only statement to me is to tap my cast with his cane as he moves about the room. My two and a half year old brother has me grounded finally to tickle my exposed toes. I can only reach the little bugger with my crutch. From the window I watch the streetcar and the tracks that gave me my unscheduled crack, and daily I count and study the people who enter the drug store across the way. I am flawlessly perfecting loneliness and boredom.

In spring, the snow melts and brings with it Chestnut and Maple leaves and early blooms of flowers, but the most important change is when I am able to remove the one-ton cast. In its atrophied state, my leg looks like a peeling, purple, dead beanpole.

So this must be what I'll look like when I decay after death.

I use a cane for quite some time while 'healing the heel'. Around April, I limp back to class. Now I must make up for all that I have missed. Nicky has turned three and I will be thirteen in a couple of weeks. I didn't realize the world would just keep progressing without me. Everything is measured in before the war or after the war.

Venera Di Bella Barles

I wonder what's in store for me the rest of this year? Too much has already happened. New ideas. New house. New kids. New uniforms. New nuns. New boy.

New boy???

Il BALLO di BARBIERE: The Barber's Dance

Paolo Dante, the barber, is one of the treasures in the old city where I grew up in upper New York State. His shop, in the economically depressed part of town, is about two blocks from grandfather's grocery store. It's not uncommon, when my father and mother visit Grandpa Valente, that we also stop and spend some time with Paolo, his kind, sweet wife Caterina, and their daughter, Gianna, my girlfriend. In their fairly small apartment over the barber store, Caterina Dante helps to keep the bills paid with her fine sewing skills. While Paolo performs in his parlor, she is hidden away most of the day with her work, makings alterations and beautiful gowns for the large weddings in the Italian community. Although he works hard and is a great tonsorial artist, he loses his way every once in awhile by taking the earnings from his shop and drinking until his pockets are empty.

The barber pole, the avenue's beacon, continuously turns and remains lit. Like Valente's store, the shop is kept open until late at night in anticipation of the occasional customer. On warm summer nights we sit on soda crates in front of the barbershop, swatting mosquitoes, drinking our Nesbitt orange sodas, while the adults have their iced coffees and homemade Italian desserts. When a customer comes, everyone turns their crates to watch, as if in a theater, the special treatment our friend, the barber, gives his male clients.

Everyday he dons an immaculately clean, starched, white jacket over a white shirt, and sets off the uniform with a black patent leather bow tie at his throat. Paolo, a dead ringer for Monsieur Poirot, stands just about five foot three. Round jovial red cheeks frame his small well-maintained mustache. His unusual hairstyle has a life of its own.

He parts his dark brown hair on the left and allows it to grow extra long on that side so it can be brought over to the right, covering the large bald area of his head. The only problem is, Paolo tends to bend his head to the left as he cuts the customer's hair, causing the long sparse mane to lie on his shoulders. Everyone waits to see how long it takes before the pomade gives way.

The *capriccio* of the wonderful dance starts as he circles and re-circles the client in the chair. Now and then, while giving his opinions and theories on life, he stops to check his work. While he pontificates, he waves the scissors and comb and every once in a while, takes out a hand mirror and we surmise a new understanding is revealed. But he is not finished. Once again the clippers barely touch the hair. Snip, snip, snip. The comb lifts the threadlike growth as the shears interact in the well-rehearsed waltz. The pigmented filaments float to the gentleman's shoulders, eventually finding their way to the floor. Finally, an electric razor brings a finishing touch to the man's neck then a soft brush appears to whisk the fine hairs. The dance continues. Paolo pushes a knob and the customer is prone. He propels his hands with precise movements encasing the relaxed patron's thoughts and countenance in a wet and thick, white, hot Turkish towel.

As the trusting patron lies motionless, Paolo slaps the straight-edge razor against the leather strop, as if to follow a hidden musical ensemble. With the grace of a baker, he whips soap and water into lather in the porcelain cup. He slowly removes the swaddle cloth. With exact placement he coats the pink face with the soft, white meringue-like substance. Carefully he holds the sharp instrument with his pinkie pointed high, as if holding an English teacup. Paolo begins to shave under the jawbone, sculpts about the 'Adams Apple' then grasps the man's nostrils to remove the hair above the upper lip. Paolo wipes the blade before each stroke. He pushes the snout from side to side, using it as a rudder, until he is satisfied he has leveled the stubble to the skin. Each lift of the razor, like a movement of a baton.

Our eyes are transfixed.

The nose and ear hairs are trimmed, followed once again with hot towels. As the man lies once again swathed, as if in a coma, Paolo sweeps the discarded hair into a receptacle. He tidies his work area, and we interpret, as we watch the flashing of his Italian hands and arm signals, that he gives the captive customer more opinions of the world. He washes his hands and peels the facial turban from the supine dozing man. We wait for Paolo to release the knob that will spring the chair to an upright position. Up it goes. Gently he slaps and applies astringent to the bright flushed face. He massages the head of the glazed-eyed fellow then combs every hair into place. With an atomizer, Paolo mists the surrounding air of his client, as after-shave cologne gently wafts over him. He removes the cape and brushes the gentleman from top to bottom.

The concert is over.

The tired chap, who came into Paolo's shop, leaves with a glow and a spring to his walk. Along with hair, ten years have been removed.

I am too young to understand the financial stresses the Dantes endure. Caterina seems to be the glue for the family, working hard to keep her daughter respectable and Paolo motivated. When he comes home from a long evening of drink, the demons take control of his senses and he strikes Caterina and destroys the shop. After the tantrum he is remorseful and stays sober for quite awhile, but the cycle eventually repeats itself.

They decide to turn the barbershop into a small counter diner. I suspect because Caterina will be assured that the dollar stays within the family. I'm sure the restaurant does fine. We know Caterina is chronically ill with diabetes; it must be a struggle to keep body and soul in harmony. They all take turns working the counter.

It is strange to see Paolo with an apron and chef's hat, flipping pancakes and grilled cheese sandwiches for the customers whose hair he once cut. Now, he is too busy to chat and fill the air with his philosophy. He seems to have lost his star quality.

The conversion makes a change in all of us. Our visits are never the same. I miss seeing Mr. Dante in his tonsorium, dispensing his miraculous changes on weary clients, and giving them, for the price of a haircut and shave, the obligatory opinions of the day.

The OTHER SIDE of PARADISE

The bar, with its brass arm and foot rail, is at least thirty feet long. Jars of pickled pigs feet and pickled eggs sit on one corner of the well-worn, oak top. As you walk through the double-swinging, leather-padded doors, old rancid smoke and liquor smells immediately claim your nostrils. The wooden, plank floor has turned a dirty black from New York Centrals sooty steam engines. The loud jukebox, playing the latest national hits, is drowned out when the mighty locomotives pass by and conversations of the three or four regulars at the bar frequently halt. Salvatore, my father, feeds coins to the colorful, lighted music box and immediately popular vocalists flood the room with their tunes. As if on cue, the Andrew Sisters step forward with their latest, 'Rum and Coca-Cola', or the Sons of the Pioneers take their turn, warbling 'Coool, clear waaater.' At one end of the immense room stands the pool table, waiting for the local young bucks to spar with their talents. A ready cigarette propped over an ear, while the other part of the pack is stored in their loose fitting shirt pockets or rolled in the sleeve of the immaculate white tee shirts. Many of the young men who now share snooker shots, have also shared foxholes; only recently returned from their war duty to resume some unknown destiny.

Soon after age thirteen, I shed the crutches used for my broken ankle, and my father buys Club Paradise. The neighborhood, near the nightclub, is a disintegrating section of Albany. Its multi-cultural and racial mix included mostly Polish, Irish, Black and Italian families. The well-maintained Catholic Church is the only significant building of worth amidst the run-down houses and apartments.

Uncle Joe, who just returned from the Army, forms a partnership with Dad. Uncle is to be the bartender. But Dad soon discovers it is an unwise decision. Uncle Joe, himself, likes to confer with friends about life and problems over a bottle.

I watch and listen as plans unfold; knowing that my life will become more hectic. After school, I take a bus to the club to help. Among my various jobs, I am to tend to my brother, keep the place clean, fold napkins, empty ashtrays and whatever else they find to keep me busy. Naturally, I have to keep up my homework from Blessed Sacrament, and my still bummed-up ankle complicates all.

I'll sure be glad when I can unload this stupid cane. Why is it when Daddy gets an idea we all have to work harder?

Mom is relegated to the kitchen as cook, while Dad sees his role more clearly as *padrone*. In his ostensible, well-dressed suits and groomed carriage, befitting a Las Vegas casino owner, he smokes and wields Cuban cigars like a baton. He declares himself most capable as Club Paradise's ambassador.

Up goes the menu over the bar's cash register; spaghetti and meatballs, veal and peppers, soups and an assortment of sandwiches—not an exotic or complicated assortment, but still requires my mother's intense labor. I'm sure the windowless kitchen, the size of a half bath, with room for solely one person, is meant only for sandwich making. My four-foot-nine inch mother stands on a stool, in high heels, in order to stir the sauces on the stove. Seven days a week. Week after week. Antonietta takes a bus, from our uptown home, to get to the new downtown family venture. I never see her out of the insignificant, claustrophobic room from the moment she arrives until she leaves late at night. Despite the long day, she is consistently and carefully groomed. Her hair is curled a la Bette Davis, fake pearl button earrings are never forgotten, and the makeup is perfectly applied to her youthful skin. Each day Salvatore comes to the kitchen to pass inspection and judgment on his marital employee.

To the left of the barroom is the dining-dance hall, a section of Club Paradise that is twice the size of the bar-area. At least fifty to sixty tables surround the enormous wooden dance floor. The stage dominates the far end, large enough for Xavier Cugat's Orchestra. Old patrons tell Dad, that this used to be a popular and lively nightspot, consistently packed with dancers, musicians and diners. Sal fantasizes ideas of how he will restore its once great name—maybe even sing an Italian song or two to help things along. But we wonder why it lost its glory.

Salvatore hires a somnolent three-piece combo for the first music act. Completely dwarfed by the large platform, they play the same ten lullabies over and over to maybe seven people sitting at tables in the audience, who stare at each other over dishes of spaghetti.

It certainly doesn't look like the nightclubs in those swell Carmen Miranda movies. Maybe Daddy will teach the tango again. Things will be better—I think.

But it's hard to believe that Club Paradise will ever recapture its acclaimed popularity.

The fact that we are only allowed to serve beer and wine adds to our poor business. When Dad applies for a liquor license, he is refused permission to sell the hard stuff. The board, run at the time, by Irish politicians, does not mince words about their dislike of this particular nightclub. With some sleuthing, little by little the reason is revealed. It seems, a few years before, a regrettable disagreement in the bar between a patron and an Irish policeman resulted in the tragic murder of the officer...now we know the rest of the story.

Friends offer opinions on how to promote business.

"Hey Sal, what you need to do is get a good loud polka band. You know there are a lot of those people that live all around here. They love that stuff. Maybe serve some of their food and a lotta good beer. It'll be great!"

My Italian, manic-depressive father swings into high gear. He contacts the Polish church for recommendations on any local and popular musical talent. A six-piece band is hired, complete with accordions, costumes, drums and a singer. We mimeograph and distribute flyers advertising the coming polka band. Our signs are in every shop window and on every telephone pole. Uncle Joe and Dad order extra kegs of draft beer and make sure the ventilation fans work. Dad hires a voluptuous, blond, waitress to serve and encourage interaction with the patrons. I dress the many tables with colorful cloth coverings and napkins. Mom is given a new food list. We all work on the Polish menu.

Saturday night is hot. The beer flows. It's a flaming success. Even the Pastor of the church pops in to check Club Paradise's new thrust. The polka couples ceaselessly twirl the dance floor as the musicians pour their hearts into the ever-popular 'Beer Barrel Polka.' Mom stirs the *Bigos* (cabbage and meat stew) and serves up the *Kielbasa* hot and juicy. At one point, we need to enlist the help of a bouncer to control the brawls and battles of dissenting ethnic joiners. Every evening, my three-year-old brother and I stand near the doorway, wide-eyed, as we watch the intense frenzied dancers circle the dance floor under the revolving mirrored light-ball. Salvatore, in a swanky suit, takes his ambassadorship to an important level as he walks from table to table, his arms and stogied hand waving good-will gestures to the returning patrons. Business is booming!

But one day, Dad does not come home or back to the club. Mom is frantic with worry and I hear her hysterical wail.

"Where is he? Oh my God, what am I going to do? What's going to happen to me? How am I going to take care of this place without help? Where did he go?"

Uncle Joe's sporadic attendance and inability to run the business is less than helpful. I don't understand nor am I encouraged to be in on the context of the disguised discussions between Mother, friends and relatives. Several days go by and still no word from Dad. But soon I pick up more pieces to the puzzle.

Our buxom Polish waitress is also missing.

My thirteen year old, uneducated, sexual mind soon puts a story together.

Oh, my goodness. It sounds like Dad has a girlfriend. Mom thinks it's the waitress. Is he coming back? Does this mean divorce? Gee, what'll happen to us? Wow!

After four days of watching my mother sob and wrench her hands to the heavens, he returns disheveled, unshaven and depressed.

I wonder what happened? Why does he look so bad? Nobody tells me anything. They must think I'm stupid.

The covetous female employee never returns.

Problems increase. We are robbed a couple of times in the early morning hours as we are closing the bar. Rex, our ferocious German Shepherd watchdog, is sound asleep. It's his bedtime. I don't think my family is prepared for all the extraordinary difficulties. I notice the shorter than usual fuse in my folks. Every new day Dad's dreams disintegrate.

Then one night, the way I hear the story, Uncle Joe leaves the bar quite drunk, picks a fight with a black man and as a result my uncle's face is slit open from cheek-bone to chin, leaving his once handsome face with a life-long disfiguring scar.

Business cycles down. We are left with a weak link in the music fare as a couple of members of the band move on to other pursuits. Eventually the Polish musicians disband and we replace them with a country-western quartette. Our two new waitresses wear western-style costumes: satin blouses, fringed short skirts, cowboy boots and hats. Mom learns to make barbecue sauce.

After many flyers and much advertising in the newspaper, customers come from great distances to see the Sons of the Hudson Valley at the new westernized Club Paradise. There is even an amateur night with harmonicas, banjos, guitars and yodelers, but they reveal the limitations of their handlers. The high is temporary. The new novelty all lacks a certain spark. Clients complain of not being able to buy mixed drinks.

The brightness of Club Paradise dwindles.

The Polish people find a new beer and dance hall, and there aren't enough cowboys on the East coast to even form a posse. The back dining room is closed.

Dad is building a trailer from an old trolley bed, and there's talk of selling the club and going to California so he can build houses all year. We're like gypsies, Mom says. What else is in store for us?

Certainly flexibility is an important ingredient in our tealeaves.

I often wonder if all the ghosts who chance to frequent Club Paradise, ever gather over an ale, chomp a pickled pigs foot, maybe even spot

Antonietta in the kitchen standing on the stool in her high heels, as she stirs the newest sauce recipe. And maybe they listen to my once handsome, Uncle Joe joking while pouring their drafts or maybe talk to Salvatore about his newest dreams and maybe they shake a little when they hear the New York Central chug through town on its way to New York City, and maybe they'll even deposit a quarter or two in the jukebox to hear 'der Bingo' sing.

> *Would you like to swing on a star?*
> *Carry moonbeams home in a jar,*
> *And be better off than you are...*

Venera Di Bella Barles

CALIFORNIA BLUES:
GOING WEST ITALIAN STYLE

ALBANY, NEW YORK

World War II is over, and everyone takes to the highways—in search of new lives and so will we.

My dad says it'll probably take a month or two to get there, and we'll see palm trees again, just like Italy, and we'll see Indians, the desert, and movie stars.

Trailers are the big fad in 1946, big beautiful shiny ones like the Spartan and Air Stream. Dad decides to take the eighteen-foot rusty trolley bed that sits on the back part of the property of our first home on Fairlawn Ave, and reshape it into our future. When he finishes building the aluminum, wheeled, cottage, it has a cast iron sink in the front end, a new stove, four Bentwood barroom chairs and a table, salvaged from the sale of Club Paradise. All our clothing, linen, and bedding are piled on top of Dad's precious tools. This is Mom and Dad's bed. Nicky sleeps between them and I have an army cot in a small area between the stove and sink.

Everything is sold. The soft velvety armchair that I curled up in when I needed hugs, the one where I rubbed the nap of the fabric and dreamed while Salvatore and Antonietta battled out life. Even my piano is gone. I can't believe it's gone. I think I will never be able to play on another one since I learned my lessons on this one. It's sold. Sold to another little girl probably. I watch as they lower the beautiful instrument over the side of the upstairs balcony. Everyone is watching the gypsies. The Di Bellas are on the move again. Mom is taking her cream, satin bedspread, the one she uses only when company comes. All our houses have been sold: Fairlawn Avenue, three on Buchanan Street, the duplex on Allen Street, and finally this duplex on Pine Avenue.

My four-year-old brother is leaving his best friend Donny, and I say good-bye to my first year in parochial high school, to Albany, Algebra and all I have known. I have spent reasonably happy early years here, but since I've moved so often I have become a loner. I don't have many close friends to miss or say good-bye. But I am excited to go forward and not look back. As usual, I am an optimist and think my life will be good and plentiful.

Dad's new, green Buick Roadmaster does the heavy work. It shows great bravery, dipping low when the trailer is hitched. Even though I have just turned fourteen, I am thrilled at the prospect of being the navigator and relief driver for my dad. Mom will sit in the back seat as is typical. I never have seen her in the front, she is always too fearful, probably with good reason. Her rosary helps. With this move she leaves her entire family, old friends and security behind. Another Di Bella chapter closes.

Most times, just before dark, we find a trailer park where we can stay the night. Mom makes dinner on the new butane stove. Usually pasta. Sometimes chops or steak. She even tries to make her spice cake in the oven. My cot is pretty hard. Dad smokes a lot and it makes me cough.

As we drive on Route sixty-six, we hear the first strains of cowboy music on the radio, and I know we are truly going west. They play Dad's favorite, The Yellow Rose of Texas. Somewhere along the way, Bobby Troup's new song, 'Get Your Kicks on Route 66' welcomes us, then we hear the wonderful sounds of Mexican brass bands and guitars.

I've never seen such night skies like these, filled with unfamiliar stars. It is all dream-like. The darkness is enveloping, and the quiet, yes the wonderful quiet, is womb-like. We do much of our driving at night. During the day it's magic when the heat ripples in the distance, as if we are coming to an oasis. We stop at the sign that says, 'See the two-headed Snake - Gila Monsters - Reptiles!!' Mom is afraid of snakes and won't get out of the car. Navajo Indians sit by the side of the road with their exquisite wares of jewelry, blankets, and baskets, the lines on their faces like a map to their souls. Most speak only their native tongue. I can't contain my excitement. I feel a special place in my heart for these impressive, gentle, gifted people.

Burma-Shave signs guide our destination. We've been on the road sightseeing for several weeks. Cactus and tumbleweed as far as we can see and the air is pungent with the smell of sage and old hot earth.

It's just like the movies. Just like the movies!

In Oklahoma City, we buy Nicky a western hat, boots, and a new fake gun in a holster. Now he's ready for the Wild West. He imagines he sees cowboys and Indians coming over the hills.

I think I see them too.

Heat waves on the highway continue to race ahead of us; the horizon glimmers like water. I have never felt such hot, dry intense temperatures, 115 degrees in Yuma, Arizona. The family suffers adjusting to the heat. I am light-headed and troubled with nosebleeds. Dad makes us sit on top of a block of ice until we are cooled. More often than not, it is Dad that nurses us. Even our Buick has a burlap bag filled with cool water hanging over the grill. Everything is so different. Each turn brings new thoughts.

I thought living in Italy and all my days before this were unique, now, this is to be our new life. An adventure I will never forget.

SAN DIEGO, CALIFORNIA

I see why my father likes this land; it looks like his native Sicily.

There they are, just like he said. Palm trees. Goodbye, Chestnut trees.

Our new home in San Diego, in a lovely manicured neighborhood, is a thirties' beauty, Spanish style, but made of solid concrete with tile floors throughout. It must be the reason we made such a good buy. It's no wonder insurance salesmen flock to our door. There is a wonderful glassed-in sunroom and although we have no furniture, I sit on a folded blanket on the floor and listen to my opera records on our phonograph player. Jussi Bjorling, the tenor, warbles as I do homework. I absolutely luck out. There is only one room upstairs and to my delight it becomes my very own bedroom. Unfortunately, now Nicky gets to sleep between Mom and Dad, instead of me. But the sweet looking home proves to be a problem. It is cold, musty, and damp. Pictures cannot be hung on the solid walls. Dad cuts down a huge Pepper tree to encourage the sunshine into the house. Maybe it will help with Nick and my bad bouts of bronchial disorders. We live with just a table and four chairs for the whole time we are there. Our silver trailer is parked in the back yard. I can feel the impermanence.

I meet Colleen and her family, the girl who lives across the street, a good, kind group, especially her older brother Buzz. I can only admire him from afar, since he has eyes only for his sweetheart. He can't be bothered with a spoony-eyed young kid. I'm not sure what those weird feelings are. But they don't feel bad.

Dad finds a friend in San Diego who previously moved from Albany with his family. For a while it is heaven to recapture some ties with our past, but a disagreement arises between the men and the friendship ends. Then we meet another family, but Dad stops that quickly before it even starts. Women seem to always follow men with their silly decisions. We are once again alone.

The move is justified as a better area in which to work. Dad can build outdoors year round in this tropical paradise, instead of the hassles attached to the horrific winter storms in the East. We construct two new houses, but not without major problems.

Dad, who believes he knows better than anyone, stubbornly decides he doesn't need to study the California building laws.

"What have you done here, Mr. Di Bella?" the Building Inspector asks. "It looks like you've dug a basement?"

"Thatsa right!"

"I'm afraid you've made a costly mistake. Didn't you check the California Building Code? We don't build houses with basements here on canyons. You know you're not in New York now. You're going to have to fill it in."

"What? I taka the dirt away all by hand. You can'ta build a house with no basament!"

"Too bad. You'll still have to fill it in."

A tough lesson. We all work wearily on that project. The family always seems to labor too hard.

Mother cries daily. She is homesick for her family. I can't console her. The depression spreads to Dad. Soon problems intensify and they argue continuously without resolve. My nightmare intensifies.

The lead ball is suffocating me each night. I dread sleep. Everybody is falling apart. Why did we leave Albany?

Dad becomes more violent with each passing day. Mom suffers most of his physical wrath and I earn my share by intervening. My brother finds comfort in his playmates and I am able to escape part of the home stress since I am occupied with my first public school experience since first grade. Adjustment is not easy. Latin is not offered, so I must replace it with Spanish. I sometimes confuse it with Italian. My first male teacher is in geometry and he gives me hope that I am not a complete imbecile when it comes to mathematics. So far, the only good thing that has come out of this school transfer is that I have left Algebra back with Sister Mary Winifred, who was convinced I was only sparking on part of my brain.

Dad allows me to work and earn money for the family. It is to be my ticket that helps to avoid home issues. I find odd jobs: as a mother's helper with twins, house cleaning, ironing and gardening. But he still manages to keep me quite busy working with him on the houses and gardens. It has always been easy for me to find outside work. Back in Albany, I washed cars and mowed lawns, but I wish I could keep the money I earn. Once in a while I save small change. If I only knew how much this situation, in regard to money, would follow me through my life. I suffer a decline in personal worth in not being able to negotiate for myself, I learn from the best, my mother. I feel the inner rumblings of dissatisfaction and aloneness. I blindly trust my parents to be fair with me.

On the main boulevard, a block from our home, is the Ken Theater where I enter the adult world with my first official job. It changes my life forever. The independence begins to free me and I can see possibilities for my future.

The library, two blocks away, becomes another tool for salvation and backbone. I discover the wondrous power of books, the escape I so desperately need. It fills my world with gifts and adventures. I bury myself in research and stories of the classics. I savor and absorb the variety. Always endeavoring to drown out the shouting isolation. I check out books and bring them home just to see them scattered about the house. "Forever Amber" starts the romantic stirrings within me. I am so drawn into exciting stories of the sea, pirates and romance, that I start writing my first story, a romantic buccaneer tale. I save money and buy a Royal typewriter and attempt my new skill of writing. It fills my fantasies and relieves solitude for a short time. Other than occasional journal keeping, I do not write again until I reach my late fifties.

I am in my second high school and Dad completes and sells the two houses. I am unaware that he is doing well financially; one would not know from the meager offerings in our Spartan home. My concerns are elsewhere. The sick unrest continues in our family.

Soon, I will meet my first love in this fair city. But, it too, will be bittersweet.

California welcomes its new pioneer.

#6 Saying goodbye to Albany. Moving west in Dad's home built trailer. (1946)

#7 Mom, Nick, and me in front of the 1946 Buick

Venera Di Bella Barles

NEVER, is a LONG DAY

"I frutti proibiti sono i piu' dolci." (It.)
"Forbidden fruits are the sweetest."

They all know the rules. Even though they met only a short while ago here in San Diego, originally they came from the same region in Sicily. Every weekend the three families that migrated from New York to California, gather to get further acquainted. A dinner is given to welcome each new family to the group. Mr. and Mrs. Tonino have not appeared for the last two weeks.

It is my family's second Christmas in San Diego and I am fifteen. Our friends' home is festively decorated and laughter is always present. My parents aren't in good spirits about trimming our house these days, so I put up a small tree and wrap gifts for Nicky. The warmth from the greenery and colored packages help the stark barren living room.

Mrs. Bonifaci's dining table is dressed with a lace linen cloth and laden with fruit, cheese, pastries and roasted chestnuts. The air is warm and fragrant. She is a confident woman. Anisette liquore adds sweetness to the dark, rich Espresso.

The discussions are usually centered on the politics of the recent end to the Second World War. They enthusiastically express their thoughts of how Mussolini lost the fight for Italy. Firmly voicing how the war should have really been fought. Then there are words of how best to survive the new post-war society. The women compare their latest skills; delighted on how good it is to finally be able to purchase products that were scarce, and how their move from the East coast is affecting their lives.

The topics flow without much of my attention until someone raises the hottest news of the evening and then I sit stoically listening to the three families discussing the disgrace that the young American-Sicilian Tonino girl has committed towards her family. In the beginning, I don't fully grasp the depth of the intensely, animated, colloquial Italian conversation. But I know it is not good.

"*Dio*, God! How could she dishonor them this way?" Mrs. Bonifaci says.

Mrs. Pistola dismally remarks, "I hear her father has disowned her. What do you think, Mrs. Di Bella?"

"I don't know what to say," my mother answers uneasily, as she moves further back in her chair.

"He won't even allow her mother or brothers to talk to her."

"That's how it should be! *Disgraziata!* Look what she has done!" Mr. Pistola says waving his fist.

"I think the family is hiding with the shame."

Mrs. Silvestri pants, "She's only eighteen. Where did she go? I understand she may have married him."

Oh! They're talking about Emilia! Ohooo. Daddy is very red. Momma looks scared.

"I hear they ran away to marry in another state," Mrs. Pistola says. "It's too bad this had to happen, isn't it, Mr. Di Bella?"

"*Signora*, if a daughter of mine did such a thing," answers my father, as he pounds the table with his palm, "I would disown her too! *Devo ammazzerei!* I would kill her!"

Mom is silent. Her eyes are glazed.

A lump comes into my throat.

Oh God! He would kill me? But, I've always known that. I know the rules.

Mrs. Silvestri waves her handkerchief to fan the emotional heat. "She didn't look like that kind of girl. She always looked so sweet and quiet. I hope she wasn't *incinta!* How could she do such a thing to her dear mother? You have to watch girls so carefully."

Everyone paints the picture of the whys and why nots.

"You know Mr. Tonino, was always strict with her. He never let her date any boys or let her go out with her friends," Mrs. Bonifaci defends. "Maybe a little too strict. I guess he was afraid she would get into trouble. Now look at this—to what happened."

"The real problem is he wasn't tough enough. She's too Americanized!" adds my father.

My heart races as I listen to the unforgiving words.

I knew it! I've always known it! I'll never be able to ask or tell them anything about men or boys.

Of course, at the time, I don't know that in four years I will do the same to my parents. I toss and turn in my bed that night, going over the terrifying statements of each of the elders. It has been two weeks since I met my first love secretly at the theater where I am employed. He is at least twice my age and I am ignorant and smitten. Although I am wise enough not to have physical involvement, emotionally I am doomed. I live each moment in absolute dread of being found out. Guilt begins to form its canker.

Will I be turned out as my friend, Emilia Tonino?

There never is a reason so strong as to be untruthful to my parents, but my needs are changing. Oh how I wish I could approach them for advice and acceptance.

Four years later this judgmental scene returns to me—the day I decide to elope. I try hard to follow the dictates of my father; to show my parents respect, but I am treated as if I were being raised in the small villages of Sicily. Between the traditions of my parent's culture and the Catholic Church, I accumulate enough guilt to rupture my mental stability. I know I must break all ties with my family. I will have to endure the stigma. Possibly to never see them again. After all, I know the rules.

Because I choose my own life, the years that follow my marriage are emotionally painful, reliving daily the injustices I feel I perpetrated upon my family. I had dishonored my mother and father. I married out of my nationality and religion, breaking all the customs and correctness that they so carefully taught me. Of my own choice, I gave up Catholicism. It abandons me as a faithful follower. I am suddenly faced with the decisions I made. But one day I awake to realize the other side of the scenario. I see the damage caused by unfairness that parents impose upon their children.

The losses are staggering on both sides.

LA VITA DOLCE PICCANTE: THE BITTERSWEET LIFE

"Il volto sciolto ed I pensieri stretti." (It.)
"The countenance open, but the thoughts withheld."

LOS ANGELES, CALIFORNIA

We move again. This time to Los Angeles, where the movie stars live. Dad is in his element. He was here in the 1920's, before he met Mother.

I wonder if he ever dreams about his being back in the movies? Maybe he'll see his old friend George Raft?

We plant our eighteen foot silver home in a beat-up trailer park in Alhambra, where we live for one year. No privacy and very cramped. The tenseness is beyond description.

Third high school. Not making friends. Mom never talks to me. Nothing feels permanent. I'm lonely. My optimism is failing. I see nothing ahead. This endless headache is so bad.

Since coming to Los Angeles, my health is in constant turmoil with migraines, distressing chronic aches, and joint pains. These stay with me until later life. I think I am being punished for having loved without permission. I didn't want to leave my first secret *innamorato* in San Diego. The older man I fell in love with, wiser than I, realized the disastrous potential in such a liaison.

We've located some friends, the Guilianos, a large Italian family from Albany. At last some familiar faces. I have hopes that visiting friends will help our sadness. But once more we move.

Fourth high school. It's getting harder and harder. It's so tough to concentrate. My grades are dropping. Migraines. Can't sleep and when I sleep, nightmares. It's all too much.

Dad does not allow me to date or even see boys. He is getting stricter than I could ever imagine. I'm convinced everyone is much smarter than I. My school chums, Laura Guiliano and Zita Swartz, are to my mind, brighter and I know happier. But I tell myself I will do just fine. As soon as I can, I will find work again and take care of my brother and parents. After all, supposedly, they are the ones who truly love me. I pledge to buy a washing machine for my mother. Sadly, I never do. She stands on a stool to reach into the sink to scrub the clothes on a washboard. Pure insanity and so unnecessary, since they can afford to make her life easier. Every penny is for pretense. We must never forget, '*far bella figura*'.

Dad has promised to send me to college to study medicine, but now he harps on how well my friend Laura is doing because when she graduates she is getting a job as a civil servant. He seems to be pushing me to do the same.

Why is he saying this? Doesn't he remember he said I could go to college to be a doctor?

111

But I still trust him. About a year before I graduate, I move one more time to another school, Hollywood High; the fifth and final. Even though I know my grades are average, I am a good, hard-working student. Five high schools do not help. Little by little, my father strongly discourages me from attending medical school. I sense his lack of confidence in me. I am afraid to ask. He confirms my secret fears when I tell him I do not have room in my class schedule for shorthand, office preparation, and typing. He says I will have to find a way to take these subjects because I will need them and besides they are more important than science, psychology and biology for a girl.

I am not going to medical school? Why? Why? Why are you cheating me? Have I disappointed you so?

The shock and blow to my spirit is unbearable. Now, I realize what is really happening. He is grooming my little brother to give him, Salvatore, title and status. Nicky is to study medicine instead.

What is happening to my life? Why should I even care?

HOLLYWOOD, LAND OF FAKE

I walk home from Hollywood High through the movie capital's streets to a duplex I share with my mother, father, seven-year-old brother and our white Persian cat, named Schnitzel. Hollywood in the late 40's is still full of the sparkle and spirit of artists who plant their creativeness in her hands. This place appears more invigorating and alive than some of the other areas I have lived.

Daily, I take a different route to get a fresh view of my new hometown, trying to absorb the habits and mannerisms of the many hopefuls that pass by me. Hoping to gain an understanding of where I might fit in or who I might be. I have suddenly lost my identity.

There are the usual repairs on the houses, forever disrupting the peace. My life always seems so temporary and unfinished. I just want to live in a completed home. Since coming West I notice more physical violence in my Dad towards us, especially Mom. He hit her with the dish of steak and fried potatoes one night. He invariably finds fault with his meal. She doesn't seem to know what to say or do that's correct.

Please Momma! Get it right! You have to learn to get it right!

I know she's afraid to answer the telephone and so am I. It feels as if we are always dodging one person or another for him. If we don't answer the way he says; he loses it. I hate the phone.

Because of the inconsistent living conditions, I lose many opportunities to make and maintain friends. I am forced more and more to turn to my inner self for companionship, building on fantasy and manufacturing an outwardly acceptable life. I establish a persona.

I come upon a stack of true crime detective magazines being discarded in a used bookstore in Hollywood. I read each tale without a break. I become obsessive, at times, with my thirst for these gory, unpleasant stories. I search for explanations in my own chaotic life as I try to understand how different I am from those people who reach their breaking point and dissolve in horrific crimes. I am always looking for answers, even to the yet unknown questions.

By now, I am reasonably attractive and look much older than my seventeen years. I learn early to dress with sophistication in second-hand clothes. It never dawns on me that I might someday walk into a retail store and buy a new dress. Despite two jobs, Dad takes my pay, gives me just enough for bus fare. I am turning into my mother, begging for coins. This is a lifelong issue for me to shake free.

I meet a wonderful girlfriend, Darcy, the only close one since San Diego. Younger than I, yet, we still share good times, books, tennis, and questionable talent. She is the only source of stability in my life. I experience a mounting loss of feelings for my parents. Dad's harsh strictness and Mom's passivity becomes too demanding to bear.

Things drop to a final low point. I sharpen my skills of survival.

HOLLYWOOD EXPOSÉ

Darcy is not considered pretty or talented like her sister. As a matter of fact she is built rather squarely, with flat feet and a well-endowed bent nose. She wears glasses as thick as the bottoms of soda bottles. But beautiful blond corn silk curls, and a giving, trusting smile contrast all of this. Even though I am sixteen and she is fourteen, in many ways we are still childishly able to dream, spending rewarding free time together in close friendship. She seems to genuinely like me and I respect her loyalty. Besides she plays a mean game of tennis.

As I understand it, her family came from England to Hollywood with the hope of getting her younger sister, a ventriloquist, into show business. When I call for her each day to walk to our school, Hollywood High, I watch the same ritual take place. Mr. Maxwell, her father, who works in a downtown Los Angeles bank, backs the Hudson out of the arched Spanish-style carport, and Mrs. Maxwell, Mum, as she is tenderly called, stands on the stucco porch surrounded by palm trees and oleanders, waving and blowing kisses good-bye. Mum, a soft, diminutive, lady, usually receives me with warmth, never neglects to offer me an invitation for tea or hot chocolate, sandwiches, and sweets. I love the genteel way she sets the dining room table with a simple starched linen cloth, and serves me on fine china, as if I am a grown-up guest of real importance. I find the quiet discipline of their home a wonderful departure from my family's chaotic fare.

It is one of those warm lazy days, one of those what-can-we-do-next type of days. We are lying across my bed thumbing through hand-me-down movie and glamour magazines from our aspiring actress neighbor, when our eyes suddenly relate to a new ad. Sanitary pads. It is a picture of a girl in a gossamer dress, running through fields of wildflowers, hair flowing and tossing a straw hat in the air. We daydream of a little fame and think about the obvious look one must have to get onto the pictorial pages of famous publications. Although we are in the two percent who have never dated, still we want to attract our teenage male counterparts. The more we dialogue concerning the picture, the more plausible the idea seems.

We can look like that girl! What should it take? Simple!

Darcy is far ahead of the game with her long golden hair, and even though I am a brunette, my dark flashing eyes are sure to come into use. All we need to do is to make our own dresses. After all, Edith Head, the movie fashion designer, had to start somewhere.

Suddenly I remember the yards of sheer yellow material I bought at the thrift shop to someday make curtains for my room, but heck it's better to do what is needed at the moment for our careers. We have never sewn anything, or for that matter even owned a sewing machine, but progress can't be cursed by stumbling blocks or inadequacies.

Our plan of action is in full swing. We move Joan Crawford's carved Louis XIV coffee table to the side of the living room. Dad recently bought Miss Crawford's suite of furniture from a local auction house. His own stab at character acting in the 1920's only adds to the thrust of my desire. The smell of celebrity is in the air. We spread the gauzy fabric on the Oriental rug along with all the tools of our new craft.

"O.K. Darcy, lie down on this material and I'll draw around you."

She is indulgent and trusts my friendship; good or bad, she usually follows my lead. Darcy puts her body on the fabric, but I realize I am not able to outline her easily, so instead I decide to cut the material around her. All is going splendidly. She is quiet and patient as she listens to my hyper-chattering of how this magnificent plan will change our lives. I am nearly through cutting the two pieces, one for the skirt and another for the blouse. I wield the shears around her arms, reassuring her I will be careful near the armpits. Since I draw no blood I confidently approach the neckline. But suddenly the scissors catch hold of Darcy's curl and before I know it I have snipped it off. A five-inch tube of flaxen locks lays next to her ear. Darcy's eyes search my face for verification of the misdeed.

"Now, don't worry, Dary. It's not too bad. I'll just even it up on the other side."

I must leave my dress designing skills for a few moments. My newfound talent as Hollywood hair stylist makes new demands. Patiently, Darcy sits on a stool while I create a new coiffure.

Within minutes the back of her hair is shoulder length and the sides end up above her ears. Darcy checks the hand mirror with a frozen look of disbelief. Her true-blue friend has butchered her mane. But I am able to solve all this upsetting stuff. I quickly find a headscarf, fold it into a band, and wrap it around her ears hiding the unpopular haircut.

"There!" I smugly say. "No one will ever know. It'll grow by the end of summer. I'll even make you a band to match the new dress," I say, absolving myself of all guilt.

We spend every waking moment hand sewing and completing the matching sets: two full-gathered skirts, two scoop neck peasant blouses with puff sleeves and two headbands. We sew rubber bands into the ends of the armholes, but when we try on the blouses our circulation is quickly cut off. We raid Darcy's mother's sewing basket and find enough elastic from old underpants, slips and pajama bottoms to piece together. We thread them into the waists, sleeves and necklines.

Saturday is a good day to go to Hollywood Boulevard to show off our sophisticated and alluring outfits. The tourists will be out and about and will undoubtedly recognize us as local talent.

Darcy irons our two-piece, actually three with headband, ensemble, then douses on the Evening In Paris, dime-store perfume, don our ballet style shoes and paint our lips with Ponds pale-pink lipstick in a gold dispenser. Lastly, we step into three crinoline petticoats and we are ready to slip into our frocks. To top it all, we manage to find straw hats. We are like the twin girls in the 'Doublemint' commercials. Like twin Scarlet O'Haras. Like twin sanitary napkin starlets. We have stepped out of Tara's halls. To comfort her ego, Darcy removes her thick glasses.

On the boulevard, at Woolworth's food service bar, we treat ourselves to an ice cream sundae, when we are further rewarded by the local color observing our fineries. There she is, the old gal who always sits at the end of the long counter with her heavy Theda Bara eyeliner and green eye shadow; widely arched, red brows. Her bright orange-red lipstick, about a half-inch larger than her actual lips, has bled into the pale-dry wrinkled pancake make-up. The orange hair-dye hasn't been close to her roots for several months. She wears every piece of costume jewelry ever owned. A heavy, cheap perfume surfaces.

"Dahlings, you both look lovely," the nicotine-coated throat bellows.

We recognize her good taste.

As we leave the soda fountain, we pass the daughter of the lady with the orange hair. They are frequently seen walking the boulevard together. In spite of the intensely warm California day, she has on her customary regalia of worn fox furs attached to a bright red, form-fitting jacket. A large brimmed apple green felt hat with Chartreuse veil conceals her left eye. A beauty mark is pasted on the right side of her upper cheek. The makeup is thicker and more exotic than her mother's. One gloved hand holds the other glove while the uncovered hand with it's long red, chipped nails, carries a big purse that totes her rodent-size, wildly yapping, bejeweled dog. He also notices us.

"If we get tired," I tell my innocent friend, "we could take in a movie; 'The Road To Utopia', with Bob Hope and Dorothy Lamour, is showing at the Pantages."

She nods dutifully.

We parade up and down the avenue walking into our favorite shops, but always keeping a keen eye on all our admirers. We near the grand size Pickwicks, my preferred used bookstore, where I find true detective magazines, a secret joy; another place to hide from my family.

As we approach the front door of the shop, Darcy lets out a squeal.

"What's the matter?" I say to my distressed companion.

But I can see. She is standing nearly nude. The elastic has broken in the neckline of her blouse. The top and all its gathers are hanging off her shoulders and back, exposing her powder blue bra to the public. I must save her. I pull her inside the doorway and shove her towards the Anthropology section. The sight is pathetic. But, we are artisans, capable of solving any and all difficulties of our trade.

"Here Dary, let me just tuck the front of the blouse into your brassiere." I calmly say. "I'll just leave the rest of the fabric to drape to the back." I carefully push some of it to conceal the backside of the bra. "There, good as new! It looks like you have a flowing cape and now you have a sweetheart neckline."

She sighs. We leave the bookshop with heads high. All is well. We are achieving stardom. Some producer is sure to be walking this very street looking for such talent. A grandmother stops us to take a photo of her grandchild sandwiched between the two of us. Somewhere in this world is a stunning picture of Darcy and me and a midget child.

We walk towards the movie house.

"Oh, Oh, Darcy, hold on a minute! I felt something snap!"

Yes, you're absolutely right. The elastic in my waistline gives way. Three yards of unraveled yellow gauze replaces all my thinking.

Ah, but relief is coming. Johnnie's Steak House looms ahead. I hold the front of my skirt and quickly advance, pulling Darcy once again into a doorway.

"Dary, hold this." I ask my twin to walk behind me and hold up the untamed material. We resemble a vaudeville act moving in unison across a stage, smiling at everyone as we closely move past tables towards the back bathroom. Our underwear is going to have to pull heavy duty. I push the top of the skirt fabric inside my underpants and hope the undergarment can handle the load.

By this time, Darcy replaces her glasses; finally seeing the reality of our appearance. It is going to take some serious coordination, on our part, to walk the three miles to our homes. As we walk past Woolworth's, the Theda Bara girls are heading out the door. They repeat their praises. But this time, senior Madame Theda remarks to Darcy, "Well dahling, I didn't notice before the lovely cape on the back of your dress."

Then she looks at me, "And oh my dahling, what an unusual drape to your skirt."

MAKE BELIEVE

It has been three years since we left Mom's family and our friends. Dad plans for us to drive back to see them during our summer vacation. Naturally, my father buys himself a new 1949 Buick. His needs are usually met even as the family goes without. The refrigerator never has extra food, except when we have company. Everything is for show.

From the very beginning the journey is bad and tense. Even my parents doing the customary sign of the cross does little to forestall the ill-fated events. A disastrous storm in Flagstaff, Arizona is one of our first encounters. We are caught in the scariest outburst of weather. A tornado propels projectiles of lumber from trucks; we dodge debris and flying chickens, without use of wings. But, we can't avoid the hailstones, the size of goose eggs, pummeling Sal Di Bella's pride and joy, the new cream-colored Buick with the extravagant hood ornament. The off-white car is beaten to a pulp. Dents everywhere. Even though we hold maps against the windshield, it is still knocked out. We are scared and shaken. Mom's rosary wears thin. We're delayed a week or more, for repairs.

We continue towards Albany, but of course, the stress filled problems gather frequency, and with my own ongoing migraines, I have a full time job as the family pacifier. The least little thing sets my exceptionally, nervous father off. Most of the trip he continues to bellow at Mom, nearly always ending with her being bashed. My intervention usually exacerbates the argument.

Why can't I stop them? Nicky is so afraid. Why is there so much unhappiness in this family? I'm so mixed up with all the miserable problems. Oh this head.

As we drive in the vicinity of Monticello, Jefferson's Memorial, I lose my ability to stay silent any longer. I am sitting next to my father in the front passenger seat. I am about to cross the line for the first time.

"God, Dad why can't you stop this? I can't stand anymore! Why can't you be civilized?"

It is like I addressed a volcano. He is completely intolerant of my criticism, and of my raised voice. At that point he lands a hard blow to my head with his right fist. His anger escalates as he drives, continuing to slap my face and pull at my hair. He is utterly out of control. I become unhinged; I need desperately to leave. The car rolls to a stop for a red light, and I open the door and jump. I run back up the road and head into the woods, towards a small house. Frantic, I knock at the door and plead with a frightened old lady to hide me from my angry father. I have stopped thinking. I am in shock. Somehow, I am allowed to hide behind the forced Samaritan's sofa, but I can hear his footsteps come up the porch. I know God has provided me with a tool sometimes given to trauma victims, amnesia. My complete memory of this horrible time is, thankfully dim. He pulls me from the house and among the trees I receive, at the age of seventeen, the worst beating of my life. I don't remember anything until I reach Albany. Mother does not speak to my anguish. She has her own upsets.

I will never love my father the same. I will always continue to show him fake respect, but it will be just a matter of time when I will leave this family. Survival has new meaning.

But we aren't through with this unforgettable trip. There continues to be tenseness. Little is said between my father, mother and I. My small brother, as usual, is witness to the barbaric and hateful moods. At seven, he has all ready formed his emotional cocoon. We reach Albany and no one will know of our discords. We all know how to make believe, how to carry off the polite, genteel agenda.

The last three years have aged my knowing eyes. They record new understandings of how my family and relatives interact. My innocence is gone. Love is changing. I see all is different. I see my fading grandparents, old age demanding their attention; they don't speak of dreams any longer. I see my uncles, past their peaks, resigned to the level of their achievements. I see how my aunt, Mom's only sister, and her three young children struggle to make a mark and to make sense in their harsh surroundings. Like my mother, Aunt Felicia makes harsh adjustments, to a turbulent marriage, always protecting the offender of peace. This will be my last sight of many of them.

On our return to the West coast, we stop for a few days at a small Eastern town, to visit a hearty, pleasant and normal Italian family. No make believe, just refinement, softness, honest love and encouragement for each other.

Why, why, why, did we miss out on normality and happiness? Can't I ever get rid of this damn nightmare? This lead ball is getting larger and heavier. Always suffocating. It is this family that suffocates.

We say our good-byes to a wonderful break, and head for California. School will soon start.

Mom, Nicky and his new kitten are in the back seat of the Buick and once again, I am in the front passenger seat, next to Dad. We are in better spirits, after our good visit with the Grassos. Typically Father drives fifteen to twenty miles over any speed limit, and today is no different. The thirty mile limit stretches to forty-five or better. On the outskirts of the town, we near the brink of a steep hill, when I see a Cadillac convertible make a swift left turn in front of us. Dad quickly applies the brakes but cannot stop. In one lightning moment we plow full force into the side of the car. The impact sends our Buick in several spins. The smell of burnt rubber sears my senses. It is an eternity before we come to a halt, facing the opposite direction. I am to spend years with this vision in dreams and panics. Our car looks like an accordion and I am wedged in my seat, with the door caved into my shoulder and head. Although we are badly bruised, thankfully we escape major injuries. My brother, unhurt, and his new kitten are thrown over the seat onto my lap. The large steering wheel has slammed my dad in the abdomen. Mom fares the best, just distraught beyond belief and utterly hysterical. Miraculously, none of the four middle-age people riding in the convertible are injured. The police find them all drunk, with open liquor bottles in the car. The irony of this terrible disaster is that we have hit, with freakish coincidence, an executive of *our* insurance company!

At this point Salvatore loses all rationality of himself. His behavior is worse than I could ever imagine. Instead of returning to our friends, we stay in the next small town until our car is repaired. He rents an odd room, with an open ceiling, that is part of a warehouse. It has one full bed and an old dresser and a couple of straight chairs. I can't even remember where the bathroom was. For some unknown reason, he keeps us virtual prisoners. Each day he locks us in and we never know when and if he will come back to bring us food. I never truly understand his anger and dementia with us.

Maybe he's afraid I will run. I can't stand this anymore. Why doesn't this all end?

All I know is that it has been an outlandish summer of terrifying events. For two weeks we haven't a clue where he goes each night and day. Mom, in a zombie-like state, cries incessantly, and as usual is unable to comfort Nicky and me. I refuse to be solicitous to my father as in the past. I am fearful of what lies ahead of us. I stay out of his way. Nicky's kitten disappears. My brother and I will be late getting back to school.

In Hollywood High, my humor develops into a usable medium, and offers a place to test the skills. Friends respond well to my laughter-producing wit and performances. I even find a method to throw people off track from knowing me better. I continue to establish a separate and secret life. I no longer feel important to my family. I refuse to tell the outside world the truth on the subject of my parents and my home life. Instead I tell a tale.

I trump up a story when asked about my family of why I don't attend various functions. I tell them that I am a refugee from the war and that my parents are lost somewhere in Europe. When asked if I have injuries, my response is only some shrapnel in my hand, pointing to a scar on the edge of my wrist, where in fact, a large wart was removed. The yarn adds convenient drama and uniqueness. I am beginning to believe it. Added to the migraine headaches that plague me daily, now, I have develop psychosomatic pains in my right hand and arm. The lot gives credence to the strength of these lies. I keep the wolf from the door, the best I know how. I have no one to turn to for guidance for any part of my life. Friends are kept at a distance. The family has their own worries and stresses. I am expected to cope.

Make believe.

I distract everyone with humor. From this point on, I take care not to give of my feelings so freely, or so quickly. But strangely I remain the optimist. I must endure and persevere. I know this early in life.

Still I need. But how do I get without injury to my heart? I remember the formula that works well in the family. Be a peacemaker. Solve the problems of others. Be their confidant. There is power in these thoughts. I learn and improve the skill to calm my family when they dissolve into frenzy. It is a revelation to note how resourceful my psyche is with adjustments. I am a master at my craft.

Make believe.

Make believe I have great shoes, always keep them polished, even though there is cardboard to cover the half-dollar sized hole in the sole. Make believe I have a full and happy life. Keep people laughing. Distract them. Draw them out, then they won't ask about me. Make believe. Tell school friends that I am too busy to go to dances, after-school functions, field trips, or dates. Make believe I have a normal home life.

Starvation comes in many forms. Some of the residue is not always understood until the spirit has been fiercely chewed. I am slowly starving. I am stripped of independence and initiative to determine the smallest of my needs. I can't even recognize the signs of deprivation. After all, my mother is my model, a woman who long ago neglected her own being and struggle.

My parents continue to quarrel. Even though Nicky is worried, I see he has his own great strength and tends towards pacifism. When other children take advantage of him, Dad loses patience and bullies Nick to fight back, demanding behavior from him, that is not his nature. I feel compelled to intervene and shield him from harm. We are good pals and I need his closeness. He is the only steady bright genuine spot in my life. He gives me reason to keep going. The best gift my parents ever gave me.

The Fine Arts Department is an important part of Hollywood High, with numerous rising actors, dancers, and performers. Many students, from wealthy families, can afford outside tutoring. The performances and presentations in our auditorium to the public, by our young artists, are usually sold out.

I join a ballet class at Hollywood High, taught by a strict, eccentric, old ballerina with flowing hands and veils. Sensing my sincerity, she encourages me and is patient with my dance. The professor proposes an ethnic variety dance program, and announces she would like me to lead and teach some Italian dances. I'm outrageous in my attempts at make believe, and I surprise myself when I tell her I can probably handle the job. I dare not let on my lack of expertise. I am to be in charge of this portion of the show. I gather a group of ten girls and teach them the Tarantella and Quadrille, in ballet form. How will I tell them I really don't know how to do any of these dances?

Make believe.

I strike a friendship with a delightful dancer who lives with her bohemian, character-actor parents. I explain my plan and she agrees to be in my troupe. Together we devise the dance routines, choose the music, and make the costumes. For weeks before classes start, Marina and I practice each morning. We work out every detail, going over and over the parts with the students. The dancers are outfitted with colorful waist girdles, tambourines, streamers, and flutes. *Signorina* Di Bella and the Italian ballet are ready for their debut.

Venera Di Bella Barles

The day arrives. I will have to do my best acting yet. Can I really fool a whole audience? Will I be laughed off the stage and be seen as a fraud? But I know my heart is honest and giving.

I peek from behind the curtain and see the seats filled in the auditorium.

My name is printed on the brochure, I cannot back out. I cannot let my friends down because of my fears. That nightmare woke me last night.

The music starts.

Make believe.

I begin to dance.
Suddenly my legs are released from their fearful bonds, and as if I had known these melodies and steps all my life, replace my dance with a sense of confidence and wanting to give to my audience.

The "Italian Fantasy" is a success. The patrons give us a standing ovation, and I am singled out for my innovative achievements. Not since I was a young child do I experience public tears. I manage to prove some vital worth to myself. I did not tell my parents of this special event. I am learning to sustain without familial support.

Make believe is becoming real.

Graduation day is almost here and I do not know what I am to do with my life. I hear friends chattering about their goals and aspirations and of parties and gifts. Once again I feel lost and dispirited. My spirit is not there. I have an overwhelming sensation of defeat that I can't shake.

Maybe I could take some classes at City College. Ballet? I am always interested in the arts, maybe piano, music classes, or even psychology.

Every afternoon I am on a school work/training program, working for a miserly dentist. At first it feels good as I wear the nurse's uniform and learn more about the profession. Momentarily I even dream that I could be a dental assistant. Dad complains that I do not make enough money. But then all is solved for me. He goads me into asking my employer, whom my father scarcely knows, to co-sign a financial note. I am dumbfounded and embarrassed at the whole matter. I quit the job. The humiliation is too great.

Then wonders of wonders. Dad allows me to go to the prom; the first and only school party or dance I ever attend. I wear the same uninspiring, peach, arnel, gown Mom and I bought at a thrift shop for the singing recital of the school Orchesis Club.

The evening arrives and my fellow students arranged to pick me up. Unfortunately a young man comes to the door to fetch me. When Dad sees the boy at the door, he explodes, and in full view of all, slaps me with both hands. The teenagers waiting in the car stare at us with slack jaws. I break away and my father comes after me with a vengeance. I run up the stairs with my father in hot pursuit. It puts an end to my big social event and prom night. I am glad I do not see my schoolmates any longer. My embarrassment is profound.

Salvatore's loving, fatherly hands will never beat me again.

8 Venera and the "Italian Fantasy" dance troupe at Hollywood High School. (1949)

ANATOMY of a PEACEMAKER

I am a pawn in my parents' stormy marriage, and I am learning the power of transaction. At a surprisingly early age I umpire between my weak, inadequate mother and my overbearing volatile father.

"Venera, go ask your father when he wants to eat."

"What's the matter, Momma? Are you and Daddy fighting again?"

I get anxious when I hear them. Immediately I have that old feeling like the caning in the bottom of my chair is about to break.

I can see her body language. She sends me whenever she's afraid and doesn't want to talk to him.

"Daddy! Momma wants to know when you want to eat?"

"I'll tell her when I'm god damn ready!"

I wish Momma wouldn't ask me to go to Daddy when he's upset. All I do is go back and forth. Then he yells at me.

"Momma. Daddy sounds pretty mad. I don't think you'd better bother him right now."

"Too bad. I don't care. He can go to hell."

"Momma, don't talk like that. He's awful upset! You know what will happen. Please Momma, try real hard not to bother Daddy."

"Oh see, you're just like him. You're always sticking up for him!"

She doesn't listen to my words. It seems easy for her to blame me. It is as if we are enemies. Each day I wait for Dad to come home from work and then, immobilized, I listen to the build-up of trouble. It can be anything.

"Sal, the lawyer called, Momma says."

"What did you tell him?"

I can hear and feel the escalation of their voices; Father calls her names.

No matter what the answer is to a situation, she doesn't seem to know how to do it right.

Mommy's crying. Daddy wants me to go to the bedroom and ask her if she wants to go to the movies. He's not mad anymore. Sometimes she says, "Go away, Venera!" But I know she'll make-up with Daddy if I try hard.

I watch the fabric of the family unravel. Always, always at mealtimes. Food hits my belly like a stone.

When I am a little girl I stand frozen between them as he shouts at the highest pitch he can muster. If I give a reaction to the terrifying argument, by attempting to intercede or plead for them to stop, I am smacked away.

For as long as I can remember I am unable to stop my need to intervene. My anxieties are never comforted or understood. Outside our home no one knows our picture.

Even in my early life I am aware and can see how little authority Mother has to defend herself. And of course then, how can she protect me? She does not. Daily the violence grows as if self-fed. Anything jars the family from its peace. Each day I detest seeing my parents together. I begin to believe our family is normal in their actions. It is only when I am in my friend's homes and see how love is handled there, do I then understand the sickness in mine.

"Ann, get the phone!"

"I can't Sal! I don't want to lie."
"I said, get the phone! Tell him I give him money next week!"

Oh, oh! It's going to start. That stupid phone always makes everybody mad. Why doesn't Momma listen so he doesn't yell?

I, too, fear the ringing phone. It typically uncovers bad news. I make myself scarce when I am little. But as I become older it is harder to dodge my father with his demanding falsehoods, which typically is about money. I hate being responsible for any agonies. Until I am a mature woman I detest phones, and invariably, I mess up messages with my inability to think clearly. It takes a miserably long time to overcome this crippling feature of my personality.

With time, I become my father's favorite. What a clever girl I am, aligning myself with the lion's tail. Unconsciously I make it my business to understand his needs, using humor, guile and charm. When I can, I negotiate for my mother's needs. My father recognizes my efforts. I feel an unspoken praise and a potent sense that I am keeping the sick marriage together. What cunning I wield.

When I am ten years of age, I am placed in charge of my new baby brother. That means I will need to guard him also. The surrogate mother role suits me fine. Another notch for peace at any price.

I am gaining power and identification.

Dad thinks I'm strong. I can do what Momma can't do.

I become good at the game. Find those with broken-wings and save them. Negotiate for them. Rescue them. Little do I know the damage this behavior holds for me in later life.

Things change dramatically when we move to California. The drama and beatings are much more intense. I daydream that Mother will suddenly be willing to take us away from the dreaded fears. But she seems incapable of taking care of herself, let alone us. At times I wish for my father's death. In my early teens I am good at deflecting some of the undesirable set-tos, but as I reach my middle teens I realize I am not going to make a difference in their lives. I can see my own life being eaten away if I stay. I feel worn by their battles and now I have my own to face. I withdraw emotionally and pretend caring for my parents' welfare. I do not confide in them for any of my personal problems or anxieties. My only concern now is for my young brother. I do not trust his ability to fend for himself in the wake of their insanity.

Most of the physical attacks, by my father, to my mother and me, are quick stinging slaps to the head and face. Thankfully, there are not knock-down-drag-outs too often. I am eighteen when I last witness an assault on Mom. It is so dramatic that I have dreams of fright for years after.

I return home at one-thirty this one morning, from my job at the movie theater near Hollywood. Nicky, my eight-year old brother, who usually wakes to greet me, tells me that Dad has been upset with Mother most of the day.

"Momma's been crying a lot, Venera. I'm scared. I didn't know what to do."

How well I know this feeling. There is no escape for us, as children. At least I am older; I can get away more often.

"I know, Nicky. I'm here now don't worry. If you get frightened just come get me. O.K.?"

In the middle of the night I hear screams coming from downstairs in the living room. I jump from my bed and see my brother standing motionless at the top of the stairs.

"Nicky, take my bed pillows. I want you to sit in my bedroom closet and cover your ears. Don't come out until I get you. Do you hear, me? Nicky, are you listening to me?"

He's fogging out. He can't hear me. He does this every time there's trouble.

His survival skills have kicked in.

I rush down the stairs to see Dad brutally knocking Mother about. He grabs her metal hair curlers and pulls them from her head and with it a clump of hair is yanked out near her ear. He picks her up bodily and flings her like a rag doll against the wall. I stand frozen in disbelief. I recover and run to grab his arms. His strength is super-human. I can't stop him.

"Please, Dad! Stop!" I plead. "You'll kill her! Stop!"

With rage so blind, he pushes her towards the front door. My adrenaline flows as I try to mediate. But in spite of my strength he puts her outside in the cold night air. I watch exhausted and defeated as she stands on the front doorstep in her night-slip and bare feet, shaking and whimpering like an abused animal.

Why? Why? Why? Why are they like this? Our lives are constantly turned upside down. I can't concentrate on school or work. He's crazy. When is she going to wake up? I don't know what to do!

He threatens me if I let her back into the house. His wildness is teaching her a lesson.

I have failed my mother. There is so much anguish in my powerlessness. Add to this my aloneness and apprehensions. It all brings me great hopelessness. The terrors escalate to new heights and remain there through most of their marriage.

I can't stand anymore. I can't help.

9 Mother, Father and the Holy Ghost (1930's)

Venera Di Bella Barles

To LOVE or NOT to LOVE

"Amor regge senza legge."(It.)
"Love rules without rules."

I dream of love.

But what do I know of love? I learn it can be taken away. I learn it can be given to someone else. I learn it can't last long. I learn there's not much of it.

Mother doesn't like to share with me; too absorbed with her own problems, frequently replacing her loving arms with anger, jealousy, and resentment. I often approach, only to be sent away. I do not trust her. When I am young, I feel admiration and affection from my father, but as I grow older I realize that his devotion is based on control, self-interest and demands.

I am unable to discuss anything intimate with my parents, especially Mother.

I recall a painful day in the latter part of my ninth year when I frantically run to Mother. My menses has begun.

"Momma, Momma!" I run into the house frantically calling her. "I must have hurt myself! I was just swinging with Betty Ann and I have blood all over me and my pants!"

What's wrong with me? I don't like blood. Am I going to bleed to death?

"Oh God!" she cries, wrenching her hands. "Wait 'til I tell your father!" She walks to her dresser and removes a cloth from a drawer and angrily tosses it to me. "Go wash yourself and put this diaper on. Here are the pins."

"But, Momma how should I put this on? Do you mean like a baby? Why are you so mad at me, Momma? Did I do something wrong? I'm sorry for getting blood on my underpants." She does not speak, but I feel the annoyance. "What did I do? Why are you going to tell, Daddy? Is he going to yell at me?"

"You're a woman now! That's all I have to say, do you hear? You can't play anymore!"

What did I do wrong? She's so mad. I feel funny. Embarrassed. What does she mean 'I'm a woman'?

Mother's hostile and bitter reaction stuns me. Not only does she neglect to explain the event, but fails to tell me it will occur again and that it happens naturally to girls and women. I feel defective when it appears each month. A few months later, my aunt realizes what is happening and she explains and comforts my fears. As a girl, I never understand Mom's unkindness towards me. She teaches by name-calling. Her favorite: *bruta putana*, ugly tramp. For as long as I live, I will remember her voice and hear the eternal refrain. Somehow, my father's harsh hand never does as much damage as my mother's toxic mouth.

"I pity the man who gets you."

What does she mean? Why does she hate me? I never seem to do anything right for her. She always says I'm dirty!

I work harder to please.

139

I am expected to act adult and I appear so much older than my actual years, but I'm not allowed to wear makeup or lipstick until I'm seventeen. As a child, I pretend the fairy tales of my day, as do most girls. At a later age, when I see romantic movies, I begin to daydream my role as the heroine.

How does one really learn of love? The only understanding I have, other than my family, comes from novels and movies, a false picture of reality.

At age fourteen, just after we arrive in San Diego, I clean house for a lady, and while dusting her vanity I pick up each of the perfume flasks to smell the glass stoppers. I'm fascinated by the collection of lovely delicate bottles. I have only seen one inexpensive dime store blue bottle on Mother's bureau.

"They smell good don't they, Venera?" my employer says.

I'm embarrassed to have been caught.

"You haven't done anything wrong. Really. Would you like this partially used bottle of White Shoulders cologne?"

I'm overjoyed and can't believe my luck. I use it sparingly. The special feeling lingers in my mind long after the delicate scent fades. Even now, when I capture that fragrance in the air, I'm immediately drawn to that day, in Mrs. Connelly's home. I begin to think more of how I look and smell, but I need to be cautious around Mother. She resents if I appear too grownup.

How can it be that she doesn't comprehend how her words are like blades to my heart?

"What are you trying to do?" she says one day as I am grooming myself. "Steal my husband?"

Does she mean my own father? My father? This is crazy! How can she think such a thing?

Then, wonder of wonders, Dad allows me to go to the State Fair for a few days with my girlfriend, Colleen. After a long bus ride from San Diego to Sacramento, we are to stay with her sister's family. On our visit, Colleen meets with different boyfriends and I must sit next to the front passenger door of their car, while she sits in the middle cuddling and smooching with her beau. I feel trapped in the cooing transactions. I feel so out of place. I burn with embarrassment and envy.

This will never happen to me. No one will ever want to kiss me. They're laughing at me because I don't have a boyfriend.

THE FAMILY MAN

At fifteen, I step into the adult world.

I find my first meaningful employment in a local foreign movie house, a block from my home. The owner, Mr. Brennan, is also the manager and besides the projectionist, I am the only other person working there. I am hired to cover all bases: sell tickets, candy, popcorn and usher. Mr. Brennan seems nice; a married family man with five grown daughters. But not too long after I start, he corners me in his office, paws at my clothes, and plants my first kiss. Astonished and confused I push him away. I've never been kissed on the lips by a man, or for that matter anyone that I can recall. My head fills with questions.

Why is he doing this? He's married. Does he love me? If I push him away will I lose my first job? I feel dirty.

Mr. Brennan gets the message swiftly to leave me alone, but I can never tell my parents what happens. It doesn't help that I look older. Oh, yes, I think I'm sophisticated and capable of handling most situations, but I lack knowledge in sexual matters. We do not discuss these subjects in my home. I learn only through subtle non-verbal messages and the make-believe world of movies.

FRENCH CONNECTION

Periodically, a French language professor at the State University, takes his class to the French films at the theater. The tall, dark, Adonis with the mythical physique captures my imagination. Each time he approaches the admission booth, he looks at me, without words, as I give him the tickets. His hand brushes against mine and a sudden flush and chill moves along my spine. Each time I see him, my heart races. I wish for more French films.

One evening as I walk up the aisle of the theater, about to go through the velvet curtain, I collide into the arms of the 'tall, dark stranger.' His mysterious sable eyes hold mine. There is a faint aroma of orange blossoms, '4711' Eau de Cologne, sears my senses. It seems an eternity until he releases me. We are alone in the small lobby. My discomfort produces a befuddled apology.

"Oh, oh, I'm so sorry!" I say.

He softly and slowly whispers, "I'm not. I've watched you for weeks."

Heart, please do not beat so loud! What is this strange eruption pulsing through me? This is what I feel when I read my novels.

We speak for a few minutes, but I hear nothing.

"When you're finished with work, may I take you home?"

Oh. This feels so very good—but I'm afraid. I can't think. Should I refuse? I must not let him know that I can't handle myself.

"I guess it will be O.K., but I only live up the block."

When I meet him at his automoble, I tell him he will need to drop me off before I reach my house because I fear my father. He parks under the dark of trees. We sit in the car and fill the air with small talk. His mind is, of course, more cultivated than the boys who are my peers. I know I can't back out. After all, I am all grown up! Most all of my youth, I make believe that I have my act together.

I look ahead. He looks ahead. He asks about my interests. I tell him I love opera, reading, writing, tennis and that I intend to study medicine. He is kind, and soft-spoken and complimentary.

"You should do fine as a med student. You have a good mind."

I've never talked to anyone like this. No one has ever asked about me. I can't believe I'm telling him so much. He likes me.

Each night under the large shade tree, within sight of my house, we sit and talk in the muskiness of his sedan. After a couple of weeks, a special evening arrives. We quietly conversed in the night-dark, with only the pale light shadows from the street lamp. Suddenly he stops speaking and his hand slowly reaches out and touches the side of my cheek and then the back of his fingertips moves down to my left breast. I am going to die. But I will not. It is all very good. He slowly leans over and gently kisses me. I think I already know all the wonderful sensations of life, but none compares to this kiss and these moments. He's aware of my inexperience.

"You've never been kissed before have you?"

"Well, yes I have. Once quickly," I say as I try to mask my abashment.

"Are you entering college this semester?"

"Oh no, I'm not old enough."

"You aren't? How old are you, Venera?"

"Fifteen." I say, timidly.

"No. Fifteen? I thought you were around twenty-two!" he moves back away from me. "I could get into a great deal of trouble with you."

I'm too young - he's too old? No. No. No. Don't move away.

He writes poems and gives me a book of love, 'The Rubaiyat', and as he holds me in his arms he tells me to educate myself about sex. I am mildly embarrassed when he lists some books for me to read. Each day I pine for his nurturing presence and loving arms. And then one day, he takes me to his home, plays some wonderful opera, and while he holds me close, he reveals he's married.

Can I be this dumb and blind not to have known? Good-bye, good-bye sweet Joseph.

I never imagine such melancholia. I now understand the meaning of a bleeding heart. The tears flow into my pillow night after night. I am alone once more and unable to share this important first moment with family or friends.

Why am I in such pain? I can't stand this sadness. Will I ever love again or be loved?

Two years pass. I think often of Joseph.

My family and I move from San Diego to Los Angeles. And after living like gypsies for a year in the small trailer, Dad buys two more houses. We again live amidst the remodeling and chaos. Eventually we settle, in yet another duplex, in Hollywood. Seventeen seems grown-up, but an opportunity to appreciate or meet the opposite sex is never part of my up bringing. I just assume my father won't let me date. I know Mom has no say in this issue. Even though I pretend non-interest, I crave the attention men show me, at times making foolish choices to nourish the void. Although I don't understand the sport of male and female interactions, I comprehend the protection of virginity. My greenness surfaces at the most inopportune time.

HOLLYWOOD BUSINESS MAN

I am dressed quite smartly, in my second hand clothes, this summer afternoon as I walk on Hollywood Boulevard towards my home near Santa Monica Boulevard, when a well-groomed, older man falls in step beside me. I blush when he asks if I mind. His flirtations are appealing. There it is again, that wonderful sensation of being complimented and flattered. As we stroll, he questions who I am, and I return the queries.

"You look Italian, are you?" he asks.

"Yes," I tell him.

"That's great! So am I. I'm out on business from Chicago. As a matter of fact this hotel we're coming to is where I'm staying." He points upward to his room.

The answer gives me further assurance.

"I'd really like to talk to you more. Will you let me buy you some lunch? There's a good restaurant in the hotel."

Once again my heart quickens, and heat rivers through my body. My palms and feet are moist with apprehension. I cannot deny the thrill of being asked and treated as a grown woman.

He looks smooth and sophisticated. He looks like Dad.
I presume a sense of safety. A fox is always well dressed.

"I suppose that'll be all right," hesitating a moment, I reply in my most confident acting voice.

I can't let on that I have had limited experience with fine restaurants, and less with men. I am careful not to reveal my lack of refinement. It is strange sitting with a man in public.

"What would you like? Order anything. What did you say your name was?"

I look at the menu and immediately am overwhelmed with the prices and choices.

I should be careful not to spend too much of his money. I wish I were smarter.

"Venera, but you can call me Vinny. Would you mind ordering for me? I'm not too sure of what to pick."

"How about a nice shrimp cocktail before our entree?"

A cocktail? Oh oh!

When the course arrives, I am slightly embarrassed that it is food instead of an alcoholic beverage. We have a good laugh and light-hearted conversation, over the fine lunch. He finds out more about me than I do about him. I am pleased at how warm and attentive he is. It feels good to have a male friend.

Our lunch is finished and he asks if he can walk me part way to my home.

"Come up with me to my room while I change my jacket. I want to get into a sport coat. I'll just be a second."

"Well, I guess it will be O.K." Again I trust, blinded by flatteries and naivety.

He goes into the bathroom and when he comes out he is still in his shirt and tie, but without his trousers. I try not to appear shocked as I avert my gaze. It doesn't take long for him to let me know what he has in mind. Seconds later I am in his forceful embrace with my lipstick being smeared by kisses. He demands payment. I push him away tearfully.

"What's the problem?" he asks.

"I, I, I'm so sorry, but I've never done anything like this before."

I can't do what he believes I am prepared to do. He shakes me angrily.

How could I have been so stupid? He's really mad. He sounds like Dad.

"What the hell is the matter with you? Don't you know you shouldn't play such grown-up games! You can get into a hellava' lot of trouble by taking such chances."

Mother's words ring in my ears.

Bruta Putana.

The escape of work and the opportunities it gives me to know people, helps take away the pain of failure. I am in twelfth grade, juggling two jobs, and I've stopped contemplating a future in medicine. A school work-program offers me an opportunity as a dental assistant in training. Each evening, I am a cashier and usher at a movie house in West Los Angeles. I often do not return home before one-thirty in the morning. Dad permits the schedule, maybe because I turn over all my money to him.

The single-post dental office feeds my ego with the variety of duties and responsibilities. Along with attending patients, I do the full office spectrum, including accounting. At first I feel proud and fool myself into thinking I am part of the medical profession. I believe because the dentist is Italian he will be fair, but he is miserly with my salary, taking advantage of my inexperience. I hate each time he calls me a peasant in front of patients.

Do I really look so bad? Does he say that because I'm not smart? How long will it take for me to feel like my own person? How long to feel important?

I work hard most of the day at difficult tasks, but he pays me only for time spent with patients.

How will I tell Dad he's not paying me right? He's going to be mad. I'm so stupid.

When I give Dad my wages he then gives me just enough for bus fare. When it comes to money Mother and I are treated as children.

Men have so much power. Why? Why are women so dumb?

During the hours after I complete my office chores and wait for the next patient, I door-knock in the neighborhood to find odd housekeeping jobs to supplement my salary.

How will I ever get ahead and live a life of my own without my own money? Why is everything so hard? Mom and Dad don't seem to care about my life. But at least when I'm at work I'm away from the crazy house.

The mental flight works for a while.

MR. BARLES, THE PATIENT

One day in the summer of 1949, a patient comes to the dental office; friendly, handsome, well built, nattily dressed, well groomed, a twinkle in his blue eyes and the most beautiful wavy, sand colored hair I'd ever seen. We make our typical patient-assistant small talk as I sit him in the dental chair and place a cloth about his neck. The doctor checks his tooth for repair of a broken crown. Mr. Barles is a good patient, a bit of a flirt, but I am getting used to having some of the men give me spoony glances while their mouths are held open. When the doctor leaves the room Mr. Barles cheekily inquires if I would go out with him (little do I know his girlfriend sits in the waiting room).

"It's really nice of you to ask, but my father is pretty strict. He won't let me date."

Why did I tell him that? Damn my luck! I wish I could get to know him better.

After a couple of visits and a little more flirting, Mr. Barles gets his new crown, but he doesn't ask me out again.

Much happens this last year of school; a foul summer is spent with my folks on a trip to the East coast. I mature ten years. While working at the Fairfax Theater, I learn about cultures and the wonderful differences in people. I continue to decline dating offers from several interesting young men. I am flattered when they sometimes ride the trolley part-way home with me, but I'm astonished when one man whom I sell weekly movie tickets to pursues me and asks me to marry him.

I can't understand why he would ask me that. I don't even know who he is and certainly he doesn't know anything about me. There are so many decisions. Everything and everyone is so enticing. I wish they would understand all I want is to be liked.

HONORABLE FRIENDS

Dr. Ferra, the dentist, plays golf on a regular basis with two close homosexual friends; virile, body-builders and pro-wrestlers. Since the gym is just a block from the dental office, I often go on my lunch break to watch them work out—a visual satisfaction and something I have never taken time to understand before. Every once in a while the two men offer to give me a ride to my next job. It has always gone fine, purely platonic. Then one day everything changes.

It is a Saturday and one of the men asks if I need a ride. I accept. He asks about my high school and the classes I am taking.

"How about showing me Hollywood High, Vinny? Maybe we can just see the grounds. I've never been there before."

"I guess. It's just a few blocks from here."

We drive and park the car on the street.

"What's that building over there?"

"The girl's gym. It's kinda deserted right now. Even summer school is out."

"Come on, let's go check it out."

He takes my hand and walks with determination towards the gym steps.

"You're hurting my hand, Mike. Not so tight! What's going on?"

He suddenly pushes me down on the secluded concrete steps of the gym.

Oh God! He's acting so strange. His eyes have changed. He's stopped talking! I can't talk. I can't scream either. Let go of my hair! He's unzipping his pants. Oh God! He's pushing my head down on him. Oh God! Oh God! How did I let this happen? I can't move. He's so strong. He knows I'm scared. I've never even seen a man like this! Why or why is he so hateful? Please oh please let me go. He's so distant. He's done with me. I want to vomit!

It is the abyss of time. I am shaking, numb and too shocked beyond belief and imagination. I can't even cry. I can't believe the revulsion. I can't get away fast enough. I slowly and painfully walk home. Mortified.

Bruta Putana.

I retreat within myself and again I feel I have done something wrong. My need for love and attention is once more punishing me.

I wish Darcy still lived close. I don't understand men as well as I thought. Their motives seem odd and unfamiliar. There's no one to talk to. I'm alone again. Work harder. Forget. Move on.

The man brazenly continues to come to the dentist's office, as if nothing has happened. I am the one who feels the shame. Trusting innocence has no place in love.

THE LAME LITTLE LAMB DOWN THE LANE

After I graduate, I find a full time job working as a PBX operator at J. C. Penney's Los Angeles' buying office. A salary. A title. Finally I am grown-up. I dress the part in heels and used clothing. I keep my position at the theater in the evenings and weekends. I also take a few classes at Los Angeles City College. So now I work seven days a week, take six buses, plus two trolleys a day. Every moment is spoken for, and I love it. I am on my own. Dad gives me just enough money for carfare and an evening meal. I buy my first taste of American cooking at a local drug store counter.

I meet an impeccably dressed, older wealthy client, an Edward J. Robinson look alike, who has been coming to the buying office for years. He limps and leans heavily on a carved wood and brass cane, and there is a decided click to his braced leg. He is always cheerful and gallant towards me. I love his harmless flirtatious spirit. He invites me to lunch with him.

Here I go again. Shouldn't be a problem. I seem to always find them older. I certainly could outrun him.

I long for company. Each time I enjoy his friendship, my humor is restored. I appreciate dining in new and exciting restaurants in downtown Los Angeles. He teaches me the finer qualities of grace and public behavior. I have a sense of warmth towards him, nothing sensual. But I am uncomfortable with his paying my bill each time, after all, we're not dating, only friends.

"You know, Jake," I say. "I've been thinking this is not fair. I enjoy the wonderful lunches but I feel funny about your paying my bill all the time. I'd better stop doing this. It just doesn't feel right."

"Don't be silly. I insisted you join me. I'm not complaining, am I? I just want your company for lunch. My kids are all grown and my wife and I don't really talk much. It has been so much fun talking about our different cultures. You must admit we've laughed quite a bit about the humorous similarities between us Jews and you Italians!"

"You're right there. But it still doesn't feel like the right thing."

I take a few more lunches with him.

Jake says. "Can I drive you to the theater where you work at night? It's right close to my home."

He is calming as he reaches below the table and places his hand on my knee. I pull back a little but don't feel threatened.

"I just shouldn't. If my father ever caught me, he would kill me. I wish I could talk better with my family like I can with you."

He drives me to the Fairfax Theater.

The next day he takes me there once again and this time he leans over and plants a hefty wet kiss on my lips.

"Why did you do that? I thought we were friends?"

"Because I like you a great deal. Don't be so stiff. No one will have to know, we can just have some fun. Right?"

The lunches and treats come to a halt.

I can't seem to learn it all. What a fool I am. Why don't young guys ask me?

MR. BARLES, STUDENT PRINCE

I decide to sandwich into my already heavy schedule, a fruit basket of classes at city college: piano, psychology, music appreciation, and modern dance.

One day, as I sit in the college quad, a door opens, and I see him.

Is that who I think it is? Can it be? Yes it is? He won't remember. Why am I so nervous?

"Hi, Mr. Barles. I'll bet you don't recognize me?"

He does! I hope he doesn't hear my heart jumping! I should be careful.

"What a surprise seeing you here." He says. "It's Vinny, isn't it?
"You're right. It's Vinny. I'm taking a couple of classes here. What are you doing here?"
"Oh, I'm taking classes at State College on the other side of this campus. Are you still working for Dr. Ferra?"
"No. I gave that up. I'm working downtown at J. C. Penney's Buying Office and then I have a night job at the Fairfax Theater."
"Do you have some time? Can I buy you a cup of coffee yet?"

Here I go again. Brain get smart.

It has been a year and half since last I saw him. He seems sweet, sensitive and he carries a demeanor of direction and spirit. He appears more mature than most other young men I meet at school. But I have become quite leery of any male interest. Days turn into weeks. Almost daily I secretly meet him in the school quad for coffee.

What's happening to me? Not again? Be careful. Did he say he taught school? I think he said he had a BA degree and is taking Psychology. I wish I understood people's education better. There's so much I don't know. I still don't know a lot about this man.

I dream about him. I look forward to seeing him each day. I can tell him things. He listens. I ask about his life. He is cautious and private. I'm impressed with his education, values and ambition.

We're getting close. Does he like me? He doesn't say. He must know I'm a little afraid, but not of him. Why would he find me interesting? I feel so inadequate and laughable.

Everyday I leave with thoughts of Mr. Barles. He doesn't press me. He knows the situation hasn't changed with my father.

He proposes a strange thing. "Vinny, I need to practice some psychological tests for classes. Would you be willing to take some for me?"

"Well, I guess so. Are they hard? I hate tests."

He invites me to his bachelor apartment. I am leery, but I feel I have a better understanding about men's ways and means. So, after I cook a rabbit dinner, he gives me the exams. Even checks my IQ! I feel like a lab rat. Maybe it's his way of weeding out the material before coming on board with his feelings.

In April, a month after we meet, on the eve of my nineteenth birthday, he takes me for a ride to Santa Monica pier. As we walk on the wharf, I dare to ask him, "Eddie, if I fell into the water, would you jump in and save me?"

Without a moment's hesitation he responds. "No."

We have a good laugh.

Ooo. Maybe I should not have laughed. I wonder if he really cares for me?

By this time, between hugs and cuddles, I know him for six months. We continue to see each other without my parents' knowledge. My job as a PBX operator, in the days of lines, cords, and switches, gives me contact with the public, a kind of personal, non-threatening form of socialization. I seem to be doing well. I feel respected. Even though the money is not mine to keep, my monthly check stub of $110.00, feels real. After my day job, I continue to take a few classes before leaving for work at the theater in the evening. In July I find an interesting position closer to home and a little better salary as a Music Clearer at Channel 13 television studio.

But one day, my new "boyfriend" picks me up from my day job in his spiffy, green Chevy, with a wolf whistle and we drive to Tiny Naylor's, a Hollywood drive-in restaurant on Sunset and La Brea.

"I've got to talk to you about something, Vin."

"What's up, Eddie? It smells like you've been drinking."

"Yeah, I had a beer for fortification. Honey, I've had this job offer." He's holding the steering wheel tightly. "It's something I've long looked forward to exploring. It'll be an opportunity to work and travel at the same time. I'm to be a Field Director for the International Red Cross." He shifts around and hesitates for a moment. "I leave in a couple of weeks for Northern California. My first assignment is up at Camp Stoneman in Pittsburg. It's a port of embarkation for the Army. You know with this Korean conflict, this job may take me overseas."

I knew it. It's over. These are the feelings he does not often share. Why couldn't he tell me this before?

"Wow, I don't know what to say, Eddie. It sure sounds like a good chance for you."

"Vinny, I've been thinking. Will you wait and marry me when I come back? Maybe in about a year. Will you wait?"

A year. God only knows where I'll be in a year. Maybe even in Italy. I don't know him. I haven't met his family and he sure as heck can't meet mine. Who is this man who has asked to marry me? But, I want to be with him.

"Absolutely. You know I would, Eddie!"

He is leaving! He'll never return to me. He'll find himself a new gal. Back to aloneness.

He understands how unstable my situation is at home. There is a great possibility my father will take me to Italy and I know his intentions are for me to meet a man there.

"Vin, I want you to have my engraved, gold pinkie ring."

"Gads, Eddie, I can't take this. It's the ring your sister gave you."

Dazed, I immediately put it on my third finger.

The weekend is nearly lethal with my parents. My usually unresponsive mother sees the gold ring and is immediately suspicious. She threatens to unravel my lies.

I meet Eddie later in the week, but as we talk I see he is torn. He admits he doesn't want to risk leaving me behind.

"Listen, Vinny, I've been concerned about leaving you. I don't want to wait. I want you to marry me now. I'll try and talk to your father."

The fervency in my heart breaks the sound barrier.

He won't leave me! I think he loves me. He really means this! Talk to my father?

157

"You must be kidding. He'll kill you and me if he knows about this. You can't even begin to imagine the craziness!"

"But I can talk to difficult people. How bad could he be?"

"You have never met anyone like this. It'll be bad enough that his Sicilian daughter wants to marry someone she picked out, but wait until he finds out you're Jewish and not Italian or Catholic! I can't let you do this."

We decide to elope to Las Vegas the forthcoming weekend. I am happy, in love and excited, but not flustered, just numb, and apprehensive for my brother Nicky.

What will he do? Will he ever forgive me for my selfishness? What should I take? I can't think.

I give notice at the TV station, collect my severance pay, and wait for Mr. Eddie Barles to pick me up outside my office. But all happens much too fast. Our plans begin to snarl. After our rapid departure for Las Vegas, my grand scheme is found out. The floodgates open.

And now I am a married lady. What did it all mean? I was not trained to look at the future. I had no thoughts about my life—what would happen, or what to expect. I was ill equipped to enter married life, given the education I receive about marriage from my parents. I fumble at many tasks. But I am determined to make a success of this chance.

I never had dreams of marriage, a husband or children, only of a career and love.

I took my chances at love...

PART II

MARRIAGE

Venera Di Bella Barles

Marriage: Enter The Russians and Italians

The Tell Tale Hat (1940's—early 1950's)

The Russian Lady

How Goliath Slew David

Oh Daniel

Bitter Root

Samuel, Gatherer of Dreams

Marriage, Kidneys, and Other Dark Organs (1951-52)

Antipasti Served With Heartburn (1955)

Love Letters?? (1957-1986)

A Dark and Fearful Thing (1958-59)

Talking Pictures

Turiddu, How Dare You Die?

Just Tell Me You Love Me

Venera Di Bella Barles

The TELL TALE HAT

Nicky is eight when he receives the wool, khaki, Marine hat. I have no idea it will play such an important part in our lives. During our short courtship, Ed gives me his old military hat as a gift to my brother. Nicky is ecstatic when I hand it to him; wears it for days on end, tipped to the side of his head.

He's always been fascinated with hats and I rarely remember him ever being without one. When he is about two he gets his first cap, a tiny brim, navy officer type. As he gets older his headgear wardrobe grows. There is a Greek style cap, a sailor's white and let me not forget, his ever-important cowboy hat. Whenever he sees anyone wearing hats on television, in the movies, or on the street, Nicky's fantasy is piqued. It is as if he makes kinship with distant identities, a sense of belonging.

In the living room, Saturday mornings, he and The Lone Ranger meet at the weekly western TV serials. He stands in front of the screen, in a complete uniform of a tee shirt, shorts, holsters, boots and the mini-ten-gallon, waiting for an opportunity to draw his gun and join the celluloid battle. When it's his turn to "die" he shoots the bad guys and with synchronized timing, falls on his back, carefully removing his felt hat and placing it on his chest after he lands. Nicky searches for the illusive buckaroos in various parts of the house, usually cornering Mom in the kitchen while in the middle of a meatball mix.

"Stick-um up! Don't move. I've got you covered."

Nicky, the ham never misses an opportunity to perform. He comes by it honestly since the family is not shy, except for Mom. Wearing his choice cap, he's quick to give us a rendition of his latest lesson on the half-his-size accordion. He usually trusts my lead as I help with the clowning, but he is not thrilled when he sees the photograph of himself after I dress him in one of my old pinafores. I pile a turban hat high with fruit, a little makeup, jewelry, and a little Carmen Miranda music and *voila*, I've created the neighborhood drag queen.

"Hey Nicky, it's Saturday. Wanna go to Hollywood Blvd. with me?" I ask. "Maybe we can see a western or a comedy. Does that sound like fun?"

"Can we go to the five and ten for some toy soldiers?"

"Whoa. We'll see how things go. O.K.? Maybe we'll even get our picture taken at the automatic photo place."

"I need my hat!"

"Why is it every time we go somewhere you have to have a hat? Which one this time? The Marine cap?"

"I need it! You don't understand." Nicky's eyes are large with excitement.

"You have hats for everything."

Off he dashes.

Father's old world tendencies do not allow me to date or see boys, even though I am nearly nineteen. But the biological urges are strong when I meet my secret boyfriend, Eddie. My relationship with him soon turns serious, and after six months he asks me to marry him. I am terrified at the prospect of explaining to Dad this deception, knowing he will never allow any marriage, let alone this one. Ed believes he can talk to my unreasonable father, but I know what's in store for him. Without my parents' permission, our only option is elopement.

I plan a cover-up story for the weekend, that I am visiting my friend Darcy, who has moved across town. We will marry and let my parents know when we return from Las Vegas. But my lie is too soon discovered and things come apart from all directions. A so called girlfriend from work, calls Dad and Mom, delighted to tell them that I have picked up my severance check. Now they are suspicious that I am doing the "big runaway."

If only their skills at parenting could match their detective talents. While rummaging through my belongings, they find photos of Ed and me romping on the beach. Now they know what the face and body of the villainous kidnapper looks like. A further search leads them to Nicky and the infamous overseas cap. They grill the kid.

"Who gave it to you? When? Did you meet him? What's his name?"

The wool hat bares the name. E. BARLES.

The cap holds the key to the hysteria that follows. My parents track us down at my mother-in-laws' house. Years later, when the furor dies down, I receive pictures of a teenage Nicky wearing the tell tale E. BARLES hat. In one picture he salutes the photographer wearing riding pants, boots and on his head is Ed's cap. And then there is a photo of him at an American military academy, wearing a full uniform and headgear.

My brother, after graduating (cap) as the youngest with high honors from medical school, joins the Army (cap) later as a doctor. He retires twenty years later as a Colonel (some cap there!) and opens his own Oncology clinic.

I often wonder what impact we make on a child when we give them tokens of our affection. And how influential is the Marine cap in Nick's choice of a military career?

And, for that matter, why didn't he become a rodeo rider instead?

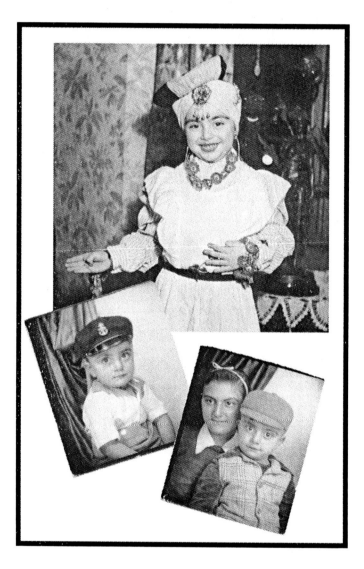

#10 Nicky in Drag; Nicky the Sailor; Nicky and me. Albany (1940's)

The RUSSIAN LADY

The first time I meet Ed's mother, she is peeling potatoes at the kitchen sink and Peter Pooper, the cockatiel, is sitting on her shoulder. He greets her each evening and after Minnie lets him out of his cage, he walks back and forth across her shoulders as she goes about her evening chores. She wears the long house dress so he can climb down to the floor. It's part of their nightly ritual. Minnie has placed a mirror on the coffee table for Peter's entertainment, but she also gets upset when the bird does a rocking dance and chants to his mirrored friend.

"Peter Pooper, Peter Pooper, Peter Pooper," he sings in rote fashion.

Minnie speaks to him as if he can return dialogue.

"Peter, Peter, don dance like dat! Peter, I told you, don do dat. Not nice. Bad boy, you'll get sick!"

Although not quite five feet tall, Minnie is solidly built. Her permed, sandy-gray hair is neatly set. She is much older looking than my mother, Antoinetta. I can see her rheumatoid fingers are thick at the joints and her face reveals the strain of her life, but still it delivers strength. She reminds me of my maternal grandmother. Sturdy with substance.

Can I make it through this first meeting and this meal? Will she undress my feelings as my mother did? She looks as if she might be fair.

Ed and I walk in through the back door, into the undersized kitchen, but I stay close to the entry studying her face for signs of rejection. I see just a little reservation.

"Ma, this is Vinny," Eddie says, as he kisses her cheek.

Kiss my mother's cheek? She would push me away. How beautiful this is.

She continues to make the meal, passively acknowledging my presence. I find myself comparing her to my mother.

I see the delicate curtains at her windows, something I never saw in my own home. There are warm invitations surrounding her decorations. Pictures and collectibles are placed with care. A crisp, colorful tablecloth adorns the small kitchen table. A bowl of her renowned, distinctively sharp tangy, coleslaw sits in the middle, and at each place setting, grapefruit halves sprinkled with sugar and topped with a cherry. She adds the onions, sautéed in chicken fat, to the mashed potatoes. The aroma is seductive. The food is different than in my home. I feel the strength of a woman in this house, not a bit like my lifeless mother. The lamb chops are broiling in the bottom of the white gas range. When she opens the refrigerator door I can see the bounty, and the multi-layered fruited Jell-O, sitting, waiting for its exit. Suddenly I feel a sense of comfort, acceptance and warmth in this room, something I never felt in my mother's kitchen. These pleasurable smells and scenes will romance my senses for the rest of my life.

"Well, Ma what do you think of her?" her son asks.

And in her distinctive style of cadence.

"Vhat's to think? I don know her." She turns to me and says, "You make my son a good wife, and ve'll see."

We chat and maintain a degree of conversation during our meal. I am nervous. Who am I to think I can convince this near five-foot Russian czarina, a clear-thinking veteran of experience, that I will be an appropriate and unique daughter-in-law?

She is refreshing. She is straight. Straight as an arrow. She sees life with clarity and simplicity. I cannot have asked for any better balm for my crippled mind. She is a woman of such profound character and strength. Little do I know she will, in the end, give me her backbone. At nineteen my life is seriously deprived of strong, assertive women. So meeting her is especially different, challenging and gratifying. I have been delivered.

Eddie tells me his mother, Manya or Minnie, her Americanized name, is a middle child, born in Russia before the turn of the century to his Jewish grandparents, Mary and Charles. Her mother, father and six siblings, come to America and settle in New York City; they leave a couple of children buried in Russia.

Minnie says. "I never liked to bodder my mother like the udder children. So she vould always ask me vhat I vant. I tell her not to vorry about me."

I have the impression, she like myself, is close to her father and feels left out of her mother's devotion. As her daughter-in-law, it is sometimes hard for me to conclude from the many conversations, around her kitchen table, how she believes she received love.

Minnie marries David, also an immigrant from Russia, and they have three children, five years apart, Daniel, Leona and Eddie, each emotionally distant from one another. Minnie's aged father, Charlie, lives with them for reasons I do not fully understand. In summer, to escape the city heat, she rents a place in the Catskills and sub-lets rooms, at the resort, to help supplement income. Minnie typically takes only the two youngest children and Grandpa Charlie, while David, her husband and Danny, her eldest son, remain in the city.

As is typical for the times, things are not always easy for the Barles'. Modern machinery replaces David's work in the garment district, and so encouraged by Minnie's adeptness as a cook, they decide to open a Jewish delicatessen. One can only imagine the delights from this shop. Much of the responsibility appears to fall on her.

Eddie would say, "I never saw her sit down or take a rest. She'd be cleaning windows in our apartment at one in the morning!"

"I vould run from store to the house, clean the children, feed the children den back to the store. A lot to do!" Minnie echoes.

Her son continues. "Then she'd cook, feed and cater to her parents and family too."

I can hear in the statements the vast physical drain as she strives to keep the familial nest intact. Besides juggling a restaurant and a home she is also the conduit for her extended family. Money is scarce during the depression, as it is for most, so she is quite miffed at David, when he is so generous to needy friends and neighbors. It puts another dimension to the strain in the marriage. The many pressures with each other, leaves a rift too wide to heal. They ultimately separate when Eddie is fourteen.

After Eddie joins the Marines at seventeen, Minnie shuts down the household and moves to California, where her eldest son has settled with his wife and young children.

Minnie, divorced, her children grown, has never owned her own home. Daily she takes a bus to her job in the Los Angeles garment district. Everyday, all day, with her ancient rings imbedded into her swollen arthritic fingers and her faded blue eyes losing their fine tuned abilities, she sews linings into women's coats. At the end of the long tiresome hours, she again boards several buses back to her modest, clean and tidy, one bedroom apartment in West Los Angeles.

Through the years, I learn of her innate humor in dealing with life. Invariably the family dissolves into tears of hysterical laughter when she relates, without trying to be funny, situations of her daily affairs. Her simple reasoning is not always charitable.

I do a great injustice to duplicate the scenarios. One day she tells us of her recent visit to the local theater. It brings a new round of applause.

"I get dere before the movie. I'm sitting, and this *alter kucker* comes with his lady friend. He says, 'Please lady, you should move over dere. Me and my miz vant to sit together.' So I say, 'Vhat dat got to do wit me, mister? No. I vant to sit here. If I vant to sit dere, I sit dere."

The couple begins to argue, but Minnie stands firm. Resigned, the two plant themselves on either side of her and continue to bicker around her the entire evening. Minnie holds her seat, ignoring them. Determination. Always determination.

We sit in on another of her stories.

One day, in her mid-eighties, while shopping in her local neighborhood, a daily chore, she is caught crossing the street in the middle of the block. A tall, young, policeman calls to her.

"Lady. Oh lady!"

Minnie does not respond. Finally he corners her.

"Lady, why didn't you stop when I called you? Didn't you hear me?"

"I hear you."

"Why didn't you answer me?"

"I don know you. Vhat business you vant with me?"

"You crossed in the middle of the street. Don't you know you broke the law? I'm going to have to give you a ticket because you jaywalked. You didn't cross at the corner at the light."

"Vhaaat?"

Minnie is mortified at the thought of a broken law and believes her only destiny is jail.

"How much do you weigh?" he asks.

"Vhat? How do I know? Do you think I veigh before I go to the street?"

Once more the officer asks, "How tall are you?"

"Come on. Vhat's the matta with you? Do you think I measure myself?"

With great indignation at this entire episode, Minnie watches him write the ticket.

"Your mother, she knows vhat you doing? Vhy don't you get bad people? You pick on old ladies? Shame on you."

She turns and walks away as he finishes.

The policeman, completely flustered by this old gal, neglects to hand her a copy of the ticket.

He runs to catch up with her once more. "Oh lady! Lady."

Minnie turns to the towering six-foot officer.

"Again? Are you starting again?"

One week after my meeting with Minnie, Ed and I are to marry. Our marriage is formed on feather pilings, without my parents' knowledge or blessing. I am Catholic, Italian and not allowed to date, and now I am about to marry a Russian Jew. I have disregarded all the rules. The week is sheer lunacy. It is one thing to have made this decision, but I impose, unintentionally, emotional turmoil at Minnie's feet. She never ostracizes me or condemns her son, as do my father and mother. I'm sure she also felt cheated by her son marrying a non-Jew.

My father's anger is unleashed. Frustrated and unable to stop our marriage he explodes into frenzy, spewing his hate and vigorous demands daily, by phone, to Minnie, who now is the object of his hatred. In later years he never asks about her or cares to learn anything about the woman. His self-centeredness always catches the limelight.

Towards the end of her life, Minnie does not want to give up her independence, to live with her children. Even in her nineties she exerts some say about her needs. She chooses a Jewish retirement home for the elderly.

While in the community dining room one day, she listens to the daily whining of other residents about their various gripes and health issues. One after the other they grumble about this ache or that pain. She sits and notes and finally cannot hold her silence any longer.

"Listen, vat's to complain? Stop the complaining! Who cares! Don you know ve're all sick in here!"

She lives until ninety-three years of age. Minnie doesn't realize she has been my mentor. We have mothered each other. She fills in areas of my life, where I felt the deprivation from my own mother and I know Minnie reaped benefits also. We become close old friends, good company, appreciative of whatever we share. She allows me to see her secrets. Whenever we are in public together, she is quick to announce proudly to everyone, as she grabs and snuggles me.

"Dis my daughter-in-law. I vish you should get such a good von!"

Little did I know what would happen once I crossed that kitchen threshold. This was my mother-in-law, Minnie, Peter Pooper's friend.

"I wish you could get such a good one!"

#11 Minnie and Vinny Barles in Los Angeles (1951)

HOW GOLIATH SLEW DAVID

"Zei gezunt Zaideh...Olov hasholem."(Heb.)
"Good-bye Grandpa...May you rest in peace."

Another life wasted—waiting for love.

How is it that we have important people in our personal lives and never get to know them?

It is 1960. The emergency phone call comes while we are on vacation in Yosemite with our two little girls, Gina and Carisa. Papa Barles is gravely ill and is not expected to live. Eddie will fly to New York to be with him, and I have to say good-bye, from afar, to a gentle man I hardly had a chance to know.

I meet him soon after I marry his son nine years before. It should have been long enough to form a solid relationship, but I leave it up to Ed to bring his father to our family. How often I regret not following my instinctive heart. I could have done a better job to seek him out. Oh, I'll give some facts as I know them, but really what truly counts is not the story, but the feelings that remain.

That first meeting is all too brief. If I had been more influential I would have at least put him into the car and bought him a cup of coffee. But, instead, Ed introduces me to my new father-in-law, David, as we stand on the sidewalk in front of his one room apartment in East Los Angeles. I'm not sure if I will be accepted, but as I search him over, I pick up immediate approval. He has Ed's twinkling, mischievous eyes and soft-spoken words. I notice he is quite portly with a troubling unhealthy redness to his complexion. His broken English brings familiarity and warmth to my ears. I understand fathers. I am ready for a good alliance.

I want to ask him many questions, but I wait until Eddie and I drive home.

"Did you like my father?" my husband asks.

"I sure did. At first I was afraid, you know, because I didn't have any idea if he was like mine. I wish I knew him better. He looks lonely. Do you know much about him?"

"I suppose he is lonely. As I've told you, he was born in Russia," Eddie replies. "He was the youngest. His family was fairly well off and educated. He spent most of his military service in Siberia."

"I wonder why he came to the U.S.?"

"I'm not really sure. I know that at that particular time in Russia it was a difficult one for Jews; many fled because of the Pogroms."

"Oh, so he came with his family? How old was he?"

"Oh no! His mother died when he was a small boy. He immigrated to the United States in his early twenties with two younger nieces."

Ed uses the pressure of his foot on the gas pedal to punctuate his sentences.

"His nieces were pretty bright. Eventually, one of them opened a business in the garment industry. You've heard me talk about them. My cousin Diana ran and owned a novelty company where she made trimming, laces and beads the kind they put on women's dresses and gowns. Very successful."

"So what did Papa do for a living?"

176

"He worked in the garment district in New York. Made good money as a cutter. But then times got so bad that he had to find other work."

"Is that when they opened the deli?"

"Yup. Mom knew a lot about cooking and how to run things. Her family ran a room and board business in Russia."

"My how their lives certainly changed. Just like my parents." I said. "I wonder if any of these labor intensive ways of earning a living ever stifled your father's curious brain? Life must have been so different and strange for them in the United States. Their dreams must have taken on new meanings."

"No kidding." Eddie said.

"I remember you said that he would stay and work in the city when Momma would take you guys to the Catskills for the summer. It's sad he didn't go with you. We never went anywhere without my father. I wonder if he liked to fish? It doesn't sound as if you had much opportunity to get to know him."

"That's the way it was. I don't recall much about him. But I know he liked animals. He'd bring home strays and Momma would give him hell. And then they would have to find another home for them."

"Did they fight much?"

"Probably some. Through the long years, along with raising the three children with general ups and downs, I'm sure there were the typical marital problems in their daily grind. Mom was just unhappy with him. Personal things she didn't want to talk about."

"You know, when you hear about someone else's family you never think they have problems like yours do. Too bad. I'd love to know if he was humorous or if he was a story teller or whatever."

"I do know no one ever complimented him or appreciated him," defends Eddie.

"But why don't you understand what they were so upset with him for?"

"Who knows? Some of Momma's complaints were that he gave away their hard earned money during the depression. He was always rescuing people."

I can only surmise what the real agonies were. Eddie doesn't seem to know too much about his family. What made them tick? I always seem to hear the same stories, but none of the feelings.

"Didn't you say he bought you your first car?"

"Yeah. This forty-nine Chevy. He paid for most of it."

"Well, that was pretty nice, I would say."

"Yeah, Dad and I took a trip soon after. We drove to Petaluma to see some of his relatives and on the way back near San Luis Obispo, you know I wasn't too competent a driver yet, I swerved, the car spun around and then I hit an embankment. The doors sprung open and we were tossed out. Ended up on the ground. They took us to the hospital and luckily released us. But the next day, poor Dad was badly bruised. Black and blue all over."

"Oh my! That was awful! What happened to the car?"

"They towed it and we took the Greyhound Bus back to L.A. A lousy kid kept kicking Pop's seat."

"Was Papa upset with you?"

"He never complained or said a bad word."

As an invited spectator, I get a tremendous sense of passivity in Papa's dealings with the family. In some ways he reminds me, as do many people, of my mother. And like my family, they are skillful with their secrets. Ed's sister, Leona, is angry with her father. For years, I try to understand what her dissatisfactions are, but I can't discern the root of the anger. I never hear her say anything loving or compassionate about him either.

She laments, "He never paid any attention to me!"

I am uncomfortable with the condemning conversations about David between my sister-in-law, Leona, and her mother. I remember at many of these gatherings, how I try to defend him, even though I don't know him. I wonder what unknown reasons there was for their unhappiness with him. I don't hear love. In these days I have all to do to understand my own family's warts and secrets. Maybe like my folks they were good at keeping false appearances. Unfortunately, I only hear one side of this saga, and it's not David's. In my Italian world I am used to males getting more praise and respect from women, rather than open denigration. But at least there wasn't physical violence in this household.

I hear one story that takes place when Minnie plans a three-month visit to California to help her eldest son Danny with his first child. Leona lives in Florida at the time.

David asks Minnie, "Who is going to take care of Eddie? I have to work."

The house is closed, as are feelings, and young Eddie and his father stay with different relatives. But there are too many loose needles flying in the wind, and David's and Minnie's marriage breaks down. When she returns, they separate, and the household never reunites. The fractured family drifts in all directions. In time, Ed joins the Marines, and Minnie makes up her mind to permanently leave New York. She sells most of the family's belongings and moves to a California apartment near her son Danny. Ed, after his service stint, moves west to live with his mother.

Does Papa Barles care? I have the impression he doesn't want to fight for his children or family. Much like my mother. At times, much like Eddie.

David is left on his own, living in boarding rooms in New York City. During the years that follow, he visits Minnie in California to see if they can get together again. But she is stern with her conditions and says she will only take him in if he will turn over all his assets to her. As an outsider, and as one who loves Minnie, I am shocked and feel terribly distressed for Papa Barles, but I also understand her harsh stand. Here she is an old woman, still working very hard daily, with very little to show for her life financially. She has had to be careful of her funds in these remaining years.

I am amazed when Eddie advises his father, "Don't do it, Dad, if things don't work out you'll be out in the street without anything. She wants to take complete control."

Papa David rents a room in Boyle Heights in East Los Angeles and spends much of his time helping Danny in his grocery store, without pay. Danny, in his consistent, despicable, needy style, borrows a significant amount of his father's savings, and hands him signed notes of promise to return the money. Maybe Minnie did have fiscal clairvoyance.

Years later, when Papa asks Danny to give back some of the loaned dollars; he gives him instead the 'great stall'. There are hard feelings and David decides to return to New York to live, but he continues to try and collect the large sum of money. Since he is unable to get Danny to honor the agreement, he contacts Minnie to at least try to redeem the signed notes for herself. But when Minnie asks her son for the borrowed funds, he has his own distortions.

"I don't owe him anything. Besides he stole from me in the store."

Why is it so hard to understand this family's fragmented lives? I think I comprehend my relatives' twisted melodramas better. What could an old zaideh (grandpa), in his late sixties, possibly want from a son's grocery store? Perhaps a little understanding and respect? He lives alone in one room, uncared for, except by strangers.

We send Grandpa Barles, the usual Father's day handkerchiefs and cards. Ed rarely calls him, and I never hear that Leona has either. Unlike my father, Salvatore, David is not a squeaking wheel. He makes no problems. And now his book is about to close. We all let him go.

It looks like Goliath has won, David.

On a day of David's last week, Leona and Eddie fly back to New York's Bellevue hospital. Their papa has suffered a heart attack. David, the gentle, little boy from Russia, is in a coma. Danny arrives on an earlier first class flight. While Eddie stands by the bedside and watches Papa Barles breathe his last few breaths in an oxygen tent, Papa's two other children wait beyond a glass partition, their angers and needs closed-in with them.

And even in the throes of death David is ripped-off. After giving his life savings away, he is then, insulted a final time. While he is being taken to the hospital, his wallet is missing from his small rented room.

Only four copper pennies are found in his shoe.

12 David and Minnie ~ Eddie's Mom and Dad

Oh, DANIEL

"Everybody likes Danny." That's what people used to say. "No matter what, he always knows how to make a living!"

"He vas up early every morning to deliver," Minnie would say, about her older son.

Everyone praised his efforts. I heard stories of how hard a worker Danny was; always energetic and resourceful. I loved being part of this family. But when it came to conversations about Danny, I heard a genuine difference of opinions and the same set of facts over and over again. But I still didn't know Danny.

I met him, soon after marrying his brother Eddie. He was thirty-five years old and the 'star', to hear his mother tell. He was her first born, five years older than his sister, Leona, and ten years older than Eddie. All were raised in the center of New York's Jewish community. The family tended towards portly midsections and Danny's was well established, topped by a large smiling, cherubic face and a salesman's approach. When you were with him, you believed him. I wanted to believe in Danny. I wanted to believe in the whole family. In those days I excused everyone without examining the facts. The warp in my own family blinded me towards others. I spent hours arguing with Ed to keep the lines of communication open to his only brother. But Eddie was running out of cheeks to turn.

What was the problem, you ask? One that seemed to cut deep for Eddie, was during our marriage Danny visited our home only one time, less than an hours drive. His excuses finally wore thin.

"What's with Danny?" I'd ask Leona, his sister. "Why is there always so much craziness when you all talk about him?"

"Oh I don't know. It's always like this. He works pretty hard and doesn't have much time."

Danny left New York City for California with his wife-to-be, Anna and her family. They then married and had the traditional large Jewish wedding. Then came three children, one girl and two boys. As was typical, Danny made a go of things. He bought a modest forties' house, and then opened a large grocery store in Central Los Angeles. He came close to losing the store in the Watts riots of 1965.

I was always trying to understand the family. Our characteristic conversations were generally like this. I remember on one visit to my mother-in-law's house, I asked my husband, "So after you got out of the Marines you came to California. Right Eddie?"

"Yeah. Mom and Dad's marriage was just about over and Leona wasn't around much anymore, so while I was in the service, Mom sold everything and went to live near my brother Danny in California. You can imagine how shocked I was when I arrived home for a short leave and everyone and everything was gone, even the locks were changed. I couldn't believe it!"

"Mom, are you making coffee?" Leona asked Minnie.

"Wow! How did you find out what happened?" I continued.

"It wasn't until I got back to the base. I got a letter that Momma had someone write for her and it explained what she had done. So I decided to join Mom, in a little apartment that my Uncle Sam owned. That's when I went to Dorsey High to finish my high school." Ed moved from the couch to the table. "Danny was doing very well with his own business and living an upscale life with his wife and kids. Anna didn't need the Barles family since she had all her relatives living close by."

"You sound pretty uptight."

"I am. Mom or me used to baby-sit for Danny. They never once invited us to sleep over or to have dinner." He turned to Minnie. "Momma the coffee is good." I could feel he was fervent. "It didn't matter what time they got in, we still had to go home! Mom worked hard at her job all day. You'd think they'd be more gracious. You can bet Anna would let her family eat and sleep there."

Momma picked up the resentment.

"She don know how to treat people nice, just her family and friends. That's all she care about! She treats us like strangers. She don let people sit in her fancy living room. Ve have to sit in da kitchen!"

Leona jumped up and stood in front of Minnie.

"Well Momma, what you don't know is that, that's an expensive frieze sofa."

"So? Ve not good enough?"

"Momma, why are you so upset?" I asked as I put my hand on her shoulder.

"I don know, Vinny. Her face was sad. "Dey always got time to see Anna's family and dere friends. Dey plays cards and fancy games. Dey takes vacations. Who knows?"

Leona shouts at her. "Momma, they play *Mahjong*! You see them. What are you complaining about?"

"Vinny, Mom and Leona take turns about favoring Danny," Eddie chimed in. "They can't find any fault in him. I don't know what Anna's problem is. Too busy with her social life," he said as he got up to get more coffee. "You'd think she'd be more hospitable."

"Eddie, it's hard for me to believe that Danny, is Momma's favorite," I said as I followed him into the kitchen. "If that's so, why doesn't he do more to encourage a better relationship with you guys? Why is Anna always blamed, never Danny? There's got to be more to what you're telling me."

"He has a hard job and no time!" Leona defended, as she joined us near the stove.

Eddie shook his head. "Look Leona, I can't tell you how many times I've gone by to see Danny at his market. Don't you think I have a busy work schedule, too?" His voice was passionate. "Why can't he come to visit us at our home?"

Leona, Eddie and I left and returned to our seats at the maple dining-room table near Minnie.

"He hasn't once been to see us!" He rose again still unsettled. "All I ever hear, 'I'll try and come sometime, Eddie, but I'm pretty busy, you know.'"

I heard the disappointment and how insulted my husband felt each time he was put off. Swept up by Danny's charms, I had a difficult time understanding my husband's grievances against him.

"You know he vorks very hard," Minnie said, in her protective voice as she sliced some coffee cake.

"Just because I go to an office, Momma," Eddie said, "doesn't mean I'm not working hard and that I don't get tired too. You think that because I don't carry boxes and I like to read, that's not work? I know, you think I'm lazy?"

Leona answered. "She always liked boys better. She doesn't think I work hard either, Eddie."

They were upset with Minnie but I knew her defensive stand. I was quickly conscious, of the toilsome life she had in the depths of New York's garment districts, plus she owned a successful deli and took care of her family. She understood manual labor well.

"Do you remember," Eddie went on, "when I hurt my back carrying Mom's TV up the steps to her apartment? Vin was in her eighth month of pregnancy with Gina. I ended up in the VA Hospital flat on my back. I didn't know what the heck was going to happen. A new job that I didn't know if I could keep. A brand new house. Vin had already stopped work with the Navy Shipyard. Talk about problems. I was in such pain and scared to death. Then Danny boy comes to visit me in the hospital and as soon as he sees me he gets faint and everybody has to pay attention to him in the next bed!"

Leona chimed in. "Well Eddie, you're not the only one! He doesn't come to see me either!"

Eddie rolled on. "See? What is his problem? Why can't he visit us once in awhile? Why does everybody always have to go to Danny?"

My husband's complaints began to ring with justification. There never was closeness between the two men.

Ed drained his coffee cup and held it up as Minnie poured more. "Does he think he's the only one who has a busy life? He has time to visit friends and go for vacations. All I ever hear is how hard things are for him, always crying about money problems. He uses everyone. Does he ever ask me how I am or how anyone is getting along? He's got the whole family snowed. Danny this and Danny that."

I remember how often Ed tried to encourage his brother to come over and visit with us. Our second child arrived two and a half years later. Still no Danny.

"That does it!" Eddie snapped. "It'll be a cold day in hell if I'll go to him again."

So Danny walked his life thinking all should listen only to his drum. As time moved by we never saw much more of Danny and his family. I felt a great loss because I couldn't understand the miserable tension. Like with their father David, Ed and Danny's relationship seemed terminal. It was hard to accept that both sides of our families were strained and distant. There was very little movement towards mutual acceptance and harmony.

We heard, that after many years of marriage, three grown children and grandchildren, Danny and his wife ended their union. He found a young, divorced, Russian emigrant sweetheart, who helped him into his old age and wiped his pockets clean.

When Minnie died, Ed completely severed all ties with his family; fed-up with the absurd and petty sibling situations. The air resounded with Danny's old refrain.

"When you get a chance, Eddie, come and see me."

Oh Daniel my brother
You are older than me
Do you still feel the pain
Of the scars that won't heal!
Your eyes have died, but you see more than I
Daniel you're a star in the face of the sky

Elton John and Bernie Taupin

BITTERROOT

"She was born bitter. Always bitter." Momma says.

It bothered me to hear this identifying allegation about my sister-in-law, Leona. Her mother, Minnie, labeled her with this remark, when she was unhappy with her.

I haven't seen Leona since 1984 when we all departed in a cool and unresolved way at Minnie's funeral. Burials have a way of unraveling spools of family threads, sometimes with great finality. But I miss her.

If alive, Leona would be an aged woman now still living alone, I presume, in greater Los Angeles. Maybe she has a cat or dog. She best related to animals. There was five years between the three siblings and not much closeness. Eddie, my husband, was the youngest, Leona, the middle child and only girl, and Danny, the eldest.

She married and divorced in her thirties. Never remarried. Never had a child. And like her mother, never owned a home. Leona was bright, intelligent, independent and quite assertive, some would even call her aggressive. She had an opinion about everything and left no doubt of her stand on issues. As a young woman, she resembled an elegant Ava Gabor, with striking, golden blond-hair and unique, high-quality clothes. Like the rest of her family, food was her weakness and with it she paid the price of weight gain. She appeared to have taken care of her financial needs with the career choice as a legal secretary.

Questions. I always have questions. Love is so difficult to get. Does anyone want to go through life miserable and bitter? What reason did she have to choose an angry road? I often saw why her family became unhappy with her. But no one is born with poison in his or her mouth. I believe it is carefully spooned.

Including the Depression that steals from everyone, her family, Russian Jewish immigrants, survived many familial changes from Russia to America. The adjustments to work, a new language and a new culture drained her struggling family. I listened to various reasons for Leona's cantankerous behavior.

I asked my mother-in-law why she felt this way about her daughter.

"She had everything—beautiful clothes. I bought her the best! Still it vuzn't enough," was the retort.

"Is it possible Momma, she needed something else besides nice clothes?"

"Vat? Who had time?" She put two matzoh balls into a soup bowl. "I had to vork in the delicatessen—I vuz a store-lady." She turned to me and asked, "Vinny, you want Kreplach?" and before I could answer. "She vuz never happy, *famished*, always sour. Who knows vhat she vants!"

If you asked Leona about her relationship with her father, David, she answered with an angry dissatisfied tone.

"He never paid any attention to me. It was like he didn't care to know me. He just didn't seem to care!"

I felt sadness for her. I only knew how important my father was for me, despite the tempestuous times. I had my own picture of Leona.

I had some of the best laughs in my lifetime with my sister-in-law. She loved music, dance, and travel and had a great drawing hand. She understood the arts and enjoyed speaking with me about them. Her homes reflected her creative thoughts. A natural. I confirmed my own ideas of style from her. Her bungled cooking and housekeeping never matched the domestic capabilities of her mother.

By all appearances, Minnie was not as complex as her daughter. I ask myself, how well did her family understand Leona's different needs and values? There was more approval doled out to her brothers. They were both married. Had homes. They both had successful livelihoods and children.

Leona also lost at love. In her early twenties, a serious romance with an accountant went to another heart. The young man went to the army, but later married someone else.

As a secretary she worked hard at her craft; employed by top-notch attorneys in Los Angeles. This led to a devastating relationship with a narcissistic scoundrel—a lawyer, who changed wives quicker than house slippers. He dated Leona for several years and finally they married. She was his third. Leona moved into his small, but tastefully furnished home in the L.A. hills. All of his belongings; none of hers. She continued to work. Mr. Groom's two ex-wives were buddy-buddy and came into Leona's life with great regularity, habitually making rounds, and meddling in her life. At first she seemed somewhat at peace in her blind state and for a while marriage appeared right. From my point of view, I longed to see healthy love matches; therefore, I kept my blinders in place.

There was tension in the union. In the middle of it all she was told she would need corrective surgery to remove fibroids in her uterus, a simple enough operation. But while in the hospital her husband instructed the doctor, without her knowledge, to remove her uterus as well. An unconscionable blatant act. He didn't want children. When she found out, Leona was damaged beyond belief. Her divorce was difficult. Her ex-knight, married the neighbor next-door; the doctor's wife.

Could this be one more notch for bitterness?

She told me she feared cancer. Curiously, she was not supportive when her elderly mother fell ill with the dread disease. To outward appearances, at the time, it seemed selfish to me, and then I remembered that for a long time she attended to most of her mother's papers, errands and needs. Why did she get angry with a feeble old lady? Why did she get angry with her younger brother, who treated her with love and civility? Her outcry was that there was a lack of caring from her mother, claiming that Minnie favored her sons rather than her. Leona behaved as if she's been robbed of life. How well I know this steal.

The argumentative side of her revealed a constant challenge to be right and heard, as if she was powerless unless she was combative. I heard an unloved woman, filled with loneliness, fears and disappointments; who made poor choices.

One day, Eddie asked her why she never continued on to college.

"I couldn't! She shouted. "I had to work to contribute to the household!"

But when he asked his mother the same question the reply was quite different.

"Nobody stop her! She could go. But she vanted a fancy private school vere her friend's ver going instead of the public college ve could afford. So, she didn't vant to go. If she didn't go to school, she had to vork and give to the family like everybody else."

By this time Leona had not been in contact with her mother for a couple of years and notified Eddie that she did not want anymore news about her ailing mom because it made her "too sick" to listen.

We unfortunately argued and for the last time, when my aging mother-in-law was to go into an assisted care home. Ed and I evacuated Minnie's apartment and brought some of her belongings to the new room. Leona came to the apartment, like a lioness in heat, after being notified by a nosy neighbor that we were taking things out of Minnie's home. Her eyes were ablaze. There were accusatory rants that we were pilfering.

"What are you screaming about, Leona?" Eddie says. "Mom has nothing! Nothing! These few things are going to her. She's still alive you know! Where have you been these past couple of years when we needed help? Suddenly, you're involved! If you think we are stealing, then take these damn keys and take care of everything yourself!"

But she would not hear of this and flung the keys back at Ed. There were mean and harsh words. Everyone parted angry at the insults. I doubt if anyone understood what the true reasons were. And if they did, no one wanted to work at healing.

We buried our dear Minnie a couple of years later. Her struggle now was over. Our two daughters, my husband and I were about to leave the gravesite.

The years left an unresolved strain between my husband, his brother, Danny, and Leona, his sister.

Danny walked over to Ed and asked him to come to his house after the memorial.

"No Danny, this is it. No more. We've been through this too many times. You know the story very well. I'm finished after today."

I saw Leona haughtily coming towards me.

"Vin, you'd better tell Eddie if he doesn't come by to Danny's house, I'll never speak to him again." Her voice had an established tone of matriarchy.

I immediately told Ed of her caveat.

"That's the best news I've heard today!" he said.

Communication also died that day.

Why am I so sad at this ending? Maybe, once again, I placed too much optimism and expectation that there would be more in the way of a family with Ed's relatives. There was so little love in my own, I didn't want to accept it in, yet, another family. I wanted so much to fix the bitterness and restore love in Leona. Once again, I didn't know how.

Ah, when the soul is young,
It is lightly filled with joy, and the taste is yet
Unknown,
Of the morsel steeped in tears, with honey
overstrown,
That leaves a bitter savor on the tongue.

Marceline Desbordes-Valmore (1786-1859)

#13 Minnie, Venera, and Leona at Santa Monica Beach in California (1953)

#14 Eddie, the Marine, with his sister, Leona (1940's)

Venera Di Bella Barles

SAMUEL, GATHERER of DREAMS

I see him as a gatherer and keeper of any and all things. Antique artifacts are one of his special talents. He turns the compulsive finds, oftentimes, into money. He does the hardest and dirtiest of jobs. He owns and runs salvage yards, hauls heavy metals, picks up the rejected accumulations of people's lives. But Samuel has become suspicious of life. Any solicitations are turned into paranoia. He suspects a hook at every turn. In his relationships he gravitates towards non-Jewish women...and he never weds again.

They are all born in Russia before World War I, and Samuel, my mother-in-law Minnie's brother, is the youngest of the seven children and the least attractive. His large bulbous nose has been operated on several times, each time just getting worse. In his youth, a devastating illness results in the removal of a lung. The operation, poorly executed, carves up his back leaving a long grotesque scar that pulls his torso down and out of alignment. Despite his malformed, five-foot body, he is strong. His eyes carry a sad twinkle.

He toils like the horses on his parents' farm in Connecticut. One can see his work ethic is well ensconced. His formal education is cast off in early years. Sam chooses the difficult role of caring for his parents, since the rest of the children leave to start their own families. I hear stories that his loyal, filial devotion unfortunately is often abused. His life takes many turns. The family eventually moves to New York City after a destructive fire levels the farm.

196

Sam's marriage faces hard times. His mother's possessive interfering, soon drives a wedge into the fragile marital union. He fathers one child, a son named Izzy, a soft and loving part of his life. His mother takes on the task of raising the little boy, after Sam's wife is, in due course, driven out by his elderly mother. But her inadequate care gives rise to the child's illnesses.

At five years of age, his young son becomes seriously ill with rheumatic fever. My husband, Ed, Sam's nephew, recalls that day his uncle came to their house, running up the stairs of the apartment house, shouting maniacally for David, his brother-in-law. Sam yells a heart-wrenching announcement.

"Izzy, died!! Izzy, died!! Izzy, died!!"

The loss of his son is too profound. Sam imagines he is destined for eternal sadness.

Samuel is living in France when I marry his nephew in the 1950's. I am told of his escapades and I'm quickly drawn to him. When we finally meet, our friendship is warm, loving, and respectful. He enjoys teasing me, the family *shiksa*, the gentile. I like his earthy, bohemian outlook on life; his rakish smiling eyes. He reminds me of my own father. Sam's family often speaks critically and unkindly of him, except when they are in need. But I see that Sam is no fool. His street smarts have taught him well.

On his return from Europe he moves to the East coast and finally back to California. We stay in touch mostly by phone. He seems to be a bird in flight.

Sam meets Elsie, a married, well-educated secretary with semi-grown daughters. She is vastly different than he with her ideas and Norwegian ancestry. Without her children, she moves in with Sam, although Elsie also comes with extra baggage. She is a heavy problem drinker. Sam's attraction for broken-winged relationships is once again fulfilled. He has an eternal struggle to bring Elsie back to herself.

197

I recall the day my family and I visit the Southern California coastal town where Sam and Elsie live in the middle of their salvage yard. We weave our way through the miscellaneous extricated debris of humanity and arrive to the center of the property where several shanty buildings are laced together. When we walk in, I can see that I have entered disturbance. Only a narrow walkway leads from one room to another; piles of boxes, pictures, statues, line the walls to the ceiling. A massive carved bed stands in a small clearing, which seems to be the hub of their warehouse living area. Propped high atop cartons are large stately candelabras. Sam clears a spot for us to sit. He is visibly happy with our visit.

"You'll have coffee, Eddie?" he asks.

"Don't go through any trouble, Sam."

"What's the trouble? We have to have coffee!" He pulls my arm to a chair. "Here Vinny, sit here."

I am distracted and fascinated by the neurotic picture that surrounds me.

My God, they live like hermits and pack rats! I wish I could understand what is going on with them? I sense his need to feel that he's still in the real world, despite the distortions. He looks so happy to see us. Just like a little boy.

He hugs us so.

I observe stashes of beautiful ornate clocks, brass candleholders, dishes, paintings of the masters, solid bronze statuary. All in disarray. As I hear the litany of how unfair he believes the family is towards him, we are served coffee in delicate china cups. His eyes reveal much. He savors the moments of sharing. Someone cares.

He hovers close as we are to leave his sanctuary.

Sam and Elsie live together for thirty years in a common law arrangement. Hard as he tries, Sam is unable to stop Elsie's need to destroy herself. He struggles to prevent her from going out alone, knowing she will buy the needed lethal alcohol. He purchases property in a less populated part of the California desert. While the house is small, it is constructed of cinder block, and appears to bring potential for a saner life. I also think that maybe this will bring some order to their disorderly lives, but I am naive in my assumptions. He voices aspirations of making the home livable, but combined with Elsie's lack of enthusiasm for betterment and his mental distractions, the house soon takes on the trash-like quality of the junk-yard dwelling.

But there is some love. A wonderful little black dog comes into their hearts. They dote on her and treat her as their child. Sweetheart. That's her name. Some years later, Sam cries a bitter tear when he tells us his "little Sweetheart" has died. It is hard for me to see and hear his deep cry.

Most times when Sam visits Los Angeles for errands, he drives by to see his sister Minnie. And then on his way back to his home in the desert, he stops to pay us a visit. The dirty old station wagon is jammed-packed with pickings. Sam arrives one day, when I am not at home, and Ed invites his uncle into the kitchen for coffee and cake.

"Eddie, where's Vinny?"

"She's gone marketing, Sam. She'll be right back."

"Whaa. I hear her in the other room."

"No honest, Sam, she's not here."

Not satisfied with his nephew's answer he asks, "When is she coming out to see me?"

By this time Ed figures out that Sam has heard, Farfel, the mynah bird, mimicking my voice to perfection, by babbling and laughing in my sound track.

"Uncle Sam, come with me, we have a bird in the other room copying Vinny's voice."

He reassures his uncle and shows him the mynah. His disbelief is squelched when he asks our feathered pal questions. Farfel laughs my laugh and sings an operatic scale for Sam.

Despite Sam's worldly experience his conversations, sometimes naive, are also laden with the perceived and not so perceived persecutions. We listen without judgment, careful not to feed into his neurotic needs or give him reason to form distrust or that we are needy. Of all the relatives, Ed seems the best able to relate and treat him the most civil. Sad to say, Eddie's older brother finds ways to manipulate Sam for money. He takes unfair advantage of his uncle, as with his own father. Sam resents these boorish behaviors.

Even though he's accumulated a reasonable sum of money, he and Elsie still live a Spartan life. We become busy with ours and do not stay in contact with them as often. As they get older, their health begins to fail. We do not hear that Sam suffers a debilitating stroke. He is placed in a nursing home, confined to a wheel chair unable to speak, leaving Elsie to fend for herself at the cinderblock cottage. While Sam is away, she and one of her daughters squirrel away money, fearing that she will be left penniless.

I move to our new home out of state, and wait for Ed to follow after his retirement. One day, soon after my transfer, my husband calls to tell me that Elsie has been found dead in the little house. The years of drunken, lonely, stupors have ended. Her heart makes its final demand.

I return to help Ed move Sam's furniture and settle his uncle's affairs. Our daughters, Carisa and Gina, and their mates Peter and William give us the needed assistance to sort through the jumbled mess. Sam is in need of a conservator, but first everything must be accounted for and the house emptied. The risk is high for an invasion of squatters and vandals in the isolated desert location. We find a will leaving the entire estate to Ed. He is told his uncle probably has buried many personal items and art objects in the barren sands around the property. There is no way to know where they are.

As we enter the house it is distressing to see its litter and chaos. Immediately, I feel as if I am invading Sam's privacy. It is difficult unearthing his and Elsie's scars of a tumultuous life.

Nothing is in order, much like their lives. Through the years, Elsie, a collector also, purchased many things through catalogs: dolls, how-to books, trinkets, and cookbooks. There are boxes upon boxes of craft kits, never opened or worked on. Sewing patterns, materials and yarns to knit. All untouched.

Did she buy these many kits and treasures to simulate normality and to placate a weakened spirit? Were Sam and Elsie's inanimate objects less likely to walk out of their lives or to cause them pain? Questions, so many questions.

Near his end, Sam sits alone in the nursing home, unable to speak and express his rage at his settlements. He must suppress his thoughts at the loss of his long-time partner, and probably he is frightened at the prospect of being preyed upon once again as a little Samuel. His lifetime gatherings, with their histories, destroyed or regarded as trash. Who will be there to understand the stories of his trappings?

Our lives end fast, flipping through like microfiche. How different than we, are they to keep hope alive in their strange manner?

How will my personality and life be known? And will my archeologists understand the artifacts peculiar to my dreams?

15 Uncle Sam and Aunt Elsie in California. (1980's)

MARRIAGE, KIDNEYS, and OTHER DARK ORGANS

Eddie and I put together our next moves soon after we decide to wed. They will not be sleek like a 007 espionage movie; more like a Keystone Cop setting.

After that first meeting with Eddie's mother, Minnie, we prepare for our elopement to Las Vegas. I have an elaborate cover-up plan for my parents. I tell them, that after work, I have been invited to visit and stay the weekend at my friend Darcy's house, who moved from Hollywood a couple of months previously. We were to let my parents know the truth, after our return.

The night before, I pack and say my farewells to all I grew up with: photographs, carved furniture, torn kitchen towels, the dented aluminum pots and chipped dishes, Dad's workshop, Nicky's accordion, my piano—and of course, no goodbye to my brother. I am sure I will never see anyone or anything again. I have no clear idea what I am doing or where my life is leading. Along with my typewriter, I pack a small, black, wooden suitcase, which once held an old phonograph. All I take are a few pieces of clothing, two promotional give-away spoons from a local bank, salad tongs, and a handmade apron from an old friend. I am ready for housekeeping. These are my sole possessions now.

Friday arrives. Eddie picks me up from the television studio to take me to his mother's apartment. I pile two suitcases; my typewriter and the wooden one holding my belongings into his Chevy. I have just kissed my past so long, or so I thought.

But everything hits the fan and nothing goes as intended. A family friend, who works in the accounting office, is onto my friendship with Ed. She waits with retaliatory salivation for me to stumble. After issuing my final check, she promptly calls my parents and tells them that I have quit my job. The situation gets sticky and our plans to marry are hurriedly pushed forward. Late that evening we leave Los Angeles for Nevada.

So here I am on my way to Las Vegas. This day, August 4th, 1951, is also Mr. Edward Barles' twenty-fifth birthday and I will soon be his nineteen-year-old bride. We drive through the Nevada desert night and early Saturday morning, in the wide-open spaces and amidst the tumbleweeds, we arrive on the outskirts of the lighted city. The temperature has already matched my father's anger. Eddie stops the car at the desolate wasteland's edge and we change into our wedding clothes. I put on a navy-blue, polka dot rayon dress with a white collar. I have no bouquet of flowers, photos or extras to mark this unforgettable day. We say our vows in front of the judge at the courthouse. His clerk is our witness. Within minutes it is over. The blur is not how I imagined my marriage ceremony would be.

Our honeymoon escape is a memorable, small motel, past the old Flamingo Hotel, the last large nightclub casino on the strip. The cement block barren walls are painted the popular early nineteen fifties dirty lime green. I'm glad the noisy window air-conditioner is there to tame the desert heat of 115 degrees. It has one setting...high/loud. We spend our wedding night cuddling in a frozen state, covered with a sheet and a lightweight overused, faded, floral bedspread. The air conditioner wins. It is a creative, fact-finding evening under the covers for our lovemaking, as we chatter and wait for the great thaw. The unlit, God knows what's in the dark, shower stall sports a moldy curtain that sticks to our bodies, but our need for love overrides our need for luxury.

After our unscheduled elopement we return the next day to Los Angeles, and Minnie's house, to face the wounded and the on-going battle. While we are gone, my father manages to trace our location. Now Minnie is caught in the middle of the *imbroglio*. Relentlessly, my parents had pursued my new mother-in-law for details, by phone, of our whereabouts. They torment her with threats and racial slurs, using every insult they can conjure to scare the wits out of her. I am mortified of the treatment to this lady. I feel uneasy about leaving her alone when we move north. How much easier it would be to have a Jewish bride for Minnie's youngest son and not have nuptials in a three-ring circus.

Ed answers another call from my father when we arrive home.

"Who do you think you're yelling at?" replies Ed.

I know exactly what Salvatore is saying without hearing the words. I've heard his intimidations all too often.

"You're right, there is no more Di Bella child. Do you understand? She's a married woman now." Ed shouts. "Such disgusting hatred! And you better stop bothering my mother too."

Not how I wanted Ed's first conversation with my father to be, but it was as I imagined.

This sets off a whole new action. We are to stay a few days with Minnie, as Eddie pulls together for his new position in Northern California. But as plans go, ours are feeble. The day we are loading our belongings into Ed's Chevy, I spot my father's car parked down the block from Minnie's house.

"Vin, get into the car and we'll drive past it to make sure."

We drive past the large cream-colored Buick with the flying winged Mercury hood ornament. Gelatin is strong compared to my knees. Every fear I theorized is in place.

"Eddie that's his car!"

"Are you sure? I don't see anyone in it."

205

"I'd know that Buick anywhere! He's going to kill us! Oh my God, I see him! He's standing on those people's lawn with my brother Nick!"

"Are you sure?" Eddie reacts. "I can't leave my mother alone if you think he's that nuts!"

"What's he going to do?" I scream as I scoot to the car's floorboard afraid he'll see me. I am cursed with every fear known to man.

We drive past them and they watch us. We circle the block and encounter a motorcycle policeman around the next corner. Ed tells him that my dad is acting erratic and won't accept the fact that we are married. We ask him to tell Dad to stop harassing Minnie. Salvatore moves on. With these new pressures we move ahead to our next adventure.

In San Francisco, Ed receives training for his new job. We live the first couple of weeks of our marriage in a San Francisco hotel. Then we have a month's stay in a motel in Pittsburg, California, a small town about fifty miles inland. Finally, two months into our coupling, we settle into a dilapidated old house owned by an equally beat-up, screaming landlady, Mrs. Balacci. Somehow I feel at home. The house, if you'll pardon the expression, is furnished. The moth-eaten sofa has a missing leg, but isn't off-balance since the floor is slanted and evens out everything. The kitchen is a sight to never forget with a refrigerator door that needs propping and refuses to stay closed. Like our honeymoon motel's air conditioner, everything is one temperature. Frozen. Not to be left out, the oven door needs a stick and a chair wedged against the handle. But I am an excited new bride filled with optimism for a grand and wonderful life. Nothing is going to deter me from proving my worth. This is my kitchen. Let the nest begin.

Ed begins his new position, with the International Red Cross, at the Army base in Pittsburg. Since this is during the Korean conflict, he has expectations that this work will take him to far corners of the world. I'm sad to say that marriage soon changes this idea for him. Every penny is carefully spent. We are one poor couple. I find a part-time job with an accountant but it leaves me bored to tears. Numbers, as the nuns will verify, is not my gig. I'm not sure what my future is all about. Everything is so new.

I can't believe how different my life suddenly becomes with a new husband. The stormy relationship with my Italian-born parents and my comprehension of marriage leaves me with poor training for my future. I was well trained by watching my mother submit to my father for every decision. I surmise this must be the way to live with a new husband. On the other hand, my man was raised by a dominant Russian-Jewish mother, who wouldn't dream of not asserting her own thinking. Consequently Ed waits for me to react independently to life. I wait for him to give me my next instruction.

Our first Thanksgiving is an opportunity to try my virginal culinary skills. My acting career has begun.

I have never made a whole meal on my own. I decide to roast Ed's favorite, a duck. During the week we stayed in his mother's apartment, the size of a thimble, I watched her make the favored poultry in a brown paper bag, which, in my uneducated cooking state, seemed unique to me. Minnie performs her food preparation duties effortlessly. But I am not afraid. I am sure I can handle this unknown feat, even with my lack of experience.

Make believe.

I buy the duck and give the fowl fellow a good bath, dose him with spices, slip him into the grocery bag, then into the hot oven with the propped door. I make the sign of the cross.

It rains all night and most of Thanksgiving Day. We have scattered pans throughout the house to catch the water coming through the well-ventilated roof. So now the rain drives the ants and their friends indoors for shelter. I seem to be drawn to one-temperature machines. The stove, which also only knows high, blasts heat, hot as a foundry furnace, into the closet-size kitchen, while I, the 'child bride', wilt in the natural smoky sauna. I prepare the side dishes. The moment arrives to remove the bagged bird from the oven. I peak into the grocery bag and see that the duck is a "Peking" knockout. Stunningly beautiful. The crispy skin and aroma reward my heart. I have conquered one gladiator in this untamed arena. I place it on the breadboard to rest while I set the table and finish last minute preparations. After ten minutes, in the poor kitchen light, I reach in to the open bag and remove the *canard sauvage*, and shriek in horror. I take a closer look at the roasted fowl. The ants have taken up residence in the game bird, dancing the tarantella on his succulent back! Amidst the tears, Ed and I make a joint decision to brush them off and trust the extra protein will not disturb our sleep pattern.

A new opportunity comes my way. I am hired as a secretary for the CID, Criminal Investigation Detachment, for the Army. Since my youth I've read true crimes avidly, but the stark reality of some of these army cases offers me quite a hair-raising, blushing education. An agent asks me to file a crime photo. It is a downright quick study. My eyes nearly pop their sockets when I see the picture of a dead officer sitting on the john with his pants down around his knees. The eye-opening, new employment opens avenues of discussions with my new groom.

Sound advice says you should get to know the person you are to marry. Ask all the qualifying questions long before you decide to join forces. We came nowhere close to this theory. Our relationship was love first, stay blind, ask no questions, and hope for the best.

Case in point. One night while cuddling in bed, in Mrs. Balacci's run down house, I tell Ed about my exciting new job; giving him my impressions of the undercover agents and detectives involved in their clandestine investigations.

Suddenly, my new groom drops a bomb.

"Vin, I kinda feel I need to tell you something," he says with some hesitation.

I answer in my softest, loving tone, "What is it, Eddie?"

"Well, it's something about my real work. I guess since you now have confidential, military clearance, I can tell you."

"What is it, Ed?" Immediately losing the soft quality in my body. "What's this real work stuff?" I sit up, aware of a different sound to his voice.

"Well, I don't know how to tell you, Vin, but I'm a secret agent."

"What? Oh yeah. No way. No way." My body springs bolt upright as if in a dentist's chair. "I don't believe you! You're always playing dumb tricks on me."

"I'm telling the truth, but that's all right, don't believe me. But don't blow my cover with anyone."

"You can't be real. Why haven't you told me? This is serious!"

"I couldn't tell you, honey, because I'm working on a top-secret case."

"Let's see your identification, Eddie," confident I have him now.

"We don't carry anything like that around. It's too easy to be discovered. Maybe I shouldn't have said anything. Anyhow I have to go to the bathroom."

I sit on the bed, astounded. Holy cats! What does this mean? I've known him for seven months and I've had no hint about this side of him. With narrowed, agitated eyes I watch as my *esposo* returns to bed.

"I don't like this one bit, Ed. What kind of malarkey is this? You must have something to identify yourself!"

"Well, aah, I do," he falters. "I have a tattoo. A hidden tattoo."

"You what?" I move to the edge of the bed. "Where? Let me see it. I still don't believe you, Ed Barles. Just show me where it is. Is it on your back?"

"Naw, they wouldn't put it where you can see it too easy."

"So where?" my speech is now in it's highest octave. "In your armpit?"

"Well. It's aaah, it's on my privates."

"What? Are you crazy? You're always trying to pull a fast one, Eddie!"

"Honest! It's a star. All the agents have a star."

"Who would do that?"

"I'm serious! Here, take a look!"

"Oh my God!"

The little blue star is definitely on his scrotum. I begin to tremble that this might be the truth. My husband is an undercover agent. But wait a second. Is that a telltale crinkle near his eye?

"Eddie, you're lying! That's why you went into the bathroom! You thought you could fool me, didn't you? How would you like to be a crippled agent with early retirement? I'll give you a secret star!"

Next we move to a barracks-type military house, a unit about the size of a thirty-five foot trailer, but much better and cozier than our slanted shanty. Things appear to fall nicely into place. We even start a family. Peter Pooper, Minnie's cockatiel, now lives with us, then we rescue a stray kitten, dumb Madeline, and our neighbor has a couple of Eurasian kids, Mei Li and Louie, who latch on to us.

Although money is tight, we resolve to save two hundred dollars and buy our first appliance, an apartment-size refrigerator to replace the icebox, which yields a continual menu of spoiled food. When the new addition arrives we buy a half-gallon of ice cream and put it into the freezer. Each night we get up from our bed to look at the light in our new cold box.

My daily question, planted indelibly in my brain by my mother, soon starts to annoy my *amore*.

"Eddie, what do you want for dinner?"

"Honey, you don't have to keep asking me every day what I want. I know you're afraid of making mistakes but I'm sure you have some great ideas and I trust you'll do your best. Why don't you surprise me?"

I set upon exploring my newfound freedom. I make the usual steak and fries. Try my hand at fried chicken and mash potatoes. I hit the mark with my spaghetti and meatballs. I'm not too familiar with American cooking, but I am willing to try. I make an effort to prepare foods I know his mother has cooked for him.

I remembered the layered and fruited gelatin dessert my talented mother-in-law served. But I've never made *Jell-O*. I buy two packages, strawberry and lime and a can of fruit cocktail. I follow directions, and that evening I present the finished course to my spouse. It smells delicious, but the fruit had sunk to the bottom and the lime had run into the strawberry, making the color a little less than perfect. I attempt to cut a gray slice to place onto Ed's dish, but the Jell-O has become a secret, rubberized weapon.

I am undaunted in my persistence to prove to my husband he has not lost two bucks on his share of our license. I decide to venture into my Italian heritage for ideas to feed my trusting and food-loving mate. I try to recall the different delicacies that delighted my gourmand father. Surely I can recapture these moments of comestible delights. A roast! Yes, an Italian roast! Damn, how clever I am!

Although I never actually saw how Mother prepared this dish, it looked easy enough and certainly inexpensive. I can do it. I imagine the table for the evening meal. A clean, freshly starched, ironed tablecloth, a few dandelions in a glass, even lighted candles, like they do in the movies. I round out the menu with Ed's favorite baked potato with sour cream, butter and cheese, a salad of red onions, tomatoes and basil with Italian dressing, and a little ice cream sundae for dessert. I can hardly wait. It is almost dinnertime. I freshen my clothes and cologne and wait for His Honor to arrive.

"Hi honey. How's it going?" Ed says, as he puts his briefcase on the chair. "Oh that looks nice, candles oooh oooh! Something smells good. What's cooking?"

"Eddie, guess what? I have an Italian surprise for dinner!"

I light the candles and turn off the main light in the undersized room. Next, I serve the salad and baked potato and then to the oven to remove my work of genius. I put the roasted meat onto a platter and place it in the middle of the table, anticipating my husband's admiration.

And with a pessimistic smile he questions.

"What is that, honey?"

"You're gonna love it Eddie, my mother used to make this for my dad. It's roasted kidney."

Silence.

"What? Roasted what?"

"Roasted whole kidney! Here, I'll slice it for you." I return, with my confidence at high peak.

In the diminished light, I cut down into the awaiting gland. It spurts some juices. I put several slices on Ed's dish and he draws back, grimacing, as he cuts into the broiled organ. Each time he sticks it with his knife and fork it releases more blood, until his dish is filled with the sanguineous fluid. With disbelief and a weak loving smile, I drain the dishes. But once again the juices return.

"Er-aa I don't think I can eat this, honey. I'll just eat the salad and potato."

However, now is the time for guilt and how much does he really love me?

In my best whining voice, "But, I worked all day on this dinner."

"I'm sorry, Chi-Chi," he consoles. "You know, Vin, you've been trying much too hard on these meals lately. How about a night out tomorrow? Maybe a Crab Louis over in Antioch?"

16 Eddie and Venera's first photo together. Santa Monica Beach. (1951)

ANTIPASTI SERVED with HEARTBURN

I've had nightmares about this day.

Following our fiery elopement, I know if I am ever to see my parents again, there will have to be much bowing and scraping to heal this relationship. It will not be easy to accept this first invitation to dine at my parent's home. Ed and I continue to be on rocky terrain with the senior Italians. The entire four years, since our marriage, is sprinkled with tense adjustments. The hardest part is the unspoken words.

We are without contact from Mom and Dad the first year in Northern California. Other than distorted words through the grapevine of their whereabouts, the information is slim. My father's disdain and hostility are constant enemies. After several months, we drive south to visit Ed's mother in Los Angeles and decide to check my old Hollywood neighborhood, secretly hoping to catch a glimpse of my parents in their garden. But I can hardly go on the street without raking up old fears. There is no sign of them. We stop to get information from an elderly neighbor.

"Well, I'm surprised," she says. "Don't you know what's happened? Your father and little brother moved away to Italy after your mother died. Any ways, that's what he told us."

My shock is profound. What happened? She gives no further details.

Oh no! Mom is dead. How? And they're gone. Why didn't you let me know Salvatore? How could you? You're teaching me another one of your many cruel lessons. Why are you so hateful and filled with spite?

After checking obituaries and city records, we find nothing. It is a week of horror.

I can't recall how I discover the truth, but in due course, I find out that Mother is alive and well. My family had, indeed, moved to Italy, leaving lies behind them.

At every turn my heart continues to grieve.

After a while, we carefully begin to correspond, but I am on constant vigil for trickery from my parents. We gingerly avoid anything that might upset the plans as we play the game with as much fake politeness that we can muster.

Make believe.

The letters are endlessly bittersweet and reveal the hostility when I don't comply with Father's demands. In Salvatore's need for power and superiority, he takes as many opportunities to jab at Ed about his background.

I guess by now it's no mystery why Father would take his ostentatious Buick to Europe. In one of the earliest pieces of mail, we receive a photo of the car after it was damaged. It seems he was trying to avoid hitting a child, on a small village road, and instead smashes into a stonewall. The instructions on the photograph are in great detail. He directs us to mail him a long piece of chrome strip, the length of the car and parts for the grill. The logistics of the deed are too difficult to accomplish. After much thought, I decide to scrap the impossible job. Once again I fall out of grace with my troublesome parent.

There are always too many ups and downs. I can't make him happy.

Ed and I work hard towards the same goals and with his veteran loan we finally purchase our first home. Thankfully, no children as yet, except a one year-old rescued pound pup, a wirehair fox terrier named Toby. But now, with the new house, we have fresh concerns and responsibilities; lawns, fences, car and furniture to buy. Daily, the list grows longer. My young spouse, raised in apartment houses in the Bronx, will now have to contend with novel unfamiliar tribulations. No more banging on the pipes for the Super to come and take care of repairs.

By the time Salvatore and Antonietta return to the United States, we move back to Southern California and into our new tract house, in Garden Grove. My twelve-year-old brother, Nick, who also works hard for his father's approval, is placed in a military academy in Albany, New York. I can't help but think of how much I miss seeing my brother grow up. I want so much for my parents to approve of the life we have made for ourselves, but I live on pins, fearful of what might go wrong. The price is high for my choices.

I am immobilized with nervousness and sheer terror with the anticipation of the initial meeting with Mother and Father. They are to come to our home, and I will have to prepare the inaugural meal for them. I agonize over each detail. After five years, Salvatore and Antonietta will meet my husband for the first time.

Why do I feel so utterly useless? What can I feed them? I know I'll do it wrong. How did this happen to me?

Ed helps with the decision.

"Listen, Vin, why don't we just take them to that nice Italian restaurant in town, instead of breaking your back trying to please them with a home cooked meal? That way we'll be on neutral ground."

"Oh I can't. I can just hear him say, 'She can't even cook us a dinner'. But it sure does sound tempting."

We did. Salvatore sulked without direct words.

I was right. I know what he's thinking. What kind of people are we? His daughter can't even make food for them. Great start. Once again, Venera fails.

After some penance, a phone invitation is arranged. Now we are being invited for dinner for the first time at their home.

Here we go again. Now I will learn how to really treat guests.

And again, I am miserable with the tension and dread.

We ask if we may bring our well-mannered dog, Toby, even though I know my mother is not fond of animals. I never do find out what she likes. Reluctantly they agree.

My parents have moved back into one of several duplexes they own and rent out while in Italy. I was sixteen when I lived in this dwelling. Many memories.

As Ed and I enter the house, the only furniture is the large carved European spinet my father bought for me years before. And here they are again, after selling all their furnishings in nineteen fifty-one, reduced to a cloth covered card table with place settings for four, two Bentwood chairs and two crates in the middle of the uncarpeted living room. The bedrooms and bath are on the second level.

When I see the stairway going to the top floor, I remember the awful day my father and I drive to a "yellow page doctor" for him to have a hemorrhoidectomy in the doctor's office. I am shaken to the bone when he comes out of the office pale and practically incoherent. He has been given Morphine. Dad insists on driving the long distance, but as we pull up to the house I can see he is just about to pass out. I drag him out of the car to the front steps. Mom is hysterical as we pull him bit by bit up the stairway to the bedroom. That night is one of the most frightening of my young life. Dad begins to bleed profusely and Mom is utterly helpless. He doesn't want me to call anyone. His delirium is dramatic and I fear he will die. It feels strange to hold my father's life in my care.

I walk further into the house and into the familiar smells of my childhood. Everyone is polite and stiff. Small talk prevails between my father and Ed. Mom is quietly somber. A frame of mind I well understand and remember, and as usual, I take the lead to engage in conversation. She answers in cautious child-like monotone monosyllables.

How much does she hate me for leaving her? Maybe she was glad. She never has had much to talk to me about. How much easier her life would have been had I not been born. There would have been no competition.

When Dad leads us outdoors to show us his garden, it helps to ease the heavy air. Again, memories immediately revive when I see the homemade aluminum trailer in the corner of the yard.

How I remember that summer and year. It is still fresh in my mind. Living in this tin tomb after our cross-country trip from the East coast. Crossing the divide, so to speak. Still another reminder of some of the stifling and smothering years spent with my parents.

Dinner is announced. We are directed to take our seats around the little table. Even Toby sits up straight. He seems to perceive the nervous tension. Antonietta remains quiet and aloof. She is in a state of suspended thinking and avoids any interaction that might set-off her spouse. I see she is focused solely on serving the wonderful homemade ravioli. Ed and I look forward to the food to further break the pressure. It is as I remember. The flavor. For a while I recall the good memories. Despite all the heartache of these past years, I am home. I did not think I would ever taste my mother's cooking again.

Oh that this day be the beginning of always!

Toby sits calmly watching us. We start our salad and antipasto. Occasionally my eyes meet my father's and quickly I look away. Talk lessens. All our topics have been used. *Keats* must have known this room, 'noiseless as fear in a wide wilderness'. Suddenly a great bang punctures the silence. A gunshot?

In unison we cry.

"Oh my God. What's that?"

Amidst the frantic spill of words, Salvatore jumps to his full five feet and runs up the stairs, two at time, to check the source of the loud sound. Meanwhile, Ed looks down to his lap, checking where he's been shot. Surely the blood will surface at any moment. Toby runs in circles. Antonietta heaves loud fearful sighs; her high heels click on the hardwood floors as she hastens to the kitchen. Down the steps comes Salvatore, wild-eyed, screaming in *any* language that will work. Ed and I stand frozen. We follow my hysterical father into the kitchen. At the door we discover the origin of the big boom. Salvatore, crowing like a rooster whose pinfeathers have just been seared off, wildly points with his palsied hand to the cabinet above the stove.

"Ann, what the hella hoppen?"

Venera Di Bella Barles

The pasta boiling beneath, heats the overhead space where the alcohol is stored and the warmed *Galiano* liqueur bottle pops its cork. Like the lava of Mt. Etna, the sweet yellow liquid flows slowly down the walls, into every crevice and down the back of the white Wedgewood gas range. Ed and I hold each other as a little nervous laugh escapes our lips. Normal tension is restored, and no one has, as yet, been shot.

It is one of those days that has forty-eight hours and we still have forty-five remaining.

LOVE LETTERS?

"Pensa molto, parla poco, e scrivi meno."(It.)
"Think much, speak little, and write less."

It is forever hard receiving these letters. Each time the postal-carrier leaves mail, I cautiously open the box and as I see the familiar envelope with the printed *Per Via Aerea*, the red and blue striped border, the canceled Italian stamps and the carefully written address, my head begins to spin and pound, my heart races, and all the old fears attached to this family comes into play. I am often asked why I save these odious missives. It is clear for me. There are times when I forget who I am, and did I just imagine all the anger and sadness in my life. When I look at these pieces of paper, I am convinced my recovery was needed and it was done well.

Most letters written are usually in my mother's handwriting. For years I watch my father stand over her shoulder giving instructions to write what he demands. Not until he dies, does Momma write and send greeting cards and letters of her own desire.

One of the first pieces of mail I receive after the fiery start of my marriage to Ed is a circuitous one from my fifteen-year-old brother, Nick, who was nine at the time we eloped. He is studying in Italy, while my parents live only forty miles from my house in California. In six years, after a few failures, this is still another ice-breaking attempt from my father.

September 03, 1957
Dear Sister Venera,

This letter will probably seem strange to you and surprise you, after all that's happened in the past.

Yesterday I received a letter from Dad, where he described all the suffering Mom is going through, and I'm sure you know why. The way Dad wrote that letter made me realize this, that Dad loves Mom immensely and that Mom is suffering too much.

I don't know what drove you or Ed to do what you did, but I'm sure of one thing, the love of a parent is much more greater than the disrespect of a child and that the readiness of a parent to forgive shows us how unworthy we are of such a love.

You may not believe me, but the way I've seen Mom cry and Dad suffer silently, sometimes make me ask myself if my sister, my own flesh-and-blood, is the cause of all this.

I think you realize, now that you're a mother, what a daughter means to her mother and how many sacrifices mother under-goes for her child.

What I'm going to ask you isn't too much and I think you should consider it a duty, and not a sacrifice: Visit Mom every once in a while and don't worry about Dad. When you want to come, just call up and tell Mom that you want to come and Dad will leave right away. The most appropriate time would be in the morning around 9 o'clock. It's up to you if you want

222

to see Dad or not, but if you could, you would make an unhappy man die happy. If, God-willing, this pacification should happen, please pay no attention to pride or prejudice and try to make Mom and Dad happy.

I beg of you, if you still have any love for your brother, I'm not saying for your parents, because it seems you've lost your love for them, but I hope it's not true, to do this.

Don't think for one moment that Mom and Dad told me to write these words; I have been wanting to do this for a long time, but I have hesitated in the hope of a spontaneous act on your part. I'm including a picture for you to remember me by. Please Answer Soon.

Your Brother Nicholas

I recognize the familiar phrases and statements, typically dictated by Dad. He now is engaging my brother to intercede on his behalf. I do not contact my parents until Nick, who turns sixteen, returns to America and pays me a visit. My wounds are still bleeding too profusely to reach out. He tells me how disappointed he is with me.

"I'm sorry, Nick, that you don't seem to understand the misery and pain they give."

I am hardly able to hold back the embittered fury.

"I can't stand their lies, manipulation and hate. One minute he's happy with us and suddenly without warning they disappear with some unknown dissatisfaction. Why must they always send an emissary to do their dirty work! I've made too many sacrifices and tried many times to make things better. I don't deserve this sort of treatment as if I am scum! Why does everyone have to bow down to Dad? You mark my words, Nick, you don't understand now, but some day you will do the same."

He stands tall and straight and with quiet deliberation says, "I will never do what you did to Mom and Dad!"

His day arrives eight years later.

The following spring, Mom and Nick come for a visit. I am nearly due with the arrival of my second baby and overwhelmed with the tension and mixed pleasure from the long awaited encounter with my parent. With guilt guiding my hands, every inch of the house is scoured, every weed pulled, my home stands at attention. I can't risk Mom seeing that I am less than perfect. I don't want her words proven.

I pity the man who marries you. You're filthy dirty.

When they arrive I see it is difficult for her to kiss or throw her arms around me, but I am not surprised. She has been injured. She doesn't know whom to blame for her misery; besides, she has always been on the light side with affection towards me. A small attempt is made to acknowledge her two-year old granddaughter, Gina. I feel sorry for my little one who is so excited and affectionate. She believes her grandmother will respond in like fashion.

I sense this gladness is only temporary. In order for the continuation of our meetings, I will need to prostitute my thinking. We make it through the next few years as if we have glass feet crossing minefields. I pay emotional duty. After our second child, I have a nervous breakdown. As I thought, my brother's marriage in 1965, to Ellen, a non-Italian, threatens the waters further, but we succeed in getting through Dad's tantrums. As in mine, he also insists on trying to steer his son's career and life, while discounting and giving much stress to Ellen.

Easter 1966. Fifteen hard years between us now. On and off. On and off. Once again they depart from our house in obscure anger.

What did we do wrong? It's always something! I can't figure out how to please him.

I can't defend myself against Dad's unreasonable requests. My fears and panic warp my thinking. Ed visits him to try and understand what are Salvatore's latest slights and commands. He demands that we be at their home on his say. We are to drop whatever other appointments or friends to accommodate his insatiable needs. He finishes our relationship once more with his written word. When the letter arrives I am prostrate with fright of my father's wrath. Even his words on paper have the ability to destroy any sensible thinking.

(Father's dictated letter to Ed.)
September 22, 1966   Monterey Park, California
Dear Son-In-Law,

I wanted to tell you on the phone yesterday, but I was afraid that I would get excited, so I might as well tell you what I feel about you, I want you to understand that I haven't got no calendar for my children, my house is open all the time and also my heart, and anytime even if it's every Sunday, they are all welcome to eat anytime they feel like, without asking me. As you told me that you are booked already for three months, don't tell me that baloney, you haven't got no friends that come in your house, or either you go to there house, you are

225

not the type to have friends. I found out Easter Sunday, when your boss friend drop in you don't even offer a glass of water, you complain to my daughter if they were going to eat there, finally they had to go themselves to Knott's Berry farm to eat.

I know dear son-in-law that my daughter goes through a lot with you, but we are Catholic, you don't find very many like my daughter. You telling me that you are booked, the only booked you have is going to Knott's Berry Farm and watch the people go by. I know you well, if you were sociable fellow, you would live with your family, but you don't know what means father and mother because you never lived with them. I should listen to my family, you try hard not to have the affection of my children, because you are jealous. You don't know what it means to be father, but someday you may find out, as I say, you are lucky that you have a wonderful girl in the world, she has everything. If she was like your sister, she wouldn't live with you one month, and let me tell you something if my son will treat his wife the same way you do I would go over and rip his face, but you know my son I'm sure he treats his wife wonderful.

Do you want to tell me when to come to your house and also where to sit down and how long I could stay? How can I feel comfortably, since you stole my daughter, you deal with criminals, you think we are all the same. You are smart enough to know good is in this life why don't you make me love my daughter and the rest of the family, and don't give me that poison. I forget to tell you dear son-in-law I'm going to Italy, but I'm going to Italy to try forget my troubles especial with you, since 1951 that I had that trouble.

Your Father-In-Law

I am not sure when my parents actually leave the United States.

It is three years since the last news, and for a bit, there is peace and quiet for us. Nick, by now, a physician in the Army, his wife, Ellen, and new baby girl, live in Colorado. It is now his turn to get hate mail. Embarrassing letters are sent to Nick's superiors, chaplains and whom ever my father can find to harm and discredit him.

In January 1968, we lose our newborn baby son and our grief is beyond repair. I don't hear anything for a long time from Dad but then he decides to write on his own. (Copies are sent to Ed's office as well.) Again I hold in my hand, a letter with their local California address. The palpitations start instantly. My joints and head begin to throb with pain like a cathedral bell. Suddenly I become aware that he can very well be sitting in his car in front of our house watching me. I am fearfully suspicious. I become a child, unable to rationally think. Will I never have peace and sanity in my life?

(Father's letter to me.)
1969 - Monterey Park, California
My Dear,

Do you thought that your sweet husband scare me? When he told me there was no more Di Bella Child? O no my dear you are absolutely mistaken.

Do you know you have an obligation? You have a brilliant and wonderful Mother in the world, you and your sweet brother been pushing around as a piece of rag, never had a sweet word. Remember my sweetheart since you ran away from the house, and treated your Mother as a bum, for 19 years, but now I am getting very tired and I won't let you get away as long as my eyes are still open.

It is indescribable. Are you bastard? O no how can you stand life thinking that you give away your Mother affection? Are you a Mother? No I tell who you are the cruelest, savage and disgraceful, you are the Creator's impostor you have humiliated and mortified this mother. Is this the philosophy that you learn to your Children?

For my concern you are filthy, your brutilism act, disgrace and devastated my name, you are not fit to be in society.

Remember I won't let you get away with that criminal act.

I am very tired.   I Warn You

Years of therapy, and I am still unable to let go or cope. The powers of these pieces of paper flatten me instantly. What is it about this old man that terrorizes me always? I do not answer the letter.

Once again they flee to Italy and I will **never** see my father again. They live there for the next seventeen years. My parents have a large apartment in Linguaglossa, Dad's village, and for a little while we are thankful for the silence. They make no inquiry into our lives. By now, Nick chooses to make his own life, but, as predicted, this does not sit well with Dad. Salvatore tries every miserable prank to get his way, making so much strife for my brother and his family. He is pretty much through with me and I am thankful for the respite. I finally begin to recognize that I don't need this diet of hate and vindictiveness.

After seven years, I receive another letter from Dad and before long, he pleads to us for help in bringing my brother back under his control. About twice a year the letters come forth spewing the venom of false love. Nick and Ellen, now feel the unending demands and pressures.

(Father's letter to me)
December 10, 1976
My Dear,

How are you? I bet that you never guess who is writing to you. I am your father don't you remember me? I enclose a picture honey so you could recognize me, just think April 30 you be 45! My my my never dream that I have a daughter that big, I bet by this time you are the best happy grand mother in the world. Of course my dear I can accuse you since those long years that you have a Mother and if she is alive or dead.

I swear in God that I am the most brutal that exist on earth, yes my dear my great mistake in my life was to marry this innocent mother of yours that she is brilliant that God ever created. No my dear I should marry a tiger that will tear apart you and that sweet brother of yours. I am at the end of my rope and I swear in God that I will deform your face that no surgeon will make you a human face; you are the worst corrupt delinquent the dishonest that dishonor my family. You are the animal that you treat your own mother as slava and throw her out of your house; no you treat your mother-in-law with respect because she was the worst immoral stink like you rotten.

I can never forget when you ran away from my house, that rotten mother-in-law keep in the house for 10 days and we were dying to find out where you are. Oh well I guess that skunk Jew of your husband he was lucky that day when your Mother call on the phone and tell him this is your Mother-in-law. Then you remember that I call and I talked for ten minutes and you rotten never say a word, and that skunk Jew on the other line he told me Mr. don't call here any more! Di Bella daughter doesn't exist here any more I could come over and make him open his dirty mouth and let him eat some of his shit. Let me warn Mrs. I am going to the top of the world to this skunk and find out if exist Barles family Di Bella daughter, don't forget I still have hot blood Sicilian. I come over and see you the skunk Jew don't forget your holidays.

Your father

In his outrageous distortion of facts, he never fails to remind me of his hatred. How much, am I to continue to pay? Where is the end of this idiocy? I do not answer.

(Father sends Nick and me the same letter.)
1977
To My Children,

I am going out of my mind thinking that I ask my own daughter my own flesh and blood for forgiveness? Because I send the Pasta Forna recipe, you remember that I cry hard, and the vile skunk Jew told me, no Di Bella daughter exist any more, no body in this world that did humiliate Salvatore Di Bella, but my children did, as if I were a criminal.

My son that I would give my blood to drop by drop, he told his mother to abandon his father, it is the worst infame that the children have inflict on their own father, it is unbelievable, if I tell to the people, they say that I am crazy. Just think the last letter of July 22, 1977, he wrote to me, I'm sorry Dad, but you are not going to live unpleasantly in Denver, he told his mother, that he try to forgive so many chances to his father, but no more now. This is the verdict that the children give to his father, because one married a traitor Jew, because the other married a dirty Irish, I try to forgive, and ask God forgiveness, but those infame children still hammer and hammer my destiny, until I commit a fracelo, and I'm sure that I will rest in peace.

Your Father

I do not answer.

I am forty-seven years old. Seven long years of therapy and psychoanalysis still aren't enough. By 1979, I begin to feel an outward anger.

Why do you think I went away Daddy? I thought you at least loved me, even though, I knew, Momma never did. You never gave me a chance to be honest with you. I was your pawn. Why don't you have room for truth? Questions. Always questions.

I decide to write back to my parents and send them copies of all the miserable pieces of mail they have sent to date.

Ed suggests, "Put the letters away in your desk for a couple of weeks and then send them, maybe by then you'll feel differently."

(Letter and copies to Mom and Dad.)
May 9, 1979
My "dear" Parents,

Well, I received another of your great loving letters today—excuse me, I mean a copy! I know you don't need a reply to them—but I've thought it over you should hear me also. I've listened to your poisoned stuff for years of what you've felt for my family and me. I've let you put me down, my husband, my in-laws, my children—you name it, you have said something unkind. Just once, I would like to have heard how proud you are of my family and me, after all it's all you have—it's true we're not perfect—but neither are you both!

Your granddaughters don't understand what you dislike about us—you have so much hate you're still talking about when we married, 27 years ago! Can't you find anything newer than that? Your marriage was not that perfect. Think!! I should have realized years ago, you had no love or forgiveness for us—it was just an act—to get what you wanted! You truly are sick people!! I've known you've used me and tried to use me in order to be closer to your son or whatever else you wanted. Not too many times do you think what anyone else needs. You should be ashamed of yourself! Selfish! Don't forget Salvatore, you walked out on us back in 1966—as usual, you didn't tell me what was bothering you or what you didn't like, maybe we could have had a chance to explain—but you don't need explanations—you need more hate!! So you ran—instead of sitting down with me and being honest. We might have had a chance as a loving family! You've missed a great deal in life by being such a hateful and selfish man. It's sad to see old men not happy—but you see **no one can make you happy**—you have to decide that—when you decide that you want happiness, the rest of the world will join you and want you. You must forgive first! In the last couple of sweet letters you've something new to "lie" about—we **never** threw Momma out of this house, so try a little harder to be unkind.

In all the years, that you've sent me these miserable letters—I have always defended you and Mom for what nice people you're really like to my children—so at least they don't hate you—they just don't think you love them!

And finally, as for your sick letters and copies sent to me and Nick and to all the different people you use—you're really too much—you must think I don't have a brain in my head—Momma writes the letters you dictate. She has **never, never, ever** written a letter by herself. Who do you think you're fooling? You're the one who talks like that, not momma!

Do me a favor—no more letter's—they mean nothing to me—You're both very crazy and you need a head Doctor! I'm sorry for you—but leave me out of your life!

Venera

P.S.: I thought you'd like copies of some of the "love" notes you've sent me!! I hope you enjoy them as much as I have.

I never send the letter and copies.

The years swiftly move ahead, each letter with promises of their return to make our family complete. I am the eternal optimist. They continually send instructions of how we should fix our two families to accommodate these wondering parents with non-bending points of views. As they age, I hear my father's disguised plea to take care of them, but always with threats, rather than love.

(Nick and I both receive this letter.)
May 26, 1980   Linguaglossa

This is a copy sent to your sweet brother, since you and your sister have buried alive this innocent mother, while you and the rest of the bunch having party and forget this mother if she still alive or dead.

Well dear, the party is gone, your mother will come there as soon as the papers are ready and certificate for the issue of a new passport. There will be a call when she reaches Denver Airport. Remember Mr. Di Bella and Mrs. Barles a false treatment to your mother will be the end of this family that been terrorized life of this two old people.

Hoping that you realize to make a stop on this insane dramatize life.

I am returning to Albany or Denver or California, that depends that you have my life in your hands.

Your father

P.S.: Francis Gulino came over to visit you, did you tell her that you been terrorize your father and mother at 48 years old? Hoping that I won't close my eyes that God give me a chance to see you again.

Your father

Mom, the emissary, arrives from Italy and stays with Nick and his family in Denver. I miss the phone communication she makes to our home in California. Ed tells her I will return her call as soon as I arrive home.

I am enraged. All the hate and unforgiving feelings return. I decide I will take the opportunity to make her hear how I feel. I will tell her the truth about everything in our unhappy lives. I will ask her why she can't be a more responsible mother? Why can't she short-circuit some of these family problems? I will ask her why she is so passive? I will ask her why she can't show grandmotherly love to her grandchildren? I will ask her why? Why she doesn't love me?

"By God, I'll tell her off!" I scream to Ed.

When I place the call and hear her voice for the first time in thirteen years, I make a reflective instant decision not to burden her. She will never understand my bitterness. She is only able to relate to her own pain and suffering. She sounds like a wounded child. It is the same sound I remember as a little girl. I suddenly determine she is a wager in this vicious game.

"Oh Venera, hello, how are you?" her voice quivers in a high falsetto.

"Hello Momma, how are you feeling?"

My heart beats loud as if it is in my ears. I hear the small insecure tone that forces me to give up my childhood in order to protect her from demons and hurts. Here I am again shielding her from the truth of my anger.

"Oh you know, Venera, how hard everything has been. I've been so sick and your father has been very sick too."

She names all of her out of order, defective parts. There always was a litany of physical complaints as long as I can remember. She seems only able to relate in ailments.

"I know, Ma, how hard it's been," I say softly in a trembling voice. I am hardly able to stand. My knees are so weak.

I manage to ask her why, in all these years, she hasn't written without Dad's knowledge.

"You know how your father is. It's not me." she whines.

She asks about the family and how things are? I tell her we lost our precious little son.

"Oh my, I didn't know that. That's too bad. I'm so sorry."

No questions about the details. She is much too afraid for details.

"Are you also coming to California to visit me?" I ask, knowing full well she will not. I am not part of the plan. She blames my father for the unending requirements. I am aware of the reason for this trip to my brother's home. She is the delegate to break ground for them to come back to America. She is afraid she will fail. How well I know this feeling.

The conversation ends after I tell my fragile mother I love her. She does not say the same.

I receive a significant card from her immediately, but I don't believe it is sincere. I am suspicious it is still with Dad's prompting.

(Mom's card.)
September 18, 1980
Dear Edward and Venera
Dear Venera

I grieve with you for the sad news of your son, for you were a good mother for your children, I only hope you will have happiness for the rest of your life.

I want you to know that I do think of you often you are my darling daughter and I love you and also your father. As I said last night on the phone it is not me, you must believe me and understand, I never mean to hurt you. I love you very much and I always will. Always remember this.

Your loving Mother

September 25, 1980
Dearest Momma,

You can't imagine how wonderful it was to read your two cards—they mean so much to me. I'm sorry we couldn't sit down together and really talk about ourselves. You sounded really good.

How about scheduling a couple of weeks in California with Eddie and me before leaving for Italy otherwise who knows how long it will be before we'd see each other again. Let us know if you can come. It was wonderful hearing about Aunt Felicia, Uncle Jimmy and Aunt Joan and the rest of the family. I haven't seen Uncle Jim and Aunt Joan since 1949.

I hope you make a point of enjoying your visit and don't only worry about doing things to make Dad happy, which we know is next to impossible. Do try to come to see us—who knows it could be two or three years before we'd make it to Europe again.

I love you.   Venera

She flies back to New York State to visit her family before leaving for Italy. Except for Mom's sister, Felicia, and her daughter Camille, I have cut-off communication with all of my relatives during most of my marriage. I cannot handle the stress of hearing news from anyone. I am embarrassed with my life; I feel they will also condemn me for my choices. I hear little from them.

On the east coast, Mom falls ill before she leaves for Italy, consequently, Dad flies to America to care for her. Once again the letters start with vitriolic substance, he forces my sickly mother to write his ravings.

(Mother's letter, once more, dictated by Salvatore.)

December 2, 1980
My Dear Daughter Venera and Eddy,

Your birthday card was the most wonderful that could happen in my life in 49 years that I am married, me and your father wishing you and Eddy the most wonderful happy Christmas and a Happy New Year.

It was a shame that your brother spoil my trip, I could of spend a few days with you and your family happy days, you know your father give me the money to come and see you. But see what happen your brother send for your father between my trip and his trip and stay in and furnished apartment and eat and the expenses of the apartment in Italy cost us $5,000.00, your brother promise before he left that he would take care all the expenses, even the operation on his eye that he needs bad, but since the Nov 12, 1980 we haven't heard if we were alive.

Yes dear after we sacrificed to support him. Through the doctor we found out that his income is $55,000.00 a year and his wife riding 7 horses all day long.

Forgive me dear but God punish your father but your father he didn't take care you that he wanted a son doctor and this is what he wanted, he didn't even give you the piano that he sold for a lousy $300.00.

Well I am closing and tell you if God wanted that we are going out of the United States 26 or Dec 27, 1980.

Please write to me and wishing you and your family a Merry Christmas and a Happy New Year to all. Answer soon Love and Kisses to you all.

Family and friends in Albany and Denver rally to help Mom, but Dad manages to alienate each and everyone. He refuses to pay medical bills; he twists facts and gives my brother insurmountable grief and embarrassment. He constantly demands so much from Nick.

(Another dictated letter, supposedly from Mother to Ellen, Nick's wife.)

239

Venera Di Bella Barles

This is a copy of the letter send to the wife of your sweet brother

December 4, 1980   Albany, N. Y.

My Dear,

Please let me confess you this horrible punishment that this Di Bella family been terrify for 49 years my life continues, I am not asking you for pity, no dear the only one I ask is the mother of God, could let me died and rest in peace. Believe me dear I didn't want to come to Denver, I beg my husband not to send me, but he forced me, and here I am in this mess of suffering because of my son.

He call his father not because I was very seriously ill, but to make his father pay for all the hospital and doctor bills, and be a free man.

But let me tell you this dear he could enjoy his stinking $55,000.00, but there's a God he wouldn't forget and you know that we support him with lots sacrifices and money, but let him enjoy his rotten stinky horses!

Well dear this is the result of the horrible mess that I am to pay. My husband found out that those bills they have to be paid, your husband told the doctor that he (my father) has lots of money in California.

That made my husband angry that he wanted to come to Denver and blow his brains up. I just wish to drop dead from his miserable horses and be happy.

I have no love for this bastata son that he destroy my living.

This is a mother terrorized by his son

P.S.: I'm sorry dear I may be discharge by the end of next week and going to your fathers apartment, might go back after Christmas, please if you want to write this is the address. Your father sends his love to every one Merry Christmas and a Happy New Year. Please send some pictures before I go to Italy.

Love, Your Mother

Please daddy, don't embarrass us. Be nice. I can't love you this way.

By 1983, my father decides to play hardball, yet again, with very little fairness. It is obvious he is aware illness and age is taking a toll on both of their bodies. Soon remembrances of birthdays and anniversaries fill the postal waves as they work overtime to get on our good side. I give it my best try ever. As always, as in childhood, peace at any price. They make plans to move back to the United States to live near my brother in Denver. Salvatore sells his lavish BMW. He constructs four involved trunks to ship their belongings.

(My letter to my parents in Italy.)

May 7, 1983
Dear Mom and Dad,

We received your last two letters and sorry we were so long in answering. Eddie thanks you both so very much for remembering his birthday, especially four months ahead. He always enjoys hearing from both of you. Ellen's birthday is July 26, the same day as your anniversary.

Dad, I'm glad your doctor in Italy said you could travel without causing complications to your medical problems. We hope Mom is also well and strong enough for the trip with all the changes. It's important to plan carefully to make the trip less confusing and therefore easier on both of you.

Be sure to let us know about the dates you have in mind for leaving Italy. Lots of love

Venera and Eddie

P.S.: I don't know if we told you in our last letter that Gina was pregnant and should have her first child in September.

(Their letter to my family.)

July 11, 1983
My Dear Venera & Eddie Gina & Carisa,

We received your letter but I am sorry to tell you why I didn't answer your letter soon, we both got so sick. Your father is under the doctor care for his heart, it got so bad with all the injections morning and night and 8 pills a day, it was too much every 20 days the doctor want to get electric (EKG) of his heart.

I been very sick with my blood pressure, the doctors are very concerned about it got so high last Wednesday when it was 210 the doctor said I almost got hemorrhage from my head he got me just in time.

So glad to hear that Gina is expecting her baby. I wish her a lot of luck and happiness with her husband and the new baby, does she live near your house, how about Carisa is she in Francisco, California, or near you.

Venera I send Ellen a gift for her Birthday. I only hope she will answer soon to let me know if she received it, are they going on their vacation this year? Let me know.

How are you & Eddie, give him our love and kisses and to you too, hoping to hear from you soon. Please Answer soon. Love to you all. Answer soon

Your Loving Father & Mother

They cancel their travel plans again. Health issues become dramatic. And then in 1984 plans resume. Letters are furiously written back and forth, concerning money, where and how he wants to live. The involved instructions and burden is placed squarely on my brother's shoulders. By May, things move faster. And now our own lives are complicated. Ed's mother is not doing well.

(My letter to my parents.)
October 20, 1984   Buena Park, California
Dear Mom and Dad,

Well this has been a very hard and sad week for Eddie, the kids and me. Eddie's mother died October 15, last Sunday and I can't tell you how much she meant to me. I feel

I've lost one of the closest people in my life—she suffered a great deal in the last three years—so in a way she at least hasn't any more pain. She had cancer and she fought to stay well and alive right up to the end—she would have been 94 this December. I wish you both could have met her—I know you would have liked her. You probably blamed her even though you had not met her, but you were angry with me when I married Eddie. It wasn't her fault at all. She was very good to the children and me. She didn't have much to give but somehow managed to care and be kind to me when I was sick or needed someone. She taught me how to be a woman. I'll miss her.

We are all O.K. just a little tired and worn down—but we will be better soon. Gina's baby, Alexia had her first birthday the 3rd of October and I gave her a little dinner party and it was fun.

Carisa and Gina have very busy lives—trying to make a living. I hope someday Carisa will move closer to us—it would be nice. Eddie and I baby-sit for Gina about 3 or 4 times a month and we have a good time with the baby—watching her grow has been wonderful—she has just started to walk.

Well enough about us—how are you both doing and feeling—are you getting things ready for your trip? Are you going to wait until spring to leave? The weather would probably be better for you in Colorado—but I suppose you and Nick have already discussed what you're going to do. What does everyone think back there about your leaving? Are they surprised or don't they talk to you about it?

Well it has been a long time since we have seen each other—17 years—a lifetime! We have all changed—so much water under the bridge. I'm sorry we wasted all those years.

How about it Dad, you're going to be 84 years old! That's terrific—Happy Birthday from all of us! Dad do you still smoke or did you finally quit? I remember when I was a little girl I would get up during the night and you'd be up smoking and drawing plans or some other things. I guess you couldn't sleep much. What have the doctors said about your health lately—both of you? Please let me know.

Well, I guess I've covered most of the things going on. Take care of yourselves—I guess you don't write anymore because of your hands—is that right Mom? I hope they improve soon. I love you both!

Venera and family

P.S.: Eddie is sad but feeling all right—it will take time—the children and I love him and we will take care of him.

(Response)
November 22, 1984
Dear Sweetheart Venera & Eddie & family,

We are so sorry to hear about Eddie mother has pass away, she must of suffer a lot, tell Eddie not to get himself so sick, we all have to go there don't matter what we do.

Dear Venera your father has been very sick again we had to take to the doctor in Taormina the one that operate on him. He gave him 3 different kinds of pills to take, then he want to see your father again on Dec. 7, 1984.

As for me I should go to the hospital to take an x-ray, but I can't leave your father he is so sick, my two arms I can't put on my dress I fell on top of my arm, it will be 7 months when I go to the post office or bank I ask to give me a table low or chair to sign my name. My left hand it got so bad with arthritis, your father has to cut fingernails for me.

Venera & Eddie could you find out what happen to Nick we didn't receive any mail from him, we just like to know about the 4 trunks if he heard from the company in New York.

Nick send us the picture of the newspaper of the 20 years he has done with the Army hospital we were so happy you should of seen your father how he was happy, tell Nick that your father is still using the old pipe that he gave 3 years ago, from Albany. Tell us how everyone is there and the baby we were glad that she start to walk. How is Gina and Louis and Carisa give them my love and kisses. Please tell Eddie we are so sorry for his mother, we only wish we were there to see Eddie. Hoping to hear from you all soon and tell Nick to write as we are so anxious to know about the 4 trunks if they arrive in New York. Give Eddie and to Venera lots of love & kisses.

Your loving father and mother,

P.S.: excuse my handwriting.

246

This is the last letter from Italy. Seven days later, November 29, 1984, Salvatore, my father, dies.

He's gone. He's gone. He's gone. My daddy is dead!

For a mere moment, I think things are going to work out. I feel a tempest in my heart. I almost get to say good-bye to my warden. Once more the loss resembles abandonment.

Once again, Salvatore, you've cheated me!

Nick leaves Denver for Sicily on a difficult journey. He is to bring our mother home. These are some of the highlights of Nick's notes from that hell week. His hectic and tiring job is fraught with too many details to list.

> **30 Nov, 1984 (Fri)**-Yesterday at the office I received word from Amino (friend) that Dad had died of a probable heart attack at the hospital in Linguaglossa.

> **3am**-Plane departure for Chicago.
> Connection New York (Newark Airport)

> **11:15**-Arrived passport office at Rockefeller Center Problem: No old passport and no good birth certificate (not from City of Albany). Temporary papers started. Walked the streets; crowded. **3:30**-Passport ready. **4:00**-Subway to JFK

Venera Di Bella Barles

6:55-Departure by TWA/Flight 840 (Boeing 747)
Pleasant trip - 8hrs.

December 1 (Sat)-(also our mother's birthday)

9:30am-Arrival Fumino Airport Rome; Italy feels strange.

1:00pm-Departure for Catania by Alitalia. Lunch of lasagne
and salad (good!) at airport.
2:20pm-Arrival Catania (Fontanarossa AP). Greeted by
Amino and Mother. Drove to Linguaglossa.

4:30pm-Arrival at parent's home. Body in wake, dusk,
candles, friends and family. Lid of casket removed.
Father looked surprisingly healthy; had been out walking
day before he died! Casket closed, loaded into funeral
limos. Streets wet, sky gray, damp and cold, windy (@ 40
degrees F)

Proceeding funeral limo was priest Father DiMouro—
an old friend—I was his altar boy—remained a friend of
family, visited parents at least once a month.

Fa. Di Mouro in cassock with 2 altar boys. I was
going to drive behind but instead walked behind limo with
friends and few relatives (20+). We walked about 1/4 mile
out of town to the church at the college dei Dominici.

Body taken out. Funeral mass by Pdre Di Mouro
with assistance by Pdre Raciti.

20-25 people, mostly women. Mom next to me. It felt
good to be there.

5:30pm-6:00pm-The decision as to where body would go (Sicily or U.S.) had not been made. I decided before mass to leave body there. After mass we all followed limo 2 miles out of town to cemetery. The casket was sealed by one of the cemetery workers with a blowtorch. Room was cold, damp, room entrance to cemetery. I paid the cemetery custodian 10,000 lire.

7:00pm-We went back to parent's apartment. Cold, dingy, actually a large apartment and nice. Most of furniture gone - Sold in last 3 months. Few tables, chairs, bed with bedroom furniture, fruit and stuff on floor, stained sheets and mattress (dad incontinent).

7:30-8:00pm-Mom and I made my bed; I discovered no hot water, and not much heat (turned off 10:30), no lights in most rooms. Decided to stay elsewhere!!

8:30-9:00pm-Dinner at Barlettas'. My Italian is coming back but not great yet!! Salvatore Barletta brought by all the bills for funeral, flowers, etc. He is old friend of Dad, also a carpenter, doing remodeling for Amino

Sunday—December 2
Awoke @ 10:00, slept like a log.

11:30-met at Barlettas'.

12:00-left for Giardini, followed Amino in his M-B, drives like a madman. I forgot streets are like alleys with hairpin turns.

1:00pm-Arrive Catania, with Mrs. Barletta, greeted by Rino—my school friend, Pharmacist, wife Maria from Veneto, schoolteacher. Have 5 children. Very nice home, beautiful old (17th century) refurbished with ceilings painted - sunken bathtub—restored 15th 16th Century furniture!! Like a museum. Enjoyable afternoon of reminiscing, Rino proud of his antiques. Rino had me drive around Catania. - What traffic!!

9:30pm-Mom soaked her foot
Busy walking always, better with some wine.

11:00-To bed, slept well despite dripping sound of aquarium and splashing ocean.

08:30am-Awake, tried to make instant coffee, what a mess. Cannot jog, raining too hard - did pushups, sit-ups.

9:30-Left Giardini

10:30-Arrive Linguaglossa, raining hard, what roads

1:30-Stopped by cemetery, laborers working on grave.

2:30-Visited old Church and Padre Di Mauro—restoring 14th Century Church of San Francisco

3:30-Saw La Cuzza @ Monument. Spent lot of time, cold and rainy - Shop looks like something from biblical times. Decided on a simple monument with cross, picture of Etna.

5:00-Stopped by Gregorio and Gina Ardizzone's Shop (wool socks—it's cold) (wear my raincoat all time)
6:00-Picked up Cannoli at Pina Azzurro
6:30-People at house, Mom visiting with them. Annetta Di Bella, cousin.

7:30-I called Ellen, long call.

8:30-Dinner at Barlettas' again. 6 course meal with trimmings. Glad I bought Cannoli and liquore. House cold.

11:00-Left for Giardini 11:30-Arrived, raining. Mom soaked feet. Could not sleep a wink!! Too much on my mind.

4 Dec Tuesday
8:15-Up out of bed. No time to jog. Left for Linguaglossa. Called Amer. Embassy in Palermo. To Bank, raining like crazy. To City Hall for Death Certificate and Certificate of Residence change for Mom. Lunch, cheese and salami. To Gregorio's for coffee.

2:15-To cemetery, finishing grave in rain (covered in plastic). Cement wet. We carry casket @ 200 yds, down 4 sets of steps to grave. Heavy, lower with ropes. I tip all 3 laborers.

2:45-Take Mom to hairdresser.

3:00-To La Cuzza Monument maker. We agree on terms (2.5 million lire $1400 for marble monument.

6:30-Back home. Called Tersa & Turiddu, neighbors, they bring truck and clean up much of apartment. Mom gave watch and radio to Mazza kid next door.

8:30-Dinner at Barlettas'. Amino's Birthday.. Amino refused $ for use of car and apartment. Pleasant evening, Amino's 45th birthday - great dinner - lasagna, falsomagro, pork loin, etc.

11:30-finally left for Giardini. Raining hard, streets empty—poor tire traction, almost got lost again in Fuimifreddo. I always get confused.

12:30-To bed. Cold and lonely

5 Dec Wednesday
6:00-Up early; no mineral water though, so we can't make coffee (water not good in apartment due to recent flooding and contamination of Giardini water supply)

7:30-I found a dolceria open so bought 4 "tiny" cups of coffee. Waiting for Amino, sea is rough, sky overcast and windy. Raining still

11:30-Arrive at Banco di Roma. Met with Dr. Costa-all very complicated. 50% for Mom, other 50% split 3 ways—Vin, Nick and Mom. Finally departed, raining hard. Dinner in Giardini. Pasta con Vongole, fresh fish, wine—the only rest all day. Bought shoes for Mom. Back to house, some more packing, disconnected TV and gave to Teresa. Dinner at Ardizzone. I'm running out of steam but dinner felt good.

10:30-Left for Giardini, finally stopped raining - Got lost on way home, ended up in Mascoli.

6 Dec Thursday

7am-Up early, lots to do hopefully my last day here. Made my list of errands for the day. Finally a day with Sun!!

While waiting for documents to be prepared I notice that Mom's a lot more relaxed. Doesn't even seemed to be depressed @ Dad's death—she worked so hard I think she is relieved he is gone and she can return to U.S. where she is more comfortable.

6pm-Finished cleaning up apartment - Mother sorted all her junk, lots of help from neighbors; all is clean.

7pm-Tearful farewell. Visit Zia Concettina and Carmelina— old and frail; (father's two sisters) Concettina lives upstairs, and Carmelina downstairs; the latter has lost a few marbles. I talked to cousin Nicola in Florence by telephone; doing OK has a 10 yr old son Alessandro; and wife has heart disease; financial problems. Tearful Good-bye. My cold is worse

7 Dec Friday

6:00am-Arrived at Catania airport. Depart for Rome. Beautiful View of Mt. Etna, covered with snow and surrounded by clouds.

11:15am-Departure for New York. While flying, I mention to Mom that we are approaching France—She strains to look out the window and asks "How do you know it's France, is it written on it?"

7:30-Denver arrival—almost 24 hrs more since we got up at 4 am in Sicily.

Ed and I fly from California to Denver to be there when Mom and Nick arrive. Much of Nick's duties that week in Sicily, involve burying our father, closing out the house, accounts, paying bills, seeing to a headstone for Dad's grave, and saying good-bye to several decades of our lives.

It is a hard miserable week.

They finally arrive in Denver on Friday, December 7th, 1984, both sick and exhausted, but Mom seems to handle Dad's death well.

Strangest of strange. The four trunks arrive the day after Nick and Mom return. Sal Di Bella's treasures arrive in massive custom-made, gold-colored, aluminum, crate-like trunks. It quickly reminds me of when we left Albany in our silver trailer, with all our possessions.

All their material life is within these containers; his tools, carved tables, lamps, and a large wooden birdcage, all wrapped carefully with Mom's very worn towels and linens. She has brought back her bent and dented pans, like our lives, have found, yet another home. The trunks travel for months to make their appearance this day.

Their master is left behind.

#17 Mom, Dad, and Nick in Pisa, Italy. (1952)

A DARK and FEARFUL THING

My madness seems to be growing.

How can I tell anyone that I hear voices coming from the vacuum cleaner? If I try to sleep the bedroom closes in on me. When the lights are out, I imagine bugs crawling the walls. The lead ball in my nightmare is suffocating me. I can't stand the living room curtains open. The babies need so much. I have to be strong. I mustn't let people see me at home. I don't want to visit with anyone. I don't want anything to do with any of my friends or neighbors. They want to know too much.

Suicide. Suicide.

Daily my agitation grows.

To admit that my children are living with a mad woman is not even in my thinking. I'm aware of the exhaustion. I feel intensely overworked since the delivery of my second daughter. My husband helps as much as he can, but other than him, I have no relief.

I can't control the crying. I feel so angry all the time. My body is sick. Why do I keep getting infections in my incision? It's taking so long to heal after this c-section! It's doubling me over with pain. What's the use of it all? No one really cares. I hate everything. Why was I born? I can't even pick up the babies. My soul is dying.

Suicide. Suicide.

I know I will overcome the physical problems, at least I believe, but it is the mushrooming emotional confusion that levels my psyche and soma. The indications are crushing. Things that used to be pleasurable reduce me to anguish; sex, music, socializing, sewing, home duties. I am suspicious of people's motives.

She thinks she's so hot! Who does she think she is? Miss hot shot! Miss has it all together! Miss degree here and degree there! I'm so stupid! No education. Nothing! Only thing I'm good for is to clean toilets! Oh God, will I ever sleep again? I can't stand to be in this bed. This room is going to choke me. It's getting smaller and smaller. Those bugs on the wall never stop moving. The nightmares are worse. Why am I still here? I can't see my worth. Without importance, of what value am I to my family? There are no more answers.
Suicide. Suicide.

I hide food and eat compulsively. These habits wreak havoc on my body.

I am disheveled and unkempt. Daily I tie a bandanna around my head rather than comb my hair. It is a major effort to go out with the family. Everyone needs to be perfectly groomed and dressed. Obsessed beyond belief. Each day, I neurotically scrub the house, even in the corners with toothbrushes. I leave little time to think. The vacuum beckons and speaks to my madness.

There are those voices again! They're in the vacuum. Who are they? Why are they back again today? I can't understand their words. Thank God for this radio. I'll turn it up...that's good.

By the time Ed arrives home, I see him as the enemy. I am bitter and resentful.

Eddie's lucky. He has freedom and independence. I would give anything to just get in the car and go away. I can't. I can't. Too much to do. Everyday there is too much to do. Babies need me. Babies need me. Where's the baby? Is she o.k? The market? I need to buy food. Dinner? What to make? Who gives a crap what I make!

He looks helpless. Why doesn't he know what to do with me? I wonder why? Why can't he help me? I need help with the work. Too much work. He's a psychologist. Can't he see I'm cracking? How I wish I were in his place. He's able to get away from all the boulders I place in our path.

Suicide. Suicide.

My sweet children take the brunt of my demented state. My oldest daughter, Gina, two and half, a quiet and undemanding child, has her own miseries to contend with. A strange malady plagues her little body. Even after series of tests, kept diaries and good follow-ups, the diagnosis is never clear enough to satisfy me.

Everyone is sick. Will we ever get better? No. No. No. Daddy you did this. It's your curse. If you would only want us. Why do you hate me so? My babies need you. Daddy I tried, please. Please Daddy.

Suicide. Suicide.

Thankfully, Carisa, our second child, escapes most of my bitter reactions to these irrational feelings. During our pre-occupation with her sister's illness, she takes a back position. But Gina is not all that lucky. My frustrations soon find an outlet on her backside. I know I am in serious trouble. I am spiraling to the final rung.

I'm frozen and can't jump away when cars are coming. I wish I could die. Everything is out of control. I can't stand any more. My head hurts all the time. Can't lose weight. Pills for everything; to lose weight, birth control, migraines. I can't sleep.
Suicide. Suicide.

I spend countless hours to make sure the world beyond our doors has a good image of the family. I'm careful that outsiders don't catch on to my inappropriate solutions. I don't know how to control my environment. It seems right. After all, this is how I was trained to be a parent by my parents.

Daddy when are you going to stop tormenting me? You are thousands of miles away and still you're sucking me dry. I am becoming you!
Suicide. Suicide.

My father and mother continue to burden my spirit beyond belief with their insatiable and ruinous needs. Ed gently tried to warn me, a few years before, of this breakdown, that I should probably look into therapy for these instabilities. But the cells of mental blindness that cloud my being able to see, also prevent me from hearing the help that is right at hand.

"There's nothing wrong with me. I'm just a little nervous. Besides all Italians are crazy. Ha, ha."

My Ob/Gyn doctor gives me meprobamate, the tranquilizer of choice in the fifties, but after several months, he doesn't see an improvement.

"Mrs. Barles, this is not doing anything for you. It's only taking the cap off your problems. I will not fill another prescription. You must get psychiatric help!"

Is he telling me I'm crazy? All I know about crazy I learned from Momma who always said, 'If you're nuts they will put you in the insane asylum and throw away the key'. I can't even ask my parents for help. If they find out they'll shun me further. I'm at the bottom. I've failed at all my choices. Failed at life. Failed at school. Failed at marriage. Failed at child rearing. I can't even bear my children normally; I need to be slit open. Why didn't my manual come with clearer instructions?

At times I want to label it as 'after-baby blues', but my symptoms go far beyond. Along with postpartum hormonal changes, most of the problems come in the legacy of my warped parental values. Little is explored in these days concerning chemical imbalances. It triggers chaos in my brain, exacerbating an already run down existence. To add acid to my peaked body, I have been on contraceptive pills for five long years, suffering every side affect contra-indicated in the PDR. I have joined the ranks of women who are used as guinea pigs to test these new drugs, not knowing what the future would hold. Today, I have a better understanding of how I arrive at this horror.

I am frozen with fear when I first see the referred psychologist. He shocks me into reality with my first visit.

He asks, "Why are you here?"

I begin to tell him the pathetic details of my life. He listens without comment. But when I say, "I'm afraid I am taking my anger out on my little daughter."

The doctor leans forward. "How do you mean?"

"Well I hit her. I mean, I just spank her hard when she gets me upset."

He practically comes out of his seat and forcefully states, "I don't care what your problems are. You will never lay another hand on that child. Is that understood?"

I never expect this unsympathetic advice. But it is the best thing he can do for me. A stranger is willing to help straighten my path.

Therapy is intense the next few years. My quest is to find out how I came to this point and in this condition. I have no concept of how these self-disclosures of my inner whispers can possibly heal me. But as I begin to gain trust, with much pain and struggle, I begin to reveal and strip away the powerful defenses I have so carefully built up. I am cautious at first. Feeling I am betraying my parents and family by telling this alien helper my comprehension of how I have stumbled this far. I begin to understand how much the pain of my existence with my parents undermines my future. I question why they did not believe in autonomy for their children, but instead replaced love with controls.

Slowly, very slowly, my ability to discern my future comes about. As the shroud of madness starts to ease, my physical health also gradually repairs. The nightmare, the lead ball on my chest, appears less and less. I begin to learn new survival tools. I see a new unrecognizable comfortable light.

I know, I will never more think of suicide as a choice.

There is a something which I dread;
It is a dark and fearful thing;
It steals along with withering tread,
Or sweeps on wild destruction's wing.
That thought comes o'er me in the hour
Of grief, of sickness, or of sadness;
'Tis not the dread of death; 'tis more.~
It is the dread of madness.

Lucretia Maria Davidson (1808-1825)

TALKING PICTURES

"Il tempo buono viene una volta sola."(It.)
"The good time comes but once."

Our lives are always intense.

I remember it from the beginning.

One unforgettable time in 1943, is when Dad invites the world to my brother Nicky's first birthday party. The guests come from all along the Hudson, as far as New York City and Long Island. We cook and prepare for days, stacking the *Cannoli* high. The basement of our old home, on Fairlawn Ave, is decorated. The one with the trapped piano. Anyone and everyone who plays an instrument arrives to render a tune. Dad dresses in Mom's wedding gown and veil, and with one of his equally hyper kinetic female cousins, in a tuxedo, performs a singing routine in drag. While Salvatore's pride and joy is slumped in his highchair, after one of the lesser brain-celled friends, slips the little guy some sips of lager.

It is as if someone has opened the gates of the asylum. The feast lasts the weekend.

But it isn't always a party.

I leave home when Nicky is nine and I do not see him again until he is sixteen. During these years Nicky is moved, like me, from one place to another. Around ten, Dad yanks him out of his American school, takes him to Italy and plunks him into an all boys, Italian-speaking middle school. As he jockeys for position in their ancient culture, the 'Idiot American,' as he is labeled, endures the clannishness and taunts of young pubescent males. But despite these social obstacles, he manages to shine as a bright and educated teen, making life-long friends in our parents' homeland. And as is typical, the roaming Salvatore then moves the family back to Albany, New York, to Nicky's and my birthplace.

My parents enroll him in the school my mother's brothers graduated from, Christian Brothers Academy, then Dad and Mom return to California leaving Nicky to fend for himself. Again he must adjust. This time in a tough school of much older lads in their late teens. Nick says it is difficult to live with our aging grandparents and unpredictable, alcoholic Uncle Joe, who lives on spent dreams. It must be a hard passage. He is silent about these years. A telling school photo shows him as he stands, smiling, looking like a mascot, amidst towering young men wearing military uniforms. After a year, at age fourteen, Nick returns to California to complete high school. He then returns to Italy on his own. Until he reaches adulthood, I hear little information of these years.

This young boy who gave me so much pleasure and love, now becomes the object of my petty jealousy and resentment. With these hollow formulas I am able to stay victimized. I turn each bit of information regarding Nicky's progress into a feeding trough of envy. This is not easy to admit. I am, after all, a master at disguising feelings in these early years.

For a long while, after my marriage, I shut out thoughts of my family, including my brother. I hear bits and pieces of how my brother Nicholas is doing. I want to write to him in Italy, but fear Dad's wrath towards Nick for any betrayal of the family with the contact. After six years of silence, at fifteen, Nicky sends me the first communication. My father, who lives in

California only forty miles away from where I live, has commandeered my brother to write a letter from Italy.

What I'm going to ask you isn't too much and I think you should consider it a duty, and not a sacrifice: Visit Mom every once in a while and don't worry about Dad. When you want to come, just call up and tell Mom that you want to come and Dad will leave right away. The most appropriate time would be in the morning around 9 o'clock. It's up to you if you want to see Dad or not, but if you could, you would make an unhappy man die happy. If, God-willing, this pacification should happen, please pay no attention to pride or prejudice and try to make Mom and Dad happy.

I beg of you, if you still have any love for your brother, I'm not saying for your parents, because it seems you've lost your love for them, but I hope it's not true, to do this.

Don't think for one moment that Mom and Dad told me to write these words; I have been wanting to do this for a long time, but I have hesitated in the hope of a spontaneous act on your part. I'm including a picture for you to remember me by.

I stare down into the photo and see an unsmiling young man. He doesn't understand the depth of my despair and my fear of Salvatore. The little cowboy is gone. Gone are his gun, holster and hat. His sandy brown hair has turned dark brown. It is well pomaded. I've lost six years in not being able to watch him develop into this handsome, tall, erect, well-groomed man. But I also

265

see he is posed as a dapper fellow in a man's suit and suede shoes. Holding a cigarette.

'To Venera, Ed and my niece, I offer this picture to remember me by'. It is signed, 'Nicholas J. Di Bella - Linguaglossa (Catania) Italy - August, 1957'.

I hear and see my father's words and grooming techniques.

Nick puts his thinking towards achievement. I marvel at his ability to rise above Salvatore's demands and to bring his career into focus. It must have taken phenomenal energy and concentration. How he screens out the bedlam that is our family boggles my mind to this day. I can hear those sentences of encouragement as Dad helped Nick with his determination to become a physician.

"If you don stay good in school, you better pick up the hammer and work!" Salvatore needs a doctor intensely.

It is a blessing that Nicholas sees his way through his father's ego. He graduates at nineteen, from UCLA with a BA in Zoology. I stay aware of my brother's exceptional educational progress during these years, even though my ability to stay levelheaded diminishes.

There are rare times when I experience pockets of decency with my parents. Ed, the children, and I attend a large graduation party given by Dad in my brother's honor. I see the glow and pride on my parent's faces as their son receives accolades from Sal's friends for his accomplishments.

My half-empty cup has an irreparable leak. I yearn for their approval also. I feel like a stranger looking in on this family, as if I never existed. I messed up my turn.

266

In my disturbed mind, I find reasons to fuel my emotional destruction. My husband, daughters and I are placed at the far end of the banquet table. We are not the favored ones.

This might have been my graduation party if only my father had not betrayed and stopped loving me. As is typical, Mother is cold and unreachable. It is as if I don't exist.

I retreat to my unidentified angers and wretchedness. I am a convincing actor with my solicitous warmth. I can never let on how bruised I feel.

Nick advances to USC Medical School. He is interested in tropical diseases and takes advantage of an opportunity to spend three months in Malawi, Africa, at the Likuni Mission Hospital near Lake Nyasa. I receive another photo of Nick. His dark brown-colored hair has turned nearly black. It is cropped short and his beard is full.

He is his own man, no longer posed by Salvatore.

Nicholas, with a reassuring face, stands at the Mission Hospital in Africa with a colleague. Both wear white laboratory smocks; stethoscopes protrude from their pockets. It brings tears to my eyes. It is a sobering picture seeing my little brother in a white medical jacket.

This is no lie. He made it. He's not in costume. My little Nicky. He's truly in medicine.

He is twenty-three when he graduates as the youngest doctor in his class. I want to shout it to the world.

Listen! Do you know what it must have taken for my little brother to learn all that stuff while Salvatore was breathing down his neck?

I never understand how incredible this feat is, until I become a grown woman. After Africa, he thinks to become a family practitioner. Nineteen hundred and sixty-five is an important year for him. A time of many changes. In his last year of medical school he joins the Army, and if that isn't enough, he marries.

Now if you think I went through crazy times with my matrimonial beginnings, we once again enter into The Land of Oz with Salvatore, The Wizard, who consistently makes life generally miserable for my husband and me. He now has new blood to add to his misery list. Nick's new wife and in-laws. My brother's decision to wed, against my father's wishes, gives Salvatore ammunition to try and destroy Nick's relationship.

How dare he have an independent desire without "Il Ambassadore's" approval? I told him to learn the rules.

Nick's bride and her parents plan a lovely wedding and Salvatore, as a wedding souvenir, has a grand-mal tantrum. This day, which should belong to the young couple, is periodically snatched by his Napoleonic selfish behavior. Ed and I are well acquainted with this dance. We're glad that we are able to ward off some of the silly maneuvers. Since this is not *Signore* Salvatore Di Bella's party, but these strange new American's gift to their daughter, he won't be having his way in these bridal decisions.

"Thisa no wedding. Thisa a funeral. What do they know? They Irish! Don forget who made him! I lika to ripa their eyes out!"

I know Dad. I remember these loving statements long ago.

Dad's unhappiness about Nick's choice, creates a stress on a level of a midget delivering sextuplets. It takes every available person to stabilize his attitude, and placate his every whim. Mother doesn't have a say. Now Salvatore has completed the set. No in-laws to ever deal with. Neither Nicks nor mine.

We gain a loyal and lovely sister-in-law. Through the years, Ellen has been instrumental in helping me bridge the faint perforation between Nick and me. Nicholas does well with this fine wife. She does not deserve the headaches she receives from my family.

He remains in the Army for twenty years as a medical doctor, completing residencies in Internal Medicine, Hematology, and Oncology. Nick rises in rank and esteem. He retires as a full colonel at forty-three.

Despite Nick's highly respected medical practice, raising a family of two daughters, Dad never lets up with demands for control over Nicks life during these long years. He continues to lay claim on his son as if Nick is still seven years of age. Dad sends a stinging letter to a high commander saying what a rotten son he has because he doesn't attend to his parents' every mandate. It is turned over to a chaplain.

I don't know if you will get the same agreement from my brother, regarding Dad's lack of respect for him and the pressures he sets in his path, but I can't help to see it as pay back for Salvatore.

I made you a doctor, now show me a good life and jump when I say. I need your titles.

I am not as tolerant of Dad as Nick seems to be. Maybe my memory serves me better on the hardships he presents. My recollections are different. I see tremendous stress. I see how my brother fights to suppress the turmoil. Perhaps he believes if he doesn't think of it, all will go away or get better. In my struggle to survive I'm sure I unleash some regretful, grievous fruit in Nicky's young life.

I can write this story much easier today, having shed the bitterness. Time and growth are good partners. To think that I held animus towards my dearest brother is hard for me to believe or consider. He battles demons of his own and has nothing to do with my laments.

One day I ask my grown brother.

"Nick, do you ever think of Mom and Dad?"

"Sometimes."

"Do you think they loved you?"

Without hesitation and with clarity he answers.

"No."

The answer pierces me with disbelief. "God! I'm so sorry."

"Yeah. Oh well."

"If you weren't a doctor, Nick, what would you like to have been?"

"Probably an architect."

"Whoa. That's something! Just like Dad. He certainly had a flair and natural abilities towards this very profession."

"Yeah."

"Nick, I want to take a picture of you. You decide where you want to sit. Hold it."

\# 18 Nick and his buddies at Christian Brothers Academy in Albany, N.Y. (1950's)

\#19 The young Di Bellas: Nick, Ellen and my nieces, Catherine and Christine

TURIDDU, HOW DARE YOU DIE?

> *"O occhi miei, occhi non gia', ma fonti!"(It.)*
> *"Oh eyes of mine, not eyes, but fountains now!"*
> *Petrarch*

Until I marry, most times I call him Daddy. Antonietta, my mother, calls him Sal while his intimate friends frequently use his nickname, Turiddu. Sal or Salvatore for business. He has as many personalities as he has names.

When I think of my father, I see his calloused hands with nails disfigured by blows of misguided hammers. They tell much of his life, and although he has an agile well-built, straight body of only five feet, his stature never inhibits his competitive spirit. Salvatore, the second eldest of four boys and two girls, migrates to America in his early twenties to find the imaginary gold-paved streets.

Before my brother is born, our love is different; unlike with Mom, I know Dad loves me. When I am with him he continually feeds me new potentials for life. He relishes teaching me skills and questioning my intellect. And even as a little girl I know I am his favored 'son.'

His workshop is a memorable sanctuary for his untapped talents. In this place I can do no wrong. It is here I watch the intensity of life this *Geppeto* gives to each piece of wood, and often I am reminded that the plank of lumber he is working on, will eventually end up with character and come alive to take its place in our home.

"You wanna sand this wood for me, sweetheart? After you finish we maka the airplane, O.K.?" He says, as the curls of planed wood float down to his well-worn pair of leather dress shoes.

"O.K. Daddy, I will." He has taught me to sand with the grain of the wood. "Is this good, Daddy?"

How I treasure these moments of love and sheer intimacy with the man who will also become my nemesis.

"Atsa nice. Atsa very nice. Maybe we finish thisa table today."

His nostrils and eyebrows are coated with the fine sawdust of his work. In my memory, I still retain the aromas; the strong smell of the glue pot cooking on the small burner, the pungent smell of the mixture of exquisite woods, his pipe and cigarettes. The Prince Albert tobacco can sits next to the radio; the radio that brings the Metropolitan Opera every Saturday to Sal's essence. What a blend of gifts that the world will never get to see. There are mounds of sawdust on the floor of the garage, an old sugar maple door waiting in the corner for transformation. On his workbench are the wood carving tools he brought from Italy. The statue of St. Joseph, the other carpenter, stands on the shelf, in attendance next to the radio. Near the bench is an olive oil can where we save mercury dimes together. What a purely sweet day it was the day we opened the filled can. We laugh heartily at the silliness of it all when we see that the coins are green and gummy.

After dinner, sometimes, long past my bedtime, we lean over the kitchen table discovering words in the dictionary or I watch him sketch new ideas. Shoulder to shoulder we put together a jigsaw puzzle of the slumped Indian Chief on his horse, each piece giving life to the warrior.

"Daddy, when you first came to America what kind of work did you do?" It was easier to answer my questions then. They were simple.

"I carve piano legs for Steinway." He shrugs his shoulder. "Ma, Germans make machine that make faster. Later, I work for New York Central Railroad and I carve special train for famous people."

After a hard day at work, he lays down on the sofa for a rest and lets me play with his hair. I comb and braid the dark straight locks. I feel a special closeness to this strong man. I am young; as yet, I do not fully fear him.

Salvatore has always been resourceful. He hates working for anyone other than himself. He easily retrains his thinking to fit the need. Later, he makes good money by buying nearly forsaken old houses; giving them new vitality, and restoring them to their grand habitats. He appreciates architectural design and works many nights until early hours of the morning drawing his next project. His lit everlasting home-rolled cigarette dangles from his mouth.

Before he meets Mom in Albany, he works in Hollywood constructing film sets and playing bit parts. I hear him talk of the suave Valentino and George Raft; two of the many stars he may have interacted with. I see how Turiddu likes to imitate their look of the day.

As I rummage through the family photos, I see a signed yellowed picture, to Dad, of Monte Banks, a well-known early movie star of the twenties. I then see the letter of recommendation from Mr. Banks' studio:

September 22, 1927

Mr. Salvatore Di Bella has worked for this company, as a character actor, and we wish to state that his work has at all times been satisfactory and well liked by the director and to myself. He has worked for us on two productions.

There are bits and pieces of faded newspaper articles, one of which is a small advertisement of Dad's Hollywood Art Dance Studio; Compagna Di Bella, located on Broadway, next to the Roxy Theater in New York City.

The tango is his specialty. His stage fame is short lived but the talent forever lingers.

I love when he holds listeners in a charismatic grasp as he tells extensive and spellbinding tales of his childhood, usually using himself as dupe. He thrives on their response.

It is fascinating to watch and hear Sal Di Bella's animated phone calls. The guys at the lumberyard, well acquainted with his lively spirit, enjoy getting him fired up. But he is not easily fooled and is aware of the ruse, and often he goes along with their nonsense.

"What? Spella my name? *Ma* how many times I buy lumber from you? O.K. Essa-ah-ella-vee-ah-tee-o-rrra-a, Salvatore! Gimme piece a lumber thisa long," his hands extend wide for measurements.

"How long, Mr. Di Bella?"

"*Ma* thisa long! Don fool around Jacka!"

Who is really being strung along?

Salvatore has a need to bend rules and a knack of testing the gods as well. As we drive, in his usual fast speed, on the main highway going north to San Francisco, a California Highway Patrolman pulls him over.

"Say mister, you were going pretty fast. Do you know the speed limit?"

"Yes sir, Ninety-nine. *Ma* officer, my car only go seventy-five!"

"Say, are you nuts? That's Highway 99. Not the speed limit sign!"

Dad loves San Diego's mild winter weather, a wonderful break from the extremes of upper New York State. I guess it is as good a reason as any to leave New York; besides, he has good memories of California. He often says it reminds him of Sicily. Without questioning, Mom, my three-year-old brother and me, follow Turiddu from New York to the Golden State. After our sad good-byes, we leave with our meager belongings, but also packed into the silver trailer, is his and my optimism. It doesn't take long to settle, once we reach our new state.

"By nexa week we finish the other house sweetheart." I had the feeling he was conferring with me. "Then we sella that one and build another one."

"Hey Daddy, I hope you won't make the same mistake as you did on the last house."

"I don make mistake. They don know how to build house in California."

"Are you kidding? You dug a complete basement on a canyon, which was against the building code. That's why the Inspector made you fill it all in. What a mess! We had to find more dirt after we got rid of the last pile. Don't you remember how hard we worked?"

He chuckles. We always banter back and forth. I can make him laugh and forget his troubles.

"Venere, you remember the flowers and palm trees in Sicily when you little?"

"Yup."

"Someday I'm gonna die there."

I don't need to ask why. I know his heart has never left Italy.

"You have a long time yet, Daddy."

"I want you trim the bushes today. Don forget."

"O.K Daddy. By the way, the house feels warmer. I think it helped when you cut that big Pepper Tree in back, but you know Mom says it's still so damp in this concrete house and we still can't get rid of the mildew in the closets."

"Thats right. I gonna fix - donchu worry."

"Are you thinking of moving again? Mom is so unhappy. She cries all the time. She says she misses Grandma and Grandpa Valente."

"Friday night we go to see new family. I meet new friend of Mr. Pesci. I want you and your mother and brother to looka nice. They come from near my village."

He doesn't answer a lot of my questions. He knows she's unhappy. I see it makes him nervous. He shakes so much when he holds a cup of coffee.

"Do they have kids, Daddy?"

"Yes, two."

Friday arrives. We put on our visiting clothes. Father is dressed to the enth. All the shades of brown match, from his silk woven suit to his camel hair topcoat and grayish tan hat and gloves.

"Ann, why don you wear the dress I buy you? Whatsa matta? Don you know how to dress?"

"Aw Daddy," I say. "She looks nice. Don't pick on her. Mom, wear that pin I gave you. It'll look good on you. Are you happy about meeting the new people?"

She likes when I fuss with her. I wish she didn't look so blue.

"I don't know."

Her eyes are so sad. I never hear her laugh since we moved west. She cries so much.

We drive to the quiet neighborhood and a modest Southern California home. I'm excited at the thought of meeting new friends for my lonely family. I hold my four-year old brother Nicky's' hand tightly as the friendly man answers the door and greets us to enter his living room. From a back room

Mrs. and her children, a young son and a daughter, two years younger than me, about twelve, appear to greet us. We are invited inside and ask us to be seated. The house is plain and simple, not many family pictures and no religious ones. Mrs. Reni begins to chat with my mother. She has a warm style. Immediately the men launch into the familiar Sicilian dialect, exchanging recognizable landmarks. Turiddu is energetic. I can see he is thrilled to have found these new people.

The round, linen dressed, dining table is set, not fancy but does include candles.

"Please come to the table and have some dessert and coffee." Mrs. Reni calls. "Here Venera, you can sit over here next to Mella. Nicky, you can sit next to your sister."

The father and mother speak without detection of an Italian accent. All are seated. All have smiles. Coffee is poured. Turiddu picks up his cup and starts to drink. The man touches my father's arm.

"Please Mr. Di Bella, wait one moment."

Dad puts down his cup, mystified by the interruption. We watch as Mr. Reni and his son place small silk caps on their heads while Mella and her Mother stand and put scarves on theirs. Mrs. Reni and her daughter next light the candles in the brass holders and place them in the middle of the table. They bow their heads. I sit entranced at the unfamiliar ceremony, straining to understand the ancient unrecognizable prayers. They are not Latin.

I look over to my father and see his flushed face. I wonder what to make of his change of mood. There is no smile on his face. I read his eyes. Anger?

The prayer is finished and the men speak suddenly with heated Italian words. Turiddu pushes his chair back and stands up.

"Ann, get up! Get your coat! Letsa go!"

What's happening? What's going on? He's embarrassing us! They are nice people. Has my father lost his mind? Why does he always have to make a scene?

As we drive home I listen and hear the reason for the shameful exit from our new friends house. The Renis are Italian-Jews.

Life in California becomes psychologically difficult for us. Dad is making a good living but each and every one of us are in pain with our separation from the East coast. It creeps into our souls. We lack friends and when we aren't working we spend most of our time alone in our concrete house. Dad holds on tighter to us. He fears losses. His rules are stricter and suffocating. Ownership is everything. Ownership of home, possessions, wife, and children. My parents fight continually and communication exists only subliminally. My ordinarily vibrant father appears disheartened and drained of life. I hear more of his disappointments. Since the war, the family in Italy is more needy.

"I justa mail big box to my brother, *ma* they never satisfy!"

Mom is inconsolable and we are unable to make her content. I never know when his inability to cope will shatter us all. My own life becomes more complicated, but I still want to make my father happy, to see him laugh, dance, and sing the wonderful Italian love songs again.

I am strong, I can save them. We'll be happy again. I just have to try harder.

Eventually, we sell the concrete house and move to Los Angeles and later to Hollywood. It brings us together with some old friends who have moved from the East. By this time much has happened between my father and me. Most of the trust between us has disappeared, but I continue to play his game.

Occasionally I wake pre-dawn, only to find Turiddu already sitting at the kitchen table. This Sunday, in our home in Hollywood 1950, I am up early as usual. I see my father already in the kitchen, a few hours of sleep interrupted by his regular insomnia. As soon as it is light he will, most likely, water the garden, his pride and joy. Whenever we drive about town and the countryside, he picks up stones for his yard. We recycle all the garbage, wood shavings, and ashes into the lush earth. The appealing rock gardens, statuary and fountains are showstoppers, admired by strangers, neighbors and friends.

I watch as his shaking, nicotine-stained hands roll a cigarette. He lights the ragged smoke and draws in long and hard.

"Hallo sweetheart."

"Hi Dad. How's it going? I see you're already up and at it."

The small beige and green chipped enamel pan waits on the drain board for his coffee. He throws in some grounds, and fills the water an inch from the top. He then sits at the chrome-legged, black Lucite kitchen table waiting for the coffee to boil. He begins to sketch new ideas and designs for a desk. It will match the handmade dining room set. But his thoughts jump to the plans for the evening.

"Venere, I told your mother to make spice cake for tonight. Don forget to rake the front and trim the bushes."

"O.K.," I say, reaching for the box of Mother's Oats. "You're pretty happy the way the cabinet turned out, aren't you?" He looks at me, and smiles.

Today is the day. Everything has to be neat, clean and just right for Turiddu's company. He has finally finished the carved television cabinet with side shelves, and he is pleased at how it looks in the living room. He has matched it well to the other Louis XIV decor. He rises from the kitchen table and picks up the wooden statue of the Chinese man carrying an umbrella and mounted on a horse. He places it on one of the side shelves of the new member of our family, along with vases and decorative bowls.

He returns to drink his hot sweetened coffee. I see on the table that he's been looking at some old photos of himself. His dark brown sensuous eyes, in a trance, are looking through the living room archway, and then he stares down again at the picture.

Dad looks so young and handsome in that photograph, with the fedora slanted at a rakish pitch over his sleek, brown hat. He knows people like and look up to him. I wonder if he's proven to himself, yet, that he made the right decision to leave Italy as a young man? He knows he is smart, even though he lacks formal education. He's always worked hard. After all, he taught himself to read and write in Italian and English. He's proud of his citizenship.

Once more he starts to draw the apparition of his newest creation on the sketchpad.

His hands are so unsteady. He says it was the mustard gas. He had many hardships in Ethiopia. The daily meal of only rice. He hates rice. He says he never wants to eat it again. This soldier Turiddu, looks so young. Why did times change so for him? Things are different here in California, not like it was in New York and Italy. He left many friends and good times. He hasn't even played the guitar and mandolin much lately. They're just gathering dust, hanging in the garage. Those were the days. He tells me that someday he'll live in Sicily again, because everything was more alive there. I sense he thinks people respected him more back then. Now that I am older, he also has plans for me to live in Italy. I fear he will probably marry me off. No Sal, not me.

Turiddu is lost in memories. A faint smile is on his face.

I remember the many times, as a youngster, we are invited to parties and weddings in Italy and Albany. He is invariably greeted warmly. He's aware his charisma enriches his friends. I still see him clearly. He walks, dressed in his finest, into a music hall filled with wedding guests. All heads turn to Turiddu. Momma and I follow. After he makes his greeting rounds, he spots the shy, box-shaped, overweight widow, Mrs. Mannino, sitting at the far end of the room. At the gatherings, she typically finds the darkest corner to sit and hide. Her crochet close at hand. But Turiddu comprehends what to do to make her come alive.

"Oh no, Signore Di Bella, I cannot," she pleads in Italian. "I don't know how to dance. Signore Di Bella, please *per piacere*, please!"

He knows he can talk her into changing her mind. And he knows what the hush is all about as he walks her slowly to the center of the dance floor. Eyes around the room wait for Turiddu to perform his magic with the intricate tango. Everything always changes when the music starts. He is capable, in control and powerful.

Slowly he bends her back, directing her deftly with his hands. All the time he observes her eyes. Their faces, lost in a dream state. Their legs understand the steps as if they'd been dance partners forever. He can tell she feels the movement and the imposing sensual energy. She has relaxed in his arms. He has taught her, once again, to be a butterfly.

He pours the last bit of coffee, smokes another cigarette, and I quickly see his expression tense.

I'll bet he's remembering how upset he was with us last night. Probably Momma won't talk to him today.

"Sometimes she's so stupid. She don help me. Why she don learn? Can't she learn?"

He hit me too. I wonder if he remembers. I was only trying to stop him? His blind rage is always so hard to pierce.

When he stops, he tearfully says in Italian, "They just don't understand me. Why don't they help me?"

I can't fully comprehend his tormented anguish then.

He looks out the window towards his workshop in the garage. The sun is almost up.

By evening, Antonietta's cake is ready. Turiddu sets the dining room table with the coffee cups and dessert dishes. He places a large platter of mixed fruit in the middle of the birch and birds-eye maple table; purchased just for this occasion. He is proud of his work and his friends surely will recognize his efforts again tonight. The lighting and the mood must be just right. At all costs we must make a good showing, *far bella figura.*

Turiddu, greets the four guests, while Mom and I take their coats upstairs and lay them on her cream, satin bedspread, the one used only when company comes. What does it matter, so long as it covers the thin blanket and the torn and worn bed sheets? I know she is glad she has this one nice treasure remaining from Albany. She leaves so much.

When we return to the living room, Dad is engaging our friends, the Giulianos and Timpanellis, in conversation.

They're lucky. They are always laughing and happy. They have their entire extended family living close by them. Why did everything change so much for us? Why did we leave New York? I hunger for those old feelings.

After dessert and coffee, Turiddu escorts everyone to the living room again. Nicky has his accordion propped near the piano waiting for the signal from Dad to entertain. Dad and the guests are animated as they recall, in Italian and English, the wonderful summer weekends spent at the lakes in the Adirondack Mountains.

"Do you remember, Turiddu? There'd be seven or eight cars with all our families." Mrs. Guiliano, bends to the coffee table to pick up a *dolce*. "We used to cook our pasta over the fires and later at night we'd roast *salsiccia*."

Mrs. Timpanelli, recalls. "And after, you and the men played the guitars and mandolins. You used to sing the Italian songs. God, you made tears come down our faces. Do you still sing, Turiddu?" But she goes on before his answer. Mom sits quietly listening. "Then you'd all play horseshoes and bocce, while we ladies had important things to catch up on. Right Nola?"

Nola Guiliano, shakes her head in affirmation and says, "I'll bet you don't remember this Nicky, but your sister, Venera, used to carry you all around and take care of you. You were heavy. There were lots of kids. Remember Venera? You used to put blankets over bent tree trunks to make tents and then you kids would wear them to make believe you were knights and princesses? Boy those were great times."

Turiddu remembers it very well.

Mother also remembers it well. It was always, a great deal of work.

I remember it well. There wasn't as much sadness.

"It brings to mind the winter dinners and card parties. They were swell times, weren't they Antonietta?"

Mom's eyes are distant as our friends continue with their pleasant memories.

"We just don't do that anymore since we came out here." Mrs. Timpanelli, nostalgically says. "I'll never forget the times at Mrs. Grasso's house, everybody liked to go there. She was a heck of cook." She starts to laugh heartily. "Do you recall the time we were all around the table playing cards and Mrs. Giusti, got into trouble, you know the real short lady with the large breasts who used to rest them on the table?" They all remembered. "Well, you recall she use to like to hide the cards under her bosom, and everybody was upset with the messed up game! All of a sudden Venera yells out that the missing cards are under Mrs. Giusti! God, I'll never forget it. Turiddu, you came out of your seat like a lion on a hot plate and you went after your little girl and gave her the business! Boy those were the days. God, what fun!"

But Antonietta is distracted. She is watching Sal. His mood is changing. That look she knows so well.

He seems nervous. He smokes a lot more this evening as he walks back and forth in front of the new cabinet. Occasionally he stops to open and close the doors or tap and rub his fingers on the finish.

It looks like everyone is getting ready to go. Dad is pretty upset with his friends. They haven't said anything yet about his new piece of furniture.

His hands shake heavily as he coolly bids them *arrivederci,* and when the door closes he vows to replace these bourgeois insensitive friends with new ones.

By the time I leave my family at the age of nineteen, I have lived in, at least, eleven homes.

Times change. I become an individual and not as easily fooled or molded by my family. When we move to Los Angeles, I see that Dad's dreams have already started to shift away from me to my brother. No matter how hard I try,

I cannot seem to prove myself to him any longer. Now, my brave little brother will have to push the boulder up the giant mountain.

The last time I am to see my father is after I'm married and it is Easter Sunday 1967. We think it's a fine visit and all is going well, but something doesn't please him and without words he leaves. Not long after, he takes Mother to Italy and they live there for the next seventeen years.

I promise myself, that if and when he comes back, I will be courageous and tell him of all the pain and sorrow he has given us. He never returns.

He always said he wanted to die in his native village, on the side of Mt. Etna, and at eighty-five he does.

His heart finally gives out - the heart that I so wanted.

My brother, Nick, goes to Linguaglossa, Italy, to help our mother bury him. On the tombstone he has engraved with Turiddu's wish...*nella terra che lui amava.*

To the land to which he loved.

#20 Salvatore, singing at an Italian gathering. (1950's)

#21 A young Salvatore in Italy (1920's)

JUST TELL ME YOU LOVE ME

"If one wished to be perfectly sincere, one would have to admit there are two kinds of love—well-fed and ill-fed. The rest is pure fiction."
Colette (1873-1888)

As she stares out of the window, I watch her sit on the pale, green Louis XIV sofa, twisting her lips with her fingers. She makes no comment about the passerby who stops to admire Dad's garden.

"Who's that old lady, Momma?"

"I don't know."

"How come you don't know her? She goes by the house all the time and talks to Daddy."

"Can't you leave me alone and let me sit here without you bothering me?" She holds the little mirror and checks her face. Her short legs and high-heeled, outfitted feet are propped up and crossed at the ankles.

Why doesn't she at least try to meet her? She seems very nice. Momma doesn't like to take time with anyone. Not even me. Why doesn't she care?

I can be in the same room with my mother, Antonietta, for what seems an eternity and she never says or shows the slightest interest that I'm even there.

If I don't speak, she doesn't speak. Each day she sits on the couch near the living room window, picks up the hand mirror and tweezers, and plucks the fine hairs of her eyebrows. I observe her carefully. She is completely enclosed in her own world.

My mother, not quite five-feet in stature, the oldest of the five children born to Carmela and Anthony Valente, is the only one born in a village near Naples, Italy. She has an attractive appearance. Like her mother, there is a premature gray streak in her light brown hair that compliments her smooth fair skin and blue eyes. Grooming and beauty are important to her. Unlike her sister, Felicia, the more creative, I view my mother's approach to life, as much more stifled. She is unwilling to try new aesthetic adventures or improve her education. Antonietta and Felicia, both highly puritanical; are concerned with modesty, to a fault. One dare not say anything off color in their presence. I sense my uncles also mask these religious precepts. My father's foul mouth must have been quite an insult to her senses.

Friends appear to enjoy her child-like qualities and shyness. Most times she is kind, but she is also, often, self-centered and without depth. There just doesn't seem to be an interest in other people or things. If you are to ask about her young life, she gives the same set of facts.

"You know, I only went to fifth grade, but I'm very good in arithmetic. You should know it, as good as me!"

"Why only fifth grade, Momma?"

"Because I had to work!" she angrily spits out. "I had to leave school to help out in Grandpa's grocery store. They always needed my help. Grandpa was so strict, you know. He wasn't easy. I suffered plenty."

I crave to be near her to learn and understand more. I wanted to know what was her suffering. I am wrong to assume, that she has the same talents and abilities of home crafts as her sister and mother. I am disappointed when I am nearly always turned down.

"Mommy, teach me how to crochet. You said you used to embroidery and crochet like Grandma and Aunt Philly. Mom, I sure would like to learn to cook. Will you let me some day?" She's not interested in anything I ask her to do. I know she doesn't like me.

There is no desire in her mothering.

She stops tweezing to close one of the metal curlers that has sprung open.

"I don't know. Stop bothering me."

If my father challenges her, there is a constant refrain.

"I'm a good woman. Don't you forget it."

What does she mean? I want to hear her definition. Will I be a good woman, Momma?

I am never sure if my father has been faithful to her. I only remember that it might have happened, at least once, during the time we own Club Paradise. I want to ask her about that time and what it meant to her, but I dare not. Maybe this infidelity, he places in her path, takes what little self-assurance she has.

Marriage is inevitable for Antonietta. Nothing else is expected of her life. In 1931, she marries at twenty-three, and nine months later, to the day, I am born. Not much time to get to know this older man of 33. Did they court? Was there love or just an arrangement? When they are young I recall Dad trying to be playful with her, but often times she seems to push him away. I hardly see tenderness between them. It's hard to be loving, with someone who strikes you.

My father's cousin, in Albany, introduces them. Salvatore's charm is compelling. He can walk into a room filled with people and the mood of the group enlivens distinctly.

Momma tells me. "Everyone told me what a good catch he was."

"Why? What did they say, Momma?"

"Oh he's such a hard worker, Ann—handsome and so smart. He'll probably make a good living."

She will find out that her husband-to-be is also self-educated, multi-talented, egocentric and most likely manic-depressive. He is a hard worker. He struggles to make his dreams come true of what he believes his life and our lives should be. Does she know if they will love each other in the beginning? One senses she is constantly filling other people's needs. I'm sure she calls it love.

And when they marry they have the largest and grandest wedding money can buy. This must have been quite an achievement at the brink of the country's depression, for my grandparents. Her parents struggle to keep their family fed, clothed and the grocery store from failing. Many times the only communication I get from her is when I ask her to tell me about her lavish bridal photos. Her eyes sparkle when she speaks of this magnificent ceremony. She points to the wedding photo, showing me the many attendants in the bridal party. I can see she feels admired as she comes alive.

Is this how women become important? Do I need a big wedding?

Could this have been her fifteen minutes? I would never get to know how this feels to have a glorious day in white.

"I could have had anybody," she tells me, with her head held high. "I was a looker. Lot's of men wanted to marry me."

291

How should I answer? Doesn't she know she's talking to her little daughter?

"Mommy, you're still pretty. Really."

"I know."

But, my father, Salvatore's, needs are demanding, self-indulgent, overbearing and filled with violent tantrums. He bamboozles his family's heart and affections.

My questions remain unanswered.

Does she ever realize her married life is a repetition of her childhood, as if she'd married her father? What does she think will be different about her marriage? What could she have changed to make her life better and why didn't she try? Why did she resign herself to her husband's plans? What happened to her self-respect? What ever happened to that part of the ceremony that he would respect and take care of her? We never have this exchange.

I observe how she allows men and even some women to dictate and take superior roles with her. At times her shyness is painful. She becomes a non-person without opinions or decisions. Through the years Momma remains quiet and withdrawn, not able to compete for attention, except in a passive-aggressive fashion.

Antonietta learns the art of survival in an abusive life.

It is easy to see why she emotionally abandons her children. She needs every ounce of inner strength to cope with the demanding lifestyle. When I start receiving my father's attention, the realization that she must contend with me for his affection becomes paramount. She is quick to denounce me, her little girl, with name-calling.

Momma is always mad at me. Momma always calls me "bruta putana". It's like a bad lady. It makes me feel dirty and sad.

It doesn't take long to realize I am my mother's enemy and although I am continually respectful, I try to avoid interaction with her.

"Sal," she complains. "She never helps me in the house." But when I do try to help she is critical.

"You don't do it that way. When I was your age I knew how to do everything. You don't know how to do anything. You don't even know how to iron clothes. Get out of here. You're dirty. Go see your father in the shop"

And that is what I do.

I gravitate to Dad for approval. There seems to be no way to have her love, no matter how hard I try. His beatings are disturbing and dramatic, but Mother's uncaring tongue lashes deep to my soul.

My father does make money but the family sees very little evidence of it; except when he decides to show-off to the outside world. We wear threadbare underclothes but he has the latest elegant new car. The heat and hot water is turned off to save money.

It's always cold. I don't like being cold. It makes me feel lonely.

Our sheets and blankets are thin. The refrigerator is nearly always empty, with the exception of, when company comes to dine, and then every food imaginable appears.

I love to go to my friends houses they always have snacks and their Moms are so friendly and fun. I wish Momma was like that. Nobody ever comes here much.

I see the same humiliating scene, daily, as Momma approaches Dad, like a cowered animal.

"Sal, I need some money. I have to buy spaghetti and a can of tomatoes."

"Don forget to bring back the change."

And if things do not go just right, the whole household pays the price with thrashings.

Be careful how you word it today, Momma. He looks upset. I'm scared. Is it going to be all right?

Is this what she thinks is acceptable to take? Is this what makes her paralyzed to her own self-respect? Now, as a woman, I understand why it is so hard for her to care for her children.

She is unable to care for herself.

Her simple pleasures come in cosmetics and food. Back East, at her parent's grocery store, they are attentive to her simple wants. Anything requested is prepared. I remember visiting Grandpa and watching her enjoy a bologna and ketchup sandwich on Wonder bread, and a cold bottle of beer. She is vulnerable away from her family. My grandparents are strong personalities. Antonietta seems to live in the moment; taking happiness when it appears.

Grandma and Grandpa sure seem to like her. She smiles more when she sees them. She likes to be the little girl.

Mother may have tried to tend and care for our home in the early years, but Dad's work, as a carpenter, moves us into many houses, which need constant repairs and remodeling. Housework is insurmountable. Our home customarily is kept clean, but without caring or passion. Curtains are never hung and there is very little warmth or inviting touches. We only eat evening meals together. She piles the chipped dishes in the middle of the table and throws the mis-matched silverware any which way. From the near-empty refrigerator, she takes an ever-present milk bottle filled with cold water and places it on the table.

I'm going to fix the table like they do in the movies. I hope she likes it. Those dandelions will make it look nice.

"Always trying to be a show-off, just like your father!"

Mealtime is the stage where all the days' problems are aired but are hardly ever resolved without a battle. My brother Nicky and I know we have to be extremely quiet and alert to our behavior, otherwise we will feel Dad's fury. Mom has perfected a passive manipulative style, the ability to catch him in a down mode. The moment he comes in the door she presents him with the bad news of the day. Even as a little girl I try to tell her not to bother him until he has rested and has had his meal, but I am not able to persuade her to change the pattern. His violence cannot be tamed. I blame my mother.

I warned her. She knows he'll be upset, but she just doesn't listen. She's always making trouble for us.

With Dad's help, Mom picks up cooking skills. He urges her to try more difficult recipes, but she prefers to cook simple Italian meals. There is no incentive. She knows her apple pies and spice cakes are good. With time she eventually produces some fine dishes.

"Can I help, Mom?"

Antonietta does not want me in the kitchen.

"I don't have any time, can't you see I'm busy. Besides you don't know how to do anything!"

She sends me away to see my father in his workshop. I willingly go. He accepts my being there. Here I feel love. As soon as I come home from school I change out of my school uniform and go with him to help on jobs. When I get home I am tired. I still have homework to do and to give Mom a hand. But Mom still complains to Dad about me.

I cannot do it right! What is the trick I have to learn in order to please her.

I am ten when my brother is born. Momma reminds me often that we were both difficult breech births.

"You know, I almost died having you."

Why do you remind me so often? I didn't mean to make your life miserable and painful. How can I make this up to you, Momma?

But now I'm needed to help her with my new brother.

Now she needs me. I'll show her what a good job I can do. Now that I'm the oldest, I guess I'm no longer the child.

I'm in love. In love with our new baby. I gladly run errands to the market or feed, hold or change Nicky. There are many runs up and down the stairs in the duplex on twenty-two Buchanan Street. Mom's health is fragile after Nicky's birth. The breech births must have truly wreaked havoc on her small body.

She continues to remind me. "I almost died having you!"

How can I ever repay my mother for such a sacrifice?

Nick and I become close. I'm passionate about having someone to love, and my affection is quickly returned. There is such great power in protecting the baby and making sure I shield him from the craziness of this family. Mom becomes more distant; never seems to involve herself emotionally with us on any level, except to feed and clean us. My father also has a new love, his long awaited son. Somewhere in the baby's first year, I wake to the fact that Salvatore doesn't love me the same anymore.

I'm not able to understand yet, that only a son can fill Salvatore's distant and primal dreams.

Meanwhile, as I grow and come into womanhood, Antonietta, is unable to offer me any security or important information regarding this passage. As a young woman I feel quite alone with no one to turn to for help. She is jealous, hysterical and childlike. But the worst is when she accuses me of trying to steal her husband.

Oh Momma! How can you say these things? Why do you feel this way? I just went to Dad because I was annoying you. Don't you remember?

I soon realize that my innocent behavior of accepting Dad's attention threatens her. I am so embarrassed by the accusation that I distance myself from him, further insuring isolation. My mother begins to imagine disastrous maladies are afflicting her. She also struggles for attention.

Decisions are always made for Antonietta; how to dress, who to see, how to think and where she will live. At thirty-seven she leaves all the support she has ever known; her family and friends. I see that the move from New York State to the West coast creates a deep fissure in her ability to adjust. Everyone works hard to make it a success. Outwardly the family adapts to the new surroundings, but loneliness permeates our lives. My brother manages to overcome his insecurities with fantasy and play and the knowledge that his family embraces him. But Mom grieves and laments daily, holding on to the 'used to be'. She never lives near her parents again and sees them only one more time before their death. I do not understand the depth of her sadness and loss, until I am older.

Life moves on. At eighteen, I fall in love with a man whom Mom and Dad never meet and furthermore will not receive well. I can never confide in my mother without her betraying me. Ed and I elope without their blessing.

I'm so torn. I must leave. I don't think Mom will care. Dad will be mad as hell. I can't leave my little brother? He won't understand. I'm giving him no warning. No goodbyes. I may never see him again. Everything is always so hard.

Years later, Mom tells me how difficult this time is for her. She said that Dad partially blamed her for the loss of his daughter and the shame that I brought on the family.

"That's when we had to move to Italy, you know. Because of you."

I will not see my parents for many years and when I do, the relationship remains civil but strained. Mom never says a word about the elopement when she sees me. Always numb. Letters, written by Mother but dictated by Father, are usually harsh, condemning and destructive, and when they are friendly; are habitually manipulative. Typically, Mother's ability is sadly lacking to reach beyond Dad's demands. I constantly wait for her to act independent, to try and restore peace or make some link between her grandchildren and me.

What fear is so great to ward off her maternal sentiments? She seems incapable of breaking through, or is it fine just the way things are? Maybe she is glad that I left. There is no more competition.

In 1980, Dad sends her back to America to pave the way for their return to the United States. She is told not to fail. She phones our home. This call is the turning point in my understanding and my forgiveness of my mother.

I am finally aware that the emotional barriers between us are too great to break down. I repress the desire to vocalize my feelings. I see clearly that to condemn her and hurt her with my past pains will serve nothing. It will be like thrashing a child. Little by little, my anger and hate ease away. Peace is eventually established between us. Without words. As if there never is a missing heartbeat.

Dad dies in Italy when he is eighty-five, and Mom, now seventy-five, returns to America. She spends one month with me in California before establishing her home in Denver close to my brother and his family. I can't believe how strange it is having my long lost mother there in the morning when I awake. It is equally bizarre to see her without her commander. I can see she is very sickly and disoriented. She has not been cared for properly in all those miserable years. I am glad she will be under Nick's care and supervision.

She grieves very little for Dad. She seems to have deadness for all that has ever happened to her. She never lets on to strangers or friends of her unhappy marriage or of her disappointments.

She settles in her own retirement apartment with her own bedroom, a common dining room and many social interactions to keep her busy. The four trunks that carry all her belongings are placed in Nick's basement. She takes a few of the items for her apartment.

During the following summer I visit her for a week.

"Momma, where did you get this folding chair? It looks like it's for outdoors."

"Oh, your father bought it in Italy. He sat in it all the time. Venera, did you see my nice curtains I brought back. They have nice embroidery on them."

"Maybe I can put them up in your bedroom for you. Would you like that?"

"Oh, that's good. It would make it look so nice. I'll show Rose."

"Do you like this modern kitchen? You'll probably make a lot of meals here."

There is a quick clear thinking answer.

"I don't want to cook. I cooked enough all my life. I'll eat in the main dining room with Rose."

When she first moves here, it's not easy to find anything that interests her.

"Maybe you could try some craft classes," I say. "Or how about bingo? You know there are loads of activities you can get involved with."

"I know. But I don't like to do those things."

Antonietta finds Rose, a lovely lady in the next-door apartment, a special good friend whom she comes to love. In all the years that I know my mother I don't recall any friendships formed without Father's input. But now, she has one of her own making. Out of the blue, I hear they are taking the senior jitney around town and playing bingo together. When I speak to her on the phone, she tells me how important Rose has become to her. A little twinge of jealousy pinches my feelings, wishing I could hear that she loved me.

Finally, I see my mother begin her road to personhood. She permits herself to reach out to my brother, our families and me. Greeting cards come more often. Conversations flow without fear. She becomes better acquainted with two of her granddaughters, Catherine and Christine. She at last is waking from her deep trance. Aware of her good, safe surroundings, she lets in love.

"Venera, I wonder when we're out today, if I could buy some makeup and maybe a new dress? Nothing too expensive, you know. Just so I'll have something nice to wear."

She still sounds like a child, as if she wants to be taken care of. I don't want to make these choices for her anymore. She is still fearful.

"Momma, you don't have to ask permission from anyone, ever again. Do you hear me? You're free now? You have money! You don't have to be afraid. You have the right to decide anything you feel is O.K. Understand?"

"Yes, Venera, I know. I know."

#22 Antonietta and Salvatore's wedding in Albany, N. Y. (1931)

23 Antonietta and Salvatore. (1931)

PART III

LA VITA DOLCE PICCANTE

Venera Di Bella Barles

La Vita Dolce Piccante, More of the Sweet and Bitter Life

Motherhood: A High Wire Act

Night of the Grunion (1960)

Mother's Day Interrupted (1968)

Death Probably Starts in the Toes (1970's)

Riverboating with the Queen (1970's)

The Business Woman (1971)

Boxing in a Kangaroo Court (1980)

Toby's Angel (1980's)

Life For Sale

Edward The Good, Are You Wearing Spats?

The Last Stand (1983)

Railroaded (1983)

The Deliverance (1986)

Venera Di Bella Barles

An Overnight Case (1986)

Watershed (1980's)

Eddie, I Have a Feeling we're Not in Kansas (1988)

Katz and More Katz (1991-93)

Fahgedaboudit, The New Car (1994)

High Rollers (1996)

Marriage, Kidneys, and Other Dark Organs

MOTHERHOOD: HIGH WIRE ACT

"Gentle ladies, you will remember till old age
what we did together in our brilliant youth."
Author Unknown

"Well, Mom, if you're supposed to be the mother, how come you make a lot of mistakes?"

"Now, you listen here, you two," I answer back, poking them in their shoulders with my index finger. "I was pretty young when I first had a baby and I had no one to show me or teach me what to do. No damn operator's manual came with you guys! No see page forty-three; How to Keep Your Children Interested in Life! I'll tell you what, we're in this fight together! All three of us are uninformed, so we're just going to have to learn this game jointly. How do you like that?"

There I was in a shouting match with my two teenage daughters who were challenging my abilities to parent. My defenses were skimpy but genuine.

Before I marry I'm not sure how much I really want to be a parent. I like playing house and dolls as a little girl but as I grow older I dream of a career instead.

Venera Di Bella Barles

(1943) What if I get married? Momma says all the time, "You're so dirty, I pity the man who get's you." Boy, Momma sure hates being a mother. I don't think she likes babies and kids. I do. But I don't think I want to do this when I grow up. I'm going to be a doctor or a business- woman just like our real estate agent. Dad always talks nice to her because she's so smart. She's pretty, wears neat clothes, has her own money and drives her own car. Dad would be so proud of me. Mom doesn't care what I do.

Since my efforts in becoming a professional whatever, are thwarted, marriage offers me an opportunity to prove that I can, at least, be the best at being a skillful and loving mother and wife. Thankfully my thoughts of motherhood turn positive.

We buy our first home after four years of apartment living, and I quit work at the Long Beach Naval Shipyard to have our first baby. Gina, middle name Cee to represent Charles, Ed's grandfather, is a sweet nine pounds three ounce baby, long and fair-skinned like the Russian and Neapolitan sides of our family.

But, all a woman has to do is get pregnant, and hell puts up a for rent sign. Now I have a new baby, surgical problems with the C-Section, a new home and a sick husband with a badly injured back on a new job. Life was bumming me out.

Into this web, two and a half years later, Carisa, from the Italian *Carisima*, 'dearest one', is born, tinier but also beautifully formed. Her olive skin barely contains her boundless energy. Sounds and changes easily disturb her intricate wiring.

I harbor a small fear when I am pregnant. What if I don't have a son for Ed? My father's needs leave an indelible message. I do feel good to realize that Ed is content with daughters and is proud of his babies.

But unknowingly, after this birth, I am in the throes of a nervous breakdown. Post-postpartum blues combined with guilt problems, about my parents, devours me. My whole body revolts. I am taking pills daily for everything: depression, diet, psychosomatic pains, migraines, and birth control. All hits the fan.

During these years my little girls take the brunt of my poor health. To add to my worries and concerns my toddler Gina experiences a strange illness of dizzy spells, nausea, and abnormal sleep that lasts until she is four or five years old. We're relieved when the symptoms cease, but even with the many tests, medications and doctors; we never truly find what causes these transient attacks. There are the typical illnesses and boo-boos, one of which brings us to our knees. While holding the handle of a toy in her mouth, Carisa falls gashing the roof of her mouth. The frightening wound narrowly misses her brain. The gods are with us this day.

I know I didn't want to parent the way I was taught, but I am clueless how to go about it.

I'll show everyone I know what I'm doing. I must not fail. Make believe. I must be perfect. I'll have a perfect home; husband and children just like the movies and magazines. Everyone will say, "How do you do all that?"

I certainly have learned this lesson well from my father that image, *La Bella Figura*, is everything and the outside world should not know how you get there. Except, it is a high price to pay.

Why is it so hard for my family to keep things neat and clean? Can't they understand it has to be perfect?

I am obsessive about everything. I stare at photos of my two little girls dressed in matching bonnets, gloves, sunglasses, purses, and polished shoes.

"Don't cross your feet. You're dirtying your socks."

"O.K., Mom."

"Careful how you sit, I don't want your hair messed up."

O.K., Mom."

"Don't take another toy out unless you put the other away!"

"O.K., Mom."

"Gina, swallow those vegetables. Didn't I tell you not to put them in your apron? Carisa, I can't braid your hair any tighter! Yes, I know you want your shoelaces and belt tight. Don't put finger marks on the piano! Are you both listening to me?"

"Sorry, Mom."

The strain of this style of nonsense parenting soon catches up to me. I am overwhelmed with frustrations. Failure continues to rear its ugly head.

Everything is about pleasing; Ed, my father, the kids and fixing the house. I'm on a roller coaster! I don't talk to anyone about adult things. Ed is hardly ever home since getting his new job. There is too much for me to do. I know he can't help because of his back, but I need a break. He doesn't understand how hard it is for me and how lonely I am. He thinks I can handle it all. I know he doesn't even understand how inadequate I feel when he says, "I never, ever, heard my mother complain. She had to go back and forth to the store and the house, feed everybody and clean the house. She'd be cleaning the windows at one a.m. in the morning!"

Everybody is better than me. Better educated. Better everything. Dottie, across the street, knows how to bake and sew. I must learn to cook and sew better. I can't let on I don't know anything. I can do it!

I learn to sew. After the daily routine, I fill the rest of my crammed day working late into the night, sewing doll clothes, baby dresses, clothes for Ed and myself, and household decorations.

How about that garden, Vinny? What will Dad say if he sees this? Better do better than this! Remember how nice his flowers, plants and rock gardens are? And fountains. Don't forget the fountains. You have a long way to go! The house needs painting! Don't mess up!

I work obsessively putting in gardens. I am afraid to waste time, afraid I will leave something undone. Clean, clean, clean. I'm not sure which is important, husband, house or children?

Sometimes I take the girls to parks or the newly discovered thrift shops. It is my only form of recreation and a lifesaver. I put the port-a-crib in the back seat of our black and white, two-door Ford Crown Victoria, belt Gina in the front seat while Carisa watches from the crib. Thinking back it sends goose bumps in my hair at just the thought of how unsafe this all was. As we get older the three of us are involved with scouts, swimming, yoga, ballet, the list never ends. The intensity of work grows.

Oh God, Oh God! Here's another letter from Dad full of hate and demands. Why are you only friendly and nice when you want something? My head hurts so badly. I feel like a rubber band pulled to its nth.

My mother-in-law, Minnie, and Ed's sister, Leona, are central and the only people active in our lives. Without question they give openly to the children and to me, and I am thankful for their involvement. And even though Jewish, they're good sports about celebrating Christmas.

When I know they will come, naturally I make everything a bigger project than is necessary. Preparations go on for weeks. My family duly criticizes me for such.

"Hi, Momma," I say to Minnie, on the phone. "How about Leona and you spending Christmas with us? We'll have a Hanukkah bush. What do think of that? Then when Leona goes home maybe you can stay for a couple of weeks. And maybe you and I can go to some 'goody' shops. Then Eddie will bring you back. O.K.?"

"O.K. Vinny. Dots good. I bring borsht. I make beef, barley soup too. I make the children more corduroy long pants."

"Oh, Momma, they'll just love them!"

See, Antonietta, that's how it's done. All you have to do is try. Your grand kids will love anything. Why is it so hard to be grandparents? It's all about you and Dad. Selfish. Absolutely selfish.

Minnie's hands are never empty. She makes everything seem normal and worthwhile. She embraces my love and attention. With her I feel validated as a mother. If it had not been for her I would have truly been in bedlam.

As a little girl, Carisa stays close to me, often times ignoring Ed for my attention. It is difficult for her to share and she fears that we will not include her in family affairs. We call this humorous, mischievous, but determined girl "Me Too". I'm sure it is quite difficult for her to see us focus so much attention on Gina during her illness. Of the two, Carisa has the more restless nature, craves to taste adventure; see the world, people and is always ready for new things. I understand this sense of urgent desire.

"What's going on? Why all the noise"

"It's O.K., Mom, we're just playing."

"Gina, I only hear your voice. Why can't you play quietly like your sister?"

"I can't help it, Mom, Carisa is always tickling me! As soon as you come in she stops and looks like an angel!"

Gina, a natural nurturer, prefers solitude. She instantly knows the situation. I can see how she mimics my moves in caring for her baby sister. And like her sister, she is bent on getting her way.

"You're missing all the sights, Gina. The point of taking a vacation is so that we can see something different! I know you love to read but can't you put your book down for a short time?"

"I'm watching, Mom."

In the early years, despite my festering emotional problems, the girls and I laugh and play wildly together. I am resolute to be the most efficient and involved mother.

(1940) I wish Momma, would take me to the park with the other kids. "Please teach me how to cook, Momma." There she goes again. "Don't bother me Venera, will you? For the last time, go see your father!"

Even with the on-going depression and exhaustion, I have an almost unnatural drive of energy, working on very little rest. It is a continuous challenge to find new games and fun to stay ahead of my sharp little girls.

Like a child, I spend hours with them on the floor, seeking new ways to entertain. I make log cabins, assemble Tinkertoys, build blocks, dress dolls, fix dollhouses, and always there is tumbling and wrestling. It begins to feel good and right to be their mother.

"Eddie, why can't you come down and play with us sometimes."

"You guys play. I'll sit here and watch you while I have my coffee."

On occasion, after much begging, we are lucky to get their dad down on the floor for a foursome of wrestling. I wish he could understand how much I love his interacting with us.

"Why is everything you do just by yourself, Eddie? It doesn't matter what it is; reading, television, stamp collecting or fishing. Don't you want to be with me? Why don't you like to join me or the kids?"

Ed responds, "You're never happy. Always complaining that I don't do enough."

The distortions are forever. This is the part of my marriage I miss greatly. It is quite visible to me that intimacy is difficult for him. But I never stop hungering for it.

It's like being with my mom. I feel so starved. He doesn't seem to understand. Constantly sits on a chair with a cup of coffee, watching the daily show.

When Carisa and Gina are ten and twelve we decide to have another child. They appear pleased with the plans and relish the thought of a new member in our family. But David, our full-term baby boy, lives only one day. I neglect to fully see the impact this may have had on the girls while nursing my own death wounds. After the loss, the family plunges into a depression. Even our little terrier dog, Toby, languishes with us.

I want them to have a taste of different cultures and understandings so I push them towards the arts. They prove their talents in music and art.

"Carisa, please come out in the living room and play the guitar for us."

"I don't want to."

"Why don't you like to share with us? You play so nicely and we never get to hear you. Com'on! Gina will play the piano to accompany you."

"No, Mom."

Besides the shyness, she doesn't enjoy competing with Gina.

They succeed in politeness and exhibit good manners. I never detect outward mistreatment or meanness towards one another.

But there are plenty of times they test the limits and we dissolve into stormy shouting matches. Carisa has ways of demanding truths and explanations, continuously testing my inadequate skills of parenting.

"What's the matter, Carisa? You look upset."

"I almost got killed just now!" she says with salivating energy. She knows I will go into a typical fearful tailspin. She is good at pressing those buttons that are loosely wired and fill me with anxieties. But usually both girls are pretty good at avoiding ticklish interactions with me. Unfortunately, as I was with my parents, they both learn how to tell the truth the way we want to hear it.

(1948) I wish I didn't have to lie to Dad. But I have to. I'm so scared. I can't ask him if I can do anything. He'll kill me. Why do other girls get to do all kinds of things? They have it so easy.

It is scary to see my young daughters grow into women. I can't shake this need to have my whole family stay together. I can't stand the idea that Gina and Carisa will go away someday to live lives of their own. If I could only keep them in closets until they are thirty.

Their teens bring true awareness of this thing called motherhood and how little control I have over two beautiful, provocative females maturing in this dysfunctional world. I will always have a need to understand them better. And with these needs, at times, I still hit pockets of helplessness and frustrations. My grown daughters remind me often now, that I used to talk and analyze topics to death. They didn't comprehend then, that talk and how understanding the truth saved my life.

I blindly think they are coming to me with all their problems, but, just like most children, many times they shield me from the facts. In my attempts at perfection did I not leave enough cracks, in my armor of denial, for them to approach me?

Carisa at age twenty-two, moves to San Francisco to seek her dreams, with college intentions. But like Gina, her life takes a road of complications, leaving her unfulfilled. She comes home, eight years later, to start fresh again.

Gina is also resourceful and invariably creative in finding work. I remember when she was in her early twenties, between jobs and nursing a sad love disappointment, she came back to live with us a short time.

"So Mom, I'm going to try and find work at the traveling circus."

"You're going to what?"

"Join Circus Vargas. They're down at the mall for a week."

"Why is that a good idea?"

"Dad thinks it is. That way I'll get to see some of the country and have a steady job. Maybe it'll get me out of the doldrums over this past relationship. I could work with the animals or be a showgirl and ride the elephants. You know."

"Do I?"

On her return.

"So, how did you do?" I ask.

"Not that good. Well, see I talked to a whole bunch of clowns and showgirls. They were all jammed in this trailer. There were also some people working with the elephants. They said they usually only hire homosexual males, families or stars. They don't hire single women."

"Huh," I say as I take a breath of weighty relief. "That's too bad."

"But I got a marriage proposal from one of the clowns. He was willing to marry me so I could go on the road with them. Oh, well. Although, I did get to ride on an elephant. That was fun."

"That's nice."
I never knew what would come next.

When Gina and Carisa, were young, I thought everything would magically be better for them and that maybe their lives would take wonderful turns and they would easily walk out from underneath their own personal black clouds. If only they had the same confidence in themselves as I had in them. With time, I recognized their different ambitions and how they were going to pilot their imaginings. I also knew that there were fears and, at times, unwise choices that would mar their paths. I began to see the baggage they accumulated for their adulthood. My teachings did not appear to reach them any longer. Now there were many new teachers in their lives.

I often wonder how much of my own stained and inadequate upbringing rubbed off onto them? What could I have done differently? Certainly I needed to be more relaxed, and less fearful and in need of control. Possibly, I think, I should have given a more positive and stronger image of my femininity and strength. How could they not help but see in those early years the uncertainties I presented? Could they see my inability to take responsibility in areas of decision making and dealing with money? And how could they not have seen the continuous battle I fought to achieve peace and happiness for myself? Or the struggle I had, to reach a satisfying relationship with their father and my parents? I wish I had pushed harder for them to go on with their education. Maybe they could have satisfied some of their ideas better.

So where does reality lie? What was I able to teach them? They saw me struggle to be my own person and absorb as many of life's gifts as possible. They saw me go down difficult paths. I kept a large ear to the feminist movement - relating to many issues that affected me. But unfortunately I raised Gina and Carisa as I was going through periods of self-loathing and enlightenment. How did they view me? Did they realize that I was struggling with many of my own mixed solutions? Did they see I needed to find a place where my emotional tapes of old-world male-dominance could be eased out and replaced with a sensible acceptance of achievements and limitations? Did they grasp that I was training and convincing myself not to wait for the approval of others, but to learn to pat my own head? How much did they hear in the unspoken messages? Did they hear, that the way to fulfillment and self-worth was through motherhood? For me it was the most satisfying but difficult of employments.

It would be easy to end here and say they lived happily ever after, but realism knows the truth.

The one thing I learned is that I cannot direct their lives. I need only to be available when the cry is heard for support and direction. My girls left my nest with their feathers still damp and curled. The drying and preening process came for them on the story branches of their lives. I can see as the years flow by, how important these women were and are to me. I savor their love and respect. I also see that the most important job each generation of parents has, especially mothers, is to quickly awaken to our own wounds so that we may make solid and healthy off-spring and not repeat the wrongs or excesses of our mothers and fathers.

#24 My daughters, Gina and Carisa, with
grandchildren, Alexia, Julian and Isabella
Upper Left: Carisa and Gina
Upper Right: Gina and Alexia
Middle: Gina and Carisa
Lower Right: Carisa, Isabella and Julian
Middle Left: Gina and Carisa
Lower Left: Alexia Cee

NIGHT of the GRUNION

"It seems as if I could do anything when I'm in a passion.
I get so savage I could hurt anyone and enjoy it."
Louisa May Alcott (1832-1888)

"Hey, Vinny, maybe we'll see if the grunion are running tonight. What do you think?"

"What the heck is a grunion?" I ask, knowing full well that I have been fooled by this gang before.

"Small silver fish."

"Am I understanding this right? You're going to watch little silver fish run? The only ones I know eat holes in my clothes."

"Honest! We're not fooling you. They look a little like smelt with silver stripes on their sides."

"Do things really get that quiet here that you have to go to the beach at night to watch fish?"

This should be a whole laugh a minute, I sarcastically thought. I can hardly wait.

"You'll have tons of fun. Really!" My friend, Mrs. Whitney, says, her eyes shining bright. "When the moon is out you can see a phosphorescent glow on the water beyond the waves, and that means it's the night when the grunion run up on the beach, stand up, wriggle their bodies, lay their eggs in the wet sand, and then they get back in the water by the next wave. We have to grab them before that wave comes."

"That's it, Jeanne, I've heard it all. Now I'm watching fish ovulate."

I knew I needed a vacation, but this sounded desperate. I had to keep reminding myself that these were my friends and that they loved me, but they also loved subjecting me to new and crazy things just to watch my reactions, always trying to loosen my controls. I guess it must have been fun to see the fire in this old broad's eyes. Here I was a grown woman, with two daughters, and I hadn't learned how to play. Always giving everyone the serious, overly responsible side.

It was in the 1960's, the first time my pre-teen daughters and I were invited to "Ladies Week at Carp", as it was lovingly called. This was the setting for the yearly Mecca of Mrs. J. Whitney, her three children, two daughters and a young teen son, who, usually, would take a male friend. Then there was Marilyn Gilbert, Jeanne's sister and her three children; a childhood girlfriend, Pat, a divorced, trauma nurse; Barbara, the unmarried Virgo and Jeanne's next door neighbor, a good-looking broad with too much starch, and her carefully groomed daughter.

We drove our loaded car up the hot highway from Los Angeles to Carpenteria, a small beach town north of L.A. and south of Santa Barbara, and as we were driving, I gave my darling daughters the usual Emily Post manners lecture, reminding them they were guests in someone else's home and that they were to be respectful and not act stupid and wild.

"Mom, whatda you think we'll do there for a week?" Gina asked.

"Oh, I'm sure Mrs. Whitney has everything planned. She'll tell us. Don't worry honey. It will probably be peaceful and you'll have plenty of reading time."

"Who's gonna to be there?" Carisa, my youngest asked. "What's the place like?"

"Well, she didn't say. I know they sit on the beach a lot. I really don't know much about the places either. We'll see."

The beach houses near the railroad tracks, two on a lot, one to the front and one set back, were wonderfully primitive, most likely held together with many coats of paint. The 'back house' had a barracks bedroom with barely room enough for two salvaged sets, of what I judged were World War I metal bunk beds. One set for each side of the small room, just large enough for claustrophobia to ferment. We usually plopped our bedrolls on the sagging, ancient thin mattresses. The mistress of this madness, Mrs. J. Whitney, had a separate bedroom. The sofa bed in the living room opened for two or more willing patrons, but not until the last guest stopped partying, playing cards and talking. Usually the women stayed in this back cottage, while the kids piled into the front one. The bathroom, at the back end of the house, was propped up. As I sat on the throne, I imagined I might, at any moment, be joining the underground tenants. The sandy shower drains cried to be released from their clogged and stuffed membranes. The lavatories of both houses were always in use and the sand level rose daily.

But back to that first time. It all broke down the minute I drove our lavender, 1961, Dodge station wagon into the dirt driveway and Gina and Carisa threw open their doors, screaming and carrying on the minute they saw their friends.

So much for the rules of etiquette I so carefully implanted in them.

How could I turn my children loose? My imagination went absolutely wild, thinking what mischief my 'polite and well behaved' young girls were willingly applying themselves to. I was soon to find out.

I had just settled in, getting to know the quirks of this household, when, without warning, a bucket of water was thrown through the front door. The Whitney kid and his friend were greeting the new females. I could hear my daughter's voices reach glass-shattering peaks, as they scrambled to escape the aqueous bombardment. Suddenly, I was in a whirlwind. Gina and Carisa and their girlfriends headed for the kitchen pans, filled them to capacity, and steered their course towards the offending bombardiers.

The pack came swiftly towards me with their load. I tried to intercept the unbalanced warriors.

"You had better not do this!" I sternly admonished. "You will regret this, Gina, I'm warning you. Are you listening, Carisa?"

But I had lost them. I knew everyone was instantly suffering from traumatic hearing impairment. Instinctively I pulled the front door open to allow them a smoother exit, but I was, in turn, smashed behind the door. I remained there for the duration of the battle, screaming my ominous threats.

At this point the floodgates of insanity were released within the breasts of all the adults and their offspring. The Whitney children, their cousins, my daughters and all invited friends, with the exception of the fool behind the door, a product of Catholic parochial schools, joined in the massive water fight. All I could think was, how will I ever be invited again to this restful retreat? I watched as water flowed into every window and onto the linoleum. Amid hysterical laughter, bodies slid over the slick floor. Some half-witted participant managed to find the A-bomb of the moment, the garden hose.

I screamed at my 'hostess', Mrs. Whitney, whose face was bright red with glee and untamed laughter, "Jeanne, for God's sake do something! I've never seen anything like this! You guys will destroy your place! What is going on? Have you all lost your mind?"

But there was no point in trying to speak to her or anyone, since their brain juices had already leaked out and they were *all* reverting to childhood, except myself, the only remaining responsible, frightened grown-up hiding behind the door.

From one end to the other, the cottage was thoroughly rinsed inside and out. When it was over and the mopping finished, all parties continued life as if nothing had occurred—that it was not a rare activity. My daughters were in hog heaven. Their mother was no longer in control. The rules were not like they thought. This would be a memorable vacation. It wasn't any wonder why they inquired if they could live with Mrs. Whitney.

I was soon to understand that the goal each day was to get to the beach. Our daily march to the sands and ocean, like large tortoises, usually took us over the railroad tracks, down the residential village roads, past old sun-bleached Mexican bungalows with giant sunflowers and vegetable gardens neatly tended. We were heavily bogged down with baskets, coolers with assorted sundries, towels and beach chairs. If we had too much equipment then we took our cars.

There appeared to be a contest to see who could turn the reddest in the sun. Even though some days were overcast, it did not deter the diehards who gladly lay in the fog waiting for the few rays of solar light. Sun or not, a thick layer of coco butter or some new exotic tanning oil of the season, guaranteed to fry you, was ritualistically applied to all uncovered virgin city skin.

My expectations of at least some rules surrounding breakfast, lunch and dinner were soon dashed. Would we take turns on cooking and serving? What hours would this take place?

The next morning I had answers. The 'Ladies' were gone. "Oh, Hi Tom! Where's your mom and the other women?"

"I donno. I think Mom went to the café for breakfast. I think I saw Patti and Barbara walking into town too."

I was left with my own thoughts of what had happened and some bruised feelings. I was going to have to find out what the routine was the hard way.

My daughters hadn't any problems adjusting to the new lifestyle. Oreos or potato chips for breakfast? Sounds like a deal to them.

Occasionally, in the mornings, a couple of adults whisked away to the 'Blue Window' Café, in town, to have a quiet breakfast without the crazed pack. Or fresh donuts.

I soon learned that junk food was the staple of the basic food group. Daily runs were made to 'The Spot' for hourly intake of hamburgers and fries. Around four in the afternoon we would leave our day in the sun, as the call of cocktails came upon the Grande Dames, maybe a Gin and Tonic or Slush, before the major decision of what to eat came about. Maybe barbecue some fresh tuna, or hit the local Mexican eatery or if we were desperate, we'd cook.

At least one day was spent at the Goleta swap meet or we would head for Santa Barbara to buy a new supply of beads for our hippie necklaces. The kids were excited about their newest creations of rock painting with profound proverbs: 'Keep America Clean - Eat A Pigeon' or 'She who indulges, bulges'.

After dinner the card games began, Blitz, Hearts, Casino and Pig, the demolisher of all egos. As usual the children were too damn smart for this old fool, from the eight to the fifteen year olds. They knew they could beat the tar out of me.

In the late evening, amidst the pall of heavy cigarette smoke, after the youngsters were down and the games were over, we solved the problems of our lives. The question continued to arise as to whether to have our fortunes told by the local colorful palmist, find Bridey Murphy or find the nearest guru or maybe to consider joining a pop psychology group. The answers never came before the wee hours of the mornings.

Sleeping? Sleeping was best done when you returned home. During the middle of the night the freight trains zoomed along the tracks and moved the houses a few more inches off their foundations. Each night the symphony of nasal harmonicas pierced the damp, sea, night air, killing any semblance of rest. No one admitted to snoring. Barbara, one of the more data gathering gals, a Virgo, as she proudly stated, resorted to recording our sleeping songs and playing the proof back for all our enjoyment and denials.

Mrs. J. Whitney and her entourage took a large inner tube to 'Carp', about the size of a ten-man raft. Folks came from near and far to check out the launching as the well endowed women and children struggled, with each wave, to stay on top of the large, unforgiving black behemoth. They appeared to have a range of goals; one of which was a determination to get me into the water, but my aversion to drowning usually won out. Along with my errant daughters, most of the clan loved to participate in the water plays. I watched. Glad to study them from a distance, coveting my secret desire to stay alive. Besides, I had an image to uphold of a disciplined adult. I had only momentary glimpses of my children since we arrived. Frightening as it sounds to my ears now, I had loosened the reins.

So back to the evening of the grunion hunt. It was a dark and non-stormy night, we loaded our picnic baskets with supplies to roast hot dogs on the beach, gathered blankets, 'ukes' and paraphernalia and off we flew to the much talked about party. I was prepared. I took my heavy, white vinyl, hooded jacket with the thick, teddy-bear liner. I felt confident I was ready for a Whitney evening.

After the sun went down, we sat around the large bon-fire strumming our ukuleles and singing the latest Beatle songs and old western favorites. About the fifth time around, of 'On Top of Old Smokey', someone announced.

"I think it's time for the grunion!"

The scramble was as good as a two for one sale on 'cross your heart bras'. We armed ourselves with buckets, plastic bags and whatever useable container we could snatch. I didn't know what to expect, but I put on my best 'I know what I'm doing act.' As I walked jauntily down to the water's edge, my long thick braid swinging in the moonlight and hanging to my *toches*, I listened carefully to the instructions.

"Now Vinny, you need to move fast to snag these fish! They're very slick!"

I was told that not many humans were lucky to bring them home. I was determined not to fail. My reputation was at stake since I'd failed so far at fun.

There it was. The fluorescent glow on the water. The first wave hit and I saw some motion across the wet beach. Suddenly a feverish movement overtook us and we all succumbed to the frenzy of the moment. Each time I caught a fish it popped out of my hand like a spring. But I would not to be defeated. I moved closer to the water, dug in my heels and waited for the next wave. I caught a grunion and stuck it into the plastic bag, but I needed both hands to hold the slippery pisces. Without thought, I found the pockets of my white teddy-bear coat convenient. I jammed the silver fish into my coat and as quick as I stuffed them in, they fell out. I lost all sense of my surroundings. My back was turned to the water. The next wave enfolded me and spit me out. I fell backwards into the gods' favorite, briny drink. My teddy-bear coat became an anchor to my soaked and wet body, the hood filled with salt water.

The grunion laughed and danced.

My sopping, salted braid, slapped me in the face. I lost all dignity. My revered compatriots convulsed with laughter at the sight of me working so hard to hold and catch my prey. I had nothing to show for the tremendous effort. But I gave my friends a rare opportunity to see another side of their comrade. I'd like to think I served a great purpose in being there for them.

I would not have changed a minute of those magical moments. How could I tell you this story if I had not tried to catch these wonderful silvery creatures, who for all I know, came into my life to give me the chance to loosen the tight cocoon I had woven myself into.

MOTHER'S DAY INTERRUPTED

"Gran dolori sono muti." (It.)
"Great griefs are silent."

TREATMENT AND HOSPITAL COURSE SUMMARY: This 35 year old Gravida III, Para II was admitted to the hospital for a repeat cesarean section having had two previous cesarean sections. On January 24, 1968 she was taken to the operating room for a low trans course cesarean section with the delivery of a full term living male child who breathed and cried immediately. The patient did well postoperatively. She ran a low-grade fever, which responded to conservative therapy. The patient was discharged on January 29, 1968. The only complication that did develop was that the patient became somewhat depressed because the infant died within 24 hours of birth, on the same day as that of delivery.

He lived eight hours and struggled for eight hours before he died. They say it was Hyaline's Membrane Disease, but it didn't matter what he succumbed to, I will always think of him and see him each year at his new stage of growth. We named him David Jason.

329

I arrived home with empty arms, walked into his nursery and looked into the brand new vacant crib, but in spite of the nothingness, I knew he would never, ever leave me. When I see young men, I imagine my David, walking their walk, thinking their thoughts, living their lives. His moment of life had touched me eternally.

I prepared my heart for this fulfillment, along with his father and two sisters. Everyone planned for this new baby. It had been ten years since our last child. At my age of thirty-five, I was concerned whether I should risk another Cesarean birth since the thinking in 1968 was more conservative regarding repeated C-Sections and births in older women. The odds were against me, but I was reasonably healthy and we felt good about our decision. The pregnancy went well, with just a few setbacks, some difficulties with circulation in my legs. The doctor said I would probably deliver in February.

David's sisters, Carisa and Gina, ages ten and twelve, were thrilled at the prospect of their new sibling, and Gina willingly gave up her bedroom for him. My excited family said it didn't matter what gender the new addition would be, but we thought it would be wonderful, if it were a boy. I harbored a small desire to have a son for my husband since he was surrounded by a harem of women. Since this was definitely to be our last child, we insured this by a tubal-ligation during the Cesarean operation.

I speculated how my girls would fit into an infant's schedule, but they were more than willing to take the chance. My eldest took her responsibilities like a little mother. I worried if she would overburden her perceived role. I knew my youngest might suffer the most from her loss of position as the last-born. I dreaded her getting lost in the shuffle. Years later, I was to find out how she truly experienced her grief.

During my pregnancy, Carisa, in her young innocence, asked, "What if the baby dies, Mom?"

She must have thought, with this remark, that she wielded great power towards the demise of her brother. I understood her fearful difficult thinking. The loss devastated us all. When David died, I was sure I had failed my family. I felt I raised their hopes and gave them nothing but melancholia to rock in their arms.

My unanswered angry questions were endless: Why could I not be normal? Why could I not be like other women and have children without risk of surgery? And now I was not able to have anymore because I had cut the last opportunity from my body. I condemned myself without mercy. I suppressed and fought my thoughts, for I could not afford depression the way I experienced ten years before.

I went about my days adjusting, to yet, another void. Days turned into years. It took nineteen years before I found myself truly grieving for my dead son. When we were asked how many children we had, our answer was always swift and wrong. Two. We kept away from including David into our thinking any longer. Oh, occasionally, when the anniversary of his birth came I remembered him for about a week or so. But he was fading into the fibers of our lives.

Around 1987, several deaths of relatives in the family triggered my need to look into David's fatal battle. I suddenly felt a pull to understand what my tiny son went through in those short hours in this world.

During the operation and delivery I heard him cry, and in my disoriented anesthetized state, someone announced.

"Mrs. Barles, it's a boy!"

I pleasured my groggy thoughts with the welcome cry of his birth, and the realization I had given my family a wonderful gift. Now I would finally see and touch him after nine months of feeling him within my womb. They raised David up to me. I looked with glazed eyes at his seemingly healthy body and heard his faint cry. That cry that remains in my memory forever. Little did I know it would be the first and last time I was to see him. I would never caress him. Not even in death did I get to hold him. Only strangers felt his small body.

On arrival in the Nursery the patient pursued a relentless downhill course characterized by grunting respirations, retractions, apnea. He continued to have difficulty from 2:00 until 5:00 pm and was on intermittent resuscitation and endotracheal breathing with a Byrd respirator. Attempts to correct acidosis were unsuccessful. Patient pronounced dead at 5:30 pm.

We laid him to rest. But it was all a blur. Nine months of anticipation and longing pulled out of our hearts and lives within hours.

How could I not count him as part of this family? His voice came back to me. That genuine primal cry.

"I'm here, Momma! Do not dismiss or forget me, Momma!"

I needed to give credence to his short existence, so I immediately went back to the hospital to search for the nineteen year old medical records. As I turned each page of the report every word seared into my brain. His autopsy. His birth and death certificate. And then I came upon the nurses' notes. Hour after hour was noted of David's feeble attempts at life.

As written; at 2:00 p.m. a nurse took it upon herself to baptize him.

Suddenly all the anger buried inside of me burst forth. This unknown person made our son's after-life her business without an understanding of his parents' desires. Her presumption enraged me. I took the report copies home and wept as I read and reread the lines within. I was finally beginning to grieve for my beloved little boy.

"David, you were brave those first and last eight hours of your life. I wish our medicine had not failed you. I'm so sorry Momma could not save you my sweet son, but, for me, you have not died. You will always be alive in my heart. Your short life was not in vain for it taught me many lessons that I might have overlooked. You have taken your place in our photo gallery with your father, mother, sisters and relatives. And yes, I often see you David, in the strong and handsome men on the street..."

Venera Di Bella Barles

DEATH PROBABLY STARTS in the TOES

I know it's a rule written somewhere that when urban people go to the woods, everything, not attached, must be taken from home.

Reason? Who knows? Maybe they believe they'll never make it back to the city again. In an instant, if need be, they can set up housekeeping wherever they land. Why do you think those pioneer wagons, going west, were heaped so high? They were probably just New Yorkers going on a camping trip. Each year our Los Angeles tribe endeavors to put trees in our lives, usually we pick the most advertised and popular site to fill our needs. Typically, it is Yosemite National Park.

It is the late 1950s when Ed and I pack our two daughters and most of the house into the fifty-eight VW Bug for a two week stay in the celebrated forest. The diminutive car groans when we load its belly with a port-a-crib, a non-folding potty chair, toys, cloth diapers and a sizable amount of clothing changes. We will not need to do laundry for at least six months. Then there is a multiplicity of game paraphernalia, fishing rods of all sizes, special jackets, shoes, hats for fishing and hiking. We are ready for whatever role we need to assume. There is so much gear attached to this ugly car that one can only see the driver and some of the vehicle. It looks like the American counterpart of Mr. Hulot's Peugeot as he traveled to the seashore. Re-packing this auto for the return trip never is quite as successful.

In these early years we rent a cabin, without bath, on the American plan. Daily a maid makes the beds and leaves clean linen. I'm in heaven. And, with this plan, we need a hefty appetite since Camp Curry Lodge provides three meals a day, in any amount. No problem. We've never shirked in this area. As is our custom, we eat everything that isn't in someone else's hands. In many ways, it is confining since we can't wander too far from the trough or we'll miss out on a meal.

Unfortunately, in later years, we graduate to housekeeping cabins by the river, where I get to cook and make beds. The labor intensity usually far surpasses the home routine, but somehow it all seems relevant. After all, we are experiencing what millions of Americans claim to be fun.

Our days are spent in leisurely long lines. Lines at the village general store, lines for breakfast, lunch and dinner, lines for snack bars, and each afternoon before dinner we stand in line at the baths, with our clean clothes, soap, towels and miscellaneous gear tucked into each of our toiletry bags. As is standard, the women's queue is longer with their appendages of unwashed children.

At Camp Curry there is a Kitty Kamp to store the children. It gives Ed and me a respite to explore all the natural wonders, like the gift shops and an occasional Ranger program. For exercise we *drive* to the village, about two miles, grab a hamburger between lunch and dinner, and buy another hat for Ed's collection. Once in awhile, we attempt to fish for trout in Mirror Lake or find a deep hole in the Merced River. About three-fourths into our vacation we ripen into a rhythm of rehearsed enjoyment.

In spite of the swarm of tourists, which we are used to from city living, it is great. At night we blissfully sit with the many urbanites at the amphitheater and watch Firefall. Yes, I know it's man-made, but it still is wonderful. They build a large fire on a high cliff, overlooking the valley, and the smoldering embers are then pushed over Glacier Point, creating an effective fiery waterfall, while down below on the outdoor rustic stage, Nelson Eddy/Jeanette MacDonald 'wannabes', sing "The Indian Love Call". In addition, even amateurs provide entertainment, while bats dive-bomb our heads and mosquitoes enjoy large doses of city blood. At the end of the evening we sing cowboy favorites around the fire. Our nightly after dinner walks take us to the garbage bins to watch whole families of bears sift through leftovers that the paying folks leave on their plates.

Inquisitive friends ask us why we return so many times to the same park. It does sound strange to admit that we don't try many other places. It is as if we are compelled to seek out this wonderful valley, each time tasting one more of her remarkable morsels. Maybe it is the homing pigeon part of us. Little by little it is becoming part of our lives as we learn its history and secrets feeling nourished with each of the trips. Besides, my *esposo* is not too inclined to try new things.

Don't get me wrong. We have plenty of miseries and near misses. The only year we take Ed's elderly mom with us, we have a great time, but it is also the year my oldest daughter nearly cracks her brain open like a melon. Gina misses her footing, despite all our warnings not to jump across log seats at the outdoor theater. She strikes her eyebrow and a hematoma forms the size of a baseball. It is a frightening and sobering addition to our holiday. Still we continue to be drawn like swallows to repeat the yearly experience.

I'm not saying that Ed's encounters with nature aren't memorable, either. One time, down at the river, on a convenient overhanging log, the good man finds a substantial fishing hole, and he has his line right at one of the noble trout's mouth, while across the water, on the opposite bank, Wayne, a young fishing friend, watches Ed as he reels in the good catch. Little does Ed know there is another party at the other end of the log interested in his angling skills. In his ecstasy to catch the trout, he misses Wayne's frantic and repeated hand motions signaling him.

"Heh, Ed! Lookout behind you!"

"What Wayne? Yeah it is a good size fish!"

Instinctually Ed suddenly turns to see a healthy upright bear eyeballing the potential meal, not on the American plan.

"Jeeesus!" he yells, about to take his only option to jump into the stream. The bear obviously accustom to tourists on logs by now, turns and leaves the scene since the pale man is only holding a fish instead of a hamburger. My husband later relates how his clean underwear nearly meets an unscheduled and unpleasant challenge.

It is during the Hippie movement, in the early seventies, when we decide to take the plunge and camp with a tent in the unconquered high country. We are now moving further and further from luxury. Ed's lovable psychologist friend, Larry, an Arthur Miller look alike, and a character lifted out of Woody Allen movies, loves hiking, personal psycho-therapy, and marriages, and is not fully successful at any of them. Ed had been the best man at Larry's weddings until my husband decides probably he is jinxing his poor friends' opportunity at happiness.

"Ed, you have to go with us. All you need to do is rent a tent and we can camp up in Tuolomne Meadows. We'll follow behind you guys in my car with Cora and her children."

Larry, at this time, is dating a wee crazy-maker, a textbook muddled, strange woman with four grown teenage children.

"Wow," I say. "It sounds groovy, but it's pretty high country. We'll get nosebleeds. We haven't been in a tent since we camped on the beach in Ensenada with Gina as a baby. That was a long time ago."

Habitually negative, Eddie is confident in his answer. "Let's do it. I have a friend who said he would loan his large tent."

By now we've traded our VW Bug for a more practical car. The 1961 Dodge Station Wagon, is packed to the brim with the borrowed *ten*-man tent and enough supplies to last through the eighties. Our long-haired teenage daughters, my equally lengthy braid, and not to be outdone, Edward's long flowing beard, adding balance to his Einstein coiffure, leaves no doubt we have identified with the Mangy Mane Movement. The New Yorkers, by way of California, are going to the highlands.

Instead of the cool coastal route we take the hot inland desert road. Larry and his clan follow in their automobile. About two-thirds of the way, the radiator overheats, on our almost ten-year-old car. The climb and the weight are too much for the old thing. The addition of water from time to time only prolongs the inevitable. We can hear it boiling. But, in our typically untalented way, we removed the cap. It spews its contents, like Vesuvius, over the hood, fenders and windows, enveloping, the now painted silver from lavender vehicle, in the rust colored liquid, which combined with the thick coat of dust, resembles a war machine from Lawrence of Arabia.

At the Tioga Pass entrance to the National Park, we become aware that many tourists are turned away because of their questionable appearance and nomadic inference. The park experiences some of the down side of the Hippie's, 'free to be,' movement. The worst vandalism ever; squatters are taking up residence, without regard to other people's rights, and the not too angelic Hell's Angels are raising hell.

"Eddie, what are we going to do?" I fret. "We look a mess. I'll bet they won't let us in. That was one damn hot drive up here! I'm so sweaty, we look as if we've been sleeping in the car for several months. Look at the kids. It looks like birds have nested in their hair. Bad news! Wait 'till they see this car!"

"It'll be all right. Let me do the talking."

It is no surprise when we are stopped with the possibility of being turned away. Wild haired, Chief Psychologist Ed, does some pretty fancy jawing to the Rangers as he flashes his correctional clinic's business card. The officer looks at the card and then back to the car rats and skeptically shakes his head.

We enter the park.

And now we must find a spot in these cold mountains to pitch our tent, something we have never done. Six foot plus Larry relinquishes his powers of thinking and turns his life over to his newfound love, the five-foot disordered broad. She has needs, big needs, mainly to direct the party. Back and forth we drive, looking for just the right spot. At dusk, running out of perfect campsites, we finally settle on a rutted, stony area. As the temperature drops, hunger starts to take over the dirty and whiny party. We spend half an evening of fits and tempers trying to erect the two canvas houses in the dark, adding to our already extensive colorful, four-letter language.

We soon find out that Larry's entourage has barely taken enough necessities and is scrambling for tools and supplies to erect the tent and to put together a meal. Because I came compulsively prepared, Larry's girlfriend is miffed when we offer to share. She is determined to endure without our help. We're off to a roaring start.

Bedtime does not come too quickly for the happy campers. Larry and his ready-made family of six, pile into their two-people tent. We suddenly become aware of how idiotic this picture looks. Six in a two-man tent and our four in a ten-man tent, large enough for a ballroom.

"Heh, guys, would you like to spend the night in our large tent there's plenty of room and we could conserve body heat?" Ed offers. "It's going to get damn cold."

We hear the raised voices of dissension in the small canvas cave.

"We'll be just fine," Larry calls out.

"What's the matter with them?" I ask. "How in the hell can you fit six sleeping bags in that small tent?"

"I don't know, Vin. Don't worry about them. They'll work it out," Ed says.

"For sure they're going to be warm at least," I say. "We are going to freeze our butts off tonight. We better wear everything we own. The altitude is already catching up with Gina and me. We both have bad headaches."

By evening, Gina's and my head are pounded into submission. Any talk or movement brings tears to our eyes. This new land is testing our pioneer spirit. We settle into our sleeping bags and now can't move because of the extra clothing. If we had to make a run for it there would be no way. No latrine breaks this night. The temperature drops to cryogenics significance. The rocks beneath our shoulder blades grow into boulders. The four of us roll towards each other and huddle to keep our body heat from disappearing.

"My head is unmerciful. Carisa, does your head hurt too, honey?"

"A little, but I'm really freezing."

"It is pretty miserable," I agree. "How long are we staying here, Ed?"

No answer.

As I lay in my mummified state, I begin my hallucinations. Where is my little rustic cabin in the valley? I seem to be slipping backwards in my pleasures. Look how far down I've come from those wonderful early days in Yosemite. Gone are the comfortable beds and clean linens. Gone is the American Plan! How I long to stand in line for a hot shower. I long for the hordes of people scrambling hither and yon. It's going to be a long miserable night.

No one sleeps. It is so cold that all we can do is get silly and talk.

"Eddie, I think we're dying."

"Feels like it."

"Eddie, how do you think death starts?"

"I don't know. Maybe it'll happen tonight."

"I think it probably starts in the toes, nose and fingers, then as they drop off, they signal to the larger parts to follow. Whatdya think?"

"You may have a theory there."

"Well, let me know if you die."

Next morning, we make a marvelous decision. We are going to pack up and find a campsite in the valley.

But another wild-goose-chase starts. Larry's friend, again, needs to find just the right spot to land. This time the requirements are more defined. She must be close to the riding stables for her children. I ask myself, how is this happening? Nine people are being led by this Pied Piper? How's this spot? How's that spot? Closer where? You want to go back where?

Once again we pitch the blasted tent, our remaining nerve is completely threadbare. Around four in the morning, we hear strong talk from the other tent. Larry and the kids are out looking for Wonder Woman in the pitch-black forest. During the night, she decides to take a walk in the wild and commune with nature, about as good an idea as to walk, after hours, in New York's Central Park. When she returns, she is not too shook that everyone is totally cuckoo with worry with the theory that a bear had enjoyed an L.A. midnight snack.

In a few days the trip from hell is nearly over. It is not unlike certain food that you find decidedly distasteful and vow never to try again. You can only imagine what happens in our household when talk of a vacation begins to surface. We have dim memories regarding stressful experiences of past travels to the forestland, much like the amnesia that accompanies childbirth. There must be worth in these trips. At least I believe there is value in subjecting ourselves to these histrionic exercises. As I see it, the real pay-off comes when we arrive home with all the mess, and the children dash for their own beds and we reveal to ourselves.

"My God we made it alive! It's so good to get home!"

RIVERBOATING with the QUEEN

The ad reads...

> This is the vacation you've dreamed about
> No experience Necessary
> Cruise Where you Want. When you Want
> It's the Vacation Thrill of a Lifetime!

House boating is the new rage for vacations in the 1970's. Big page advertisements beckon the unwary with delights of sailing on the Sacramento River Delta.

Ed and I pour over the advertisement.

"Whatdaya think, Vin?" Eddie says. "Do you wanna try this?"

"Sure, It'll be a break from Yosemite." Even though we don't know a thing about navigation, I am game for most things. "How hard is it to sail a houseboat? What's the big deal?"

Ed's demanding job counseling psychiatric tenants of the penal system gives him reason enough to shed tie and briefcase, and I'm back into the work force, selling real estate, after many years of doing the mom and wife thing. So the break sounds quite appealing.

Gina and Carisa, now ages fourteen and twelve, are at a point in their lives, that to be seen anywhere with their parents brings on orphan-like behavior. We pick our vacations carefully. We sell them a possible package: they can hide and sun themselves on board the boat's top deck, leave their beds unmade, just like they do at home, and not have much to do with us, just like they do at home. They agree. We restore the gleam in their eyes. Who knows, there could even be boys floating somewhere on those waters.

We include in our plans, Ed's older divorced sister, Leona, also a slave to the work force, who is in need of rest and quiet to heal a nasty stiff bursitis shoulder. Her nautical skills? Probably equal to ours. We have yet to find her talents, but we know she's a true Barles. She's a good eater.

We finally make the decision to contract for a full week on a forty-two foot ten-sleeper houseboat, called the Delta Queen. Our excitement and joy cannot be contained. These transplanted New Yorkers to the Wild West, have never tried anything like this before. But now, I suddenly have a severe case of angst rising to the surface, my fear of water.

"Is it necessary to know how to swim, Eddie? You know I swim fine in five feet of water, but once I am in six, I drown." There are too many questions, but I'm assured all will be explained in great detail once we arrive.

"Don't worry, Vin. There will be life jackets. Besides how much problem can you get into with a boat that only goes five to ten miles an hour?"

I prepare several casseroles of our favorite foods, and bring an assortment of deli meats and cheeses. I purchase the latest processed foods my family normally doesn't get to try. Junk food will reign supreme this vacation. This will be a holiday no one will want for anything or ever forget.

We load the 1961 Dodge station wagon to the last inch.

After spending most of the day traveling we finally come to the road that leads to the Sacramento River Delta and the houseboat marina. When I see the vessels lined up ready for their occupants, my imagination begins to bloom of adventures on the high seas. Number 253 awaits; our assigned boat. Our instructions are to put our belongings on board and appear for a short orientation.

"Ed, do you think we brought too much stuff?" weak and frail Leona asks.

"Nah," he answers with an air of leadership. "Why? Leona don't try and carry all of that."

"I'm all right, but Eddie, look over there at that man and his two German Shepherds. He's only taking two sacks of groceries."

"So?"

"I heard he's going for two weeks!" Leona exclaims. "But we're going to be gone for only one week and look at all this stuff!"

"You know Ed, she's right," I said, as I juggle two, man-size, meal-in-one dishes. "We look like worker ants on a safari. We've made about ten trips from the car all ready!" We resume to carry; canned foods, cases of soft drinks, beer, more cooked casseroles, every form of cold cuts, fresh fruits and vegetables, sandwich material, boxes of clothing, blankets, bath linens, games radio, and medical supplies.

As soon as we settle, my husband and I leave for orientation and enter a room with other wide-eyes sea-faring adventurers. We are promptly given ranks. Ed is Captain, and I, am singled out as his First Mate. No great surprise. The personnel endeavor to explain, in a quick half hour, some of the different problems that could arise, but it is all said in fast talking technical terms. I nudge Ed with a questioned look.

"What did he say?"

"Did you catch that, Vin?" He grinds out brusquely.

I can tell we are all ready losing that 'loving feeling' amidst the squabbling. We are in serious trouble. Neither of us can comprehend three-fourths of the information and no one has asked any questions. The head guy continues to tell us about some things that can go wrong.

"Wha. What did he say?" Ed whispers.

"I don't know. Something about 'if a cotter pin breaks and the motor bursts into flames."

"Jeesus, it's coming at us too fast!"

"Eddie, how many packages of that stuff are you supposed to put into the toilet, and where are we supposed to empty it?" I ask, as my heart plays bongos on my chest. "For crying out loud, did you get all that?"

The one page brochure reads: 'Each houseboat is fully equipped'. Among the gear, is an eight-foot long hook, probably the single most precious item a houseboat rookie should have, often used to push away from docks or whatever else you need to get away from. Ours will be well worn. In the bedroom closet, stands a ladder to reach the water from the boat. The toilet requires chemicals to dissolve the unmentionables and our instructions are to empty our holding tank at least once during the week. No problem. The large map of the sloughs and deltas is pinned to the wall. All looks good.

The vessels are lined up in the marina. We have the option to come back each day, or dock and anchor somewhere along the waterway. Boat number 253 is eager to go.

Our first day and we're raring to get started. Captain Ed sizes up the situation. Obviously, we will need to back out of our tie-up position, but because of the large numbers of speed boats racing back and forth, moving is difficult.

Ed directs his sister. "Leona, you stand on the back deck to warn Vin of traffic, and Vin, you relay it to me. Those jet-skiers move pretty damn fast. O.K.?"

Ed starts the motor. It roars so loud I can't hear directives from Leona. She changes the status depending on cross-water traffic, so by the time I receive the instructions to give to Ed, they have changed again. This keeps up for a time, by now taxing our new Captain and raising the color gradation in his neck and face. Finally, in exasperation, our esteemed first Officer, turns the motor off for a much needed rest.

We're moored next to a quiet and respectable looking couple with two soft-spoken children. It's obvious it is also their first time. They decide to take a crack at backing out. We wait and watch. Suddenly, there are frantic movements on their deck.

"Whoa!" I exclaim. "Is that them swearing? Look, the boat is making a complete U-turn and is headed right back here. Oh, oh, they're really yelling now. Obviously they must have a defective cotter pin or whatever."

Once more we try, this time with relieved success. Down the river we float.

Ah! This is so serene and beautiful. Haven't seen the girls since we started. This is going to be a noteworthy and great week. I've needed this rest. Leona looks happy too. Maybe her shoulder will get better.

We pass little towns surrounded by orchards of pears and apples; appreciating and sampling the pleasures this potent river has to offer. After a favorable, but vigilant sail, we decide to cut our day short; return to the marina, have a casserole and relax. Our long drive from the Southland has left us exhausted. We all agree, it is a great idea to start fresh tomorrow.

As we cruise towards our destination, there is a fork in the river and Captain Ed asks.

"Vin, quick! Which way do I go? Right or left?"

Swiftly, I attempt to interpret the 'Houseboat Pleasure Map' on the wall, with its '1000 miles of peaceful waterway'.

"I think it's left," comes my dyslexic reply.

He turns his wheel to the left and my eyes spot our marina's location on the map.

"No no, Ed! Quick, turn to the right, instead! Can't you go faster?"

"What the f—k? Are you sure? Jeesus Christ, there's a damn speedboat making a big wake. It's shoving against the boat! I can't go faster with this thing."

"Eddie! Look out! You're heading towards that island! God! Look at all those downed trees and branches!"

Ed tries to rectify the error – but the boat, on its determined course, can't respond in time. The water swell shoves us toward the entangled land. We stand frozen with our future before us.

"Look out!" Leona yells. "We're going to crash into that island!"

"We're going to hit that tree, Ed. Oh Gooooooooood!"

The boat slams to its resting place. The sounds of crunching metal and broken tree limbs fill my head.

Stunned, we cautiously peer over the railing.

"Can you believe this?" Eddie exclaims. "It looks like we're impaled. Impaled on a fallen tree!"

"Oh my, God! There's a large gaping hole in our side. Are we gonna sink?"

Leona has gone to be with the food in the kitchen for solace. She shouts out. "Hey you guys. It looks like the trunk of the tree has pierced the boats innards. It's sticking out of the lower kitchen cabinets, and it's knocked out cans of diet sodas and beers."

All the years of yoga and meditation does not prepare me for this anxiety. I'm certain this is the end of our week at sea, all in one day. I don't remember if the children ever came off of their bunk beds. Ed and I try the trusty 'hook' to free ourselves, but no luck...when all of a sudden we begin to push out. We look over the side again and there is wild-eyed, bursitis ridden, Leona, at the back end of the boat; her body half over the barrier, pulling at the large log. Single-handedly, she manages to work the tree out of the Queen. Bad shoulder and all! The boat slips back into the water.

We limp back to the marina with our sober tenants. As we arrive in Walnut Grove, our home base, our heads are filled with thoughts of having to mortgage the house to pay for the repairs on the Delta Queen. But the personnel don't even flinch.

"No big deal," they say, as they bang a piece of fiberboard over the hole. "Stuff happens."

Our first day is not to be forgotten. A few unscheduled sandwiches help to calm our nerves. Our heroine, Leona, has developed a severe attack of nerves and runs to the refrigerator each time Ed starts the motor. I am not far behind.

We brace ourselves for day two.

Captain Ed decides that after our frightful time the day before, we probably shouldn't attempt anything too daring. He offers that we take a quiet trip into one of the many smaller waterways, maybe Hog Slough, traffic should be minimal and the likelihood of problems nil.

We find a serene, secluded, picturesque cove, and agree. This is it. A quiet and safe *cul-de-sac* for needed recuperation after yesterday's harrowing disaster.

Ed, Gina and Carisa, jump ashore and tie the vessel to a tree. We will stay the night and head for the marina in the morning. It is magnificent. The delicious smell of steaks barbecuing on deck, triggers our out of control ravenous appetites. I might add, nothing new for the three adults on this cruise, just added padding for our all ready Rubenesque bodies. In spite of all our fears, we manage to eke out a few laughs at our good fortune of having escaped living out the summer on the brier island. But, today gives us confidence that we can handle new vistas tomorrow. Later that evening, as we soak up the peace and quiet with just crickets and bullfrogs filling the night air with song, we settle in for an enjoyable game of Casino.

It's hot and sticky this dark, moonless night, and our cabin lights are beginning to get exceedingly dim, and before too long we play cards by flashlights. This boat seems to know when our guard is down and getting too self-assured.

"What's that sound?" I ask, as I deal a lucky hand.

Eddie answers, "I don't hear anything. Stop worrying, Vin, it's just your imagination."

We continue to play.

"Leona, don't you hear that? It sounds like trees breaking." Leona's eyes have reached the limit of openness.

Soon, the cracking, snapping and crunching noises get louder. Suddenly, the window screens begin to fall into the room, whacking our heads and covering the gambling table. We bend, but remain as statues, like the ash encased Pompeians; now fruit tree branches plow through, pushing themselves into our little space, as if devouring our Queen.

"What the hell is happening now?" I shriek. I finally awake to our new fiasco. "My God, we're in the trees! Can you believe this? It's a tree house!"

"I guess we didn't consider the rising tide." The Captain says, as he looks at his stunned silent daughters; convinced their father is trying to kill them.

"The rising tide?" Leona apes. "What the heck is a rising tide doing in a weed infested pond?"

"So much for a calm and peaceful evening!" I say.

The 'African Queen' will not be out of the pear branches until morning. It's a long, sleepless night, cutting away twigs and limbs with kitchen knives and swatting large carnivorous mosquitoes, who must think this is the greatest event since their last get-together at the swamp. What to do? Ah! Food. Finally, we crash into our beds, bleary-eyed and apprehensive at the prospect of a new day.

Venera Di Bella Barles

On our return trip, out of the tree jungle, we find another slough, quiet, pleasant and far from shore, far from those pesky trees. Before we left, my seafaring husband had purchased from the big guys store, a large, yellow, two-man raft, (all nicely folded; never taken out of the box). When we arrived, he had it inflated at the dock. It grew half as large as our houseboat.

Now the yellow dinghy is about to go on her maiden voyage. We lower the swim ladder over the side of the Delta Queen.

"Dad, we're going in for a swim. Are you coming?" squeal, Gina and Carisa, anxious to start a chronicle of their own.

"Yeah, as soon as I get this thing in the water."

In they plunge, like beavers leaving the marshes. Ed carefully lowers himself into the rubberized container, but as he talks and laughs with us, I realize a strange thing is happening.

"Eddie! You're folding in half! You're going to sink!! Oh, my God, that damn boat is swallowing you!"

Too many pies, cakes and deli-sandwiches take their toll. We now have one large, useless, wet, deflated, yellow boat and officer. Leona and I, haul the dead dinghy aboard. It is its first and last voyage.

Ed, and the two bikini-clad recreation directors decide, instead, to have a good swim in the beautiful Sacramento River. It is not until later, do we become aware that this was not a wise idea. The river is highly polluted, no doubt from allowing houseboats to empty their toilets without restrictions. It's probably just as well, we don't have this bit of information.

Ed helps our daughters onto the deck, and then attempts to get himself out, but nervously discovers the ladder is too short and doesn't reach the water. His leg can't reach high enough to get to the first step.

Leona, by now, sharp enough to sense ill luck ahead, fortifies herself with several reachable snacks. The kitchen, is never out of use, and stays as busy and alive as a New York deli. The daily high drama is often soothed deliciously, in this arena.

"Eddie, I can't get you out!" I yell. "Leona, come out here and give me a hand. Maybe your super android arm can help me pull him up."

Leona puts down her food and runs to help. We sweat up enough steam to run an engine, but still. "Eddie, we can't do it! It can't be done."

He is too engorged. The Captain circles the Queen like a porpoise as he checks for a spot to embark. No luck.

The houseboat, built on pontoons, has its rim high off the water. We have two options, to throw a line and tow him back to the marina or try to heave him out once again.

By this time, my sister-in-law, has acquired special agility with her bursitis-ridden, plump body. She rolls into action. With great huffing and desperation we pull at anything we can grab onto, while our teenagers hold Leona and me. Several armpits are involved, and his new boxer swim trunks are yanked beyond belief. The waters churn with Ed's thrashes; slowly he loses faith in his rescuers. Eventually the four of us drag his pruned carcass aboard.

Thank God, we have our leader back. So far, this vacation has been nothing but work. A good meal is definitely in order.

But the thought of waking up the next day and starting all over again leaves us a little wary. I now understand why there is much drinking on board pleasure boats. A few AA meetings at sea could prove to be quite handy and necessary. Whenever Ed starts the motor he has taken to getting himself a beer to steady his nerves. But, I need to have more faith. This will be a much better day. Besides, it is our wedding anniversary and my Captain's birthday. We will give it another try. We intend to celebrate, as long as it involves food.

Fellow mariners tell us of a pleasant restaurant in the main channel of the river. So, we rev everyone up for the sail down the waters. It is a picturesque, and thankfully, uneventful trip and there is still plenty of daylight to enjoy the local scenery. The Cliff House gleams in the late afternoon sunlight as we tie the Queen up to the eatery's dock.

We find our humor slowly restoring; we enjoy our meal, and our family is intact. After all, I tell myself, we have lived through nineteen anniversaries and Ed's forty-four birthdays. And besides, we'll work all this chaos out in psychoanalysis. This is a year of challenges and changes. But, I ramble. Even Gina and Carisa, momentarily out of their bikinis, seem to be relaxed, though, ever attentive to the on going search for heedless males. However, our peaceful evening is soon interrupted with a loud bellow from the next table.

"Holy cats!" someone shouts. "There's a houseboat loose. Look! It's floating away!"

We leap from our chairs, nearly knocking the precious spread to the floor, and strain to see what number is on the side of this boat, but, we also notice a very strange thing. Everyone in the dining room is standing at the windows with fear on their faces, their bodies stretching to see whose houseboat has decided to leave them. How does one catch a forty-two foot boat, floating down the swift Sacramento River, out to the Pacific Ocean?

A woman screams and screeches, "I don't believe it! It's ours! It's ours! Oh no. Not again. Harry, I just knew we couldn't get through this meal without more trouble with that god damn boat!"

Her voice, though shrill and fretful, is music to my ears. The Queen is safe! Our anguish is assuaged, for the moment. We devour our meal. Thankfully, the rest of the evening is serene, and we are smug that we have escaped unpleasantries for the moment.

"You know, Vin," Ed, the older, proudly says, "We need gas and I spotted fuel pumps on that dock down a bit. I think we can probably stay there overnight, then in the morning all I have to do is fire up the engine and pull the boat ahead. We'll be right in line to fill up without turning the houseboat around."

"Good. Whatever gives us a smooth time," I say, leery of any new suggestions.

After dinner, we sail the short distance to the overnight dock. So, to sleep we go, peaceful with the attitude that we are finally getting a grip on this trip.

With breakfast over, everyone is ready for the new day. We check our maps. Talk over our plans then pay the wharfage.

There is an increasing awareness, amidst the denial, of a need to attend to the odiferous latrine. The air dominates the pear blossoms. As the food supply diminishes, the toilet gets a decided work out. The chemicals are not doing an efficient job. We definitely have been having a 'Scarlet moment' with our avoidance. Maybe tomorrow!

We vote to go back up the river; to find and conquer some new bogs and quagmires. As yet we haven't tried to fish, but, first we need to gas up.

"Is everyone ready?" Ed asks. "Vin, where is, Leona?"

"I'm here. In the kitchen."

Ed directs our course for the next dock with the fuel tanks. The attendant, on the dock, stands and waits with a big smile on his youthful face. He watches my husband as he nears. Then the man hollers to Ed.

"Whip it in, mister!"

"Whip it in? Whadda ya mean, whip it in?"

"Your gas tank is on the other side, mister! You have to turn it around!"

Venera Di Bella Barles

Oh no. Here we go again. Nothing is easy with this miserable boat! This isn't in Ed's plans. He's going to be a maniac. Damn what luck!

Tension is restored.

Captain Ed braces himself to pivot the Queen. Leona runs to the refrigerator to grab a last minute bagel, our young ladies hide in their bunks and play a game of Pig, and I resign myself to the fine print in my marriage contract.

Ed sails forward, and strives for a short right angle turn, without success. The water current, I realize by this time, is working for the Queen, slams us full force into the wharf. We helplessly watch, as parts of the pier, boards, railroad size spikes and posts, soar in all directions into the air, like roman candles...jolting, all the wide-eyed people standing on the dock who were out for their morning stroll. Titanic's sister ship, the Delta Queen, has met her iceberg.

The ashen, faced, speechless, slack jaw attendant jumps back aghast!

The Captain manages the best refutation statement he can create.

"Fill'er up, please!"

This river must have wonderful stories to tell. We are just simple people, needing a break from the Naked City. Brave, Edward the Good, who administers to some of the toughest prisoners in the states' penal system is being whipped and battered by this ark and these waters.

We can't help but see the damage on many of the houseboats of our fellow suburban sailors. The list is lengthy; sun decks sheared, missing sides, broken railings and these are only the visible disfigurements. There is no doubt that these dents and bruises have touched many psyches. Lord knows what their stories are.

Never quite knowing where and when this ship will meet its end, our daughters feverishly work on their suntans on the top deck. They surround themselves with all their necessities; Nancy Drew novels, lotion, ice tea, lounge chairs, and of course, a battery radio blaring the latest, 'Sugar, Sugar' by the Archies. The fact that they do not have to be a part of the mutinous crew below, makes it all the more enjoyable and besides by this time they have also locked eyeballs with the boys on neighbor boats.

Along about mid-week into our adventure on the high seas, one of the small bridges spanning the many inlets comes into view, and as we near it, we realize we may not make it under without forfeiting our upper deck.

"*Marona Mia!*" I scream to Ed and Leona, as she sensually runs her hand over the refrigerator. "We need to let the kids know. There is no time to stop! It looks like we're going to smash our top!" I scream. "Gina! Carisa! Hit the deck! Bridge ahead!"

As we go under the overpass, I hear the sound of breaking glass, then chairs and bodies smack the roof. But I don't detect any broken body or boat sounds. Leona and I run up the steps to examine the ruins. The craft is intact, but our nymphs are shaking and fuming. Their articles of rest and pleasure are strewn about the deck.

Will they ever be able to face the young guys who saw them from the other houseboat? What are their parents trying to do to them?

"Vin?" Leona asks. "Did you see this on the wall?" She adjusts her glasses and takes a closer look. "It says you have to be very careful about the changing tides. It says it can affect going under bridges. My God this boat is trying to kill us!"

"No kidding?" I respond.

Our lives are definitely being shortened and we still have two or three days left of this relaxing fun in the sun, this 'get away from it all' wonder.

We console ourselves with several small snacks.

The larder is almost empty. Our sandwiches are unquestionably smaller. Our casseroles are gone. We have consumed most of our beverages and snacks. It does not seem conceivable that three adults and two children have devoured enough food for fifteen people. This night we return to the marina to stay and recuperate.

Stress is upon me. My need to organize is imminent.

"O.K., Eddie, we definitely have to discuss a plan of action regarding dumping the toilets!" I nag to my glazed eye spouse. "There is just so much air freshener we can use. It's not working any more."

It is agreed we will evacuate the Monomatic toilet (like on jet airliners) at the dock in the morning.

We learn that the boat, The Delta Roamer, with its large simpatico Mexican family, has docked next to the Delta Queen. They plan to return home today. It has been pleasant watching the elderly parents sit daily on the deck chairs, warmly waving at people as they drift by. And now, this is their final day.

Captain Ed's wondrous imagination immediately comes into play.

"Listen, I've got an idea. We'll empty the toilet when the people next to us start their motors."

I wince as he lays out the caper. Leona moves towards the table and as I look over to our daughters they have already installed their headphones.

"Vin, you can let me know when they begin to back out of the marina. Then, I'll release the inside discharge valve. Then the churning waters will suck the sewage and gunk down below and no one will be embarrassed or the wiser. Right? You remember this is the way the guys at the rental office said to do it. Right?"

Suddenly the vision comes to mind of my family merrily and innocently swimming in Beaver Slough. My, oh my.

The moment arrives. My instructions are to stand on deck and wave good-bye to the Garcias, and at the right moment I am to give our captain the signal to pull the plug. Our daughters, who at this point have developed a sixth sense about our maneuvers, decide to jump ship and hide in the wild grasses. Leona, well, we all know where she is.

Grandma and Grandpa Garcia, their married daughters, sons and in-laws smile broadly as they tell me to be careful, but have a good time. They speak wisely because they were instrumental in getting help for our rescue calls a couple of times. Arms are open wide for their departing *adios*. The Delta Roamer, starts to leave the dock. I wave farewell smiling cheerily, but with trepidation. And to Ed I shout between my clenched teeth.

"Now!"

He pulls the plug.

It is done.

From the side of the Queen, five feet **above** the water, a spout of feculent blue sewage is released. It shoots and fans, in a continuous gush, out across our noble neighbor's deck, with a force equal to a firefighter's hose.

They are engulfed, erasing the wholesome grins from their faces. Adults and children watch the muck unfold with stunned, frozen stares. Bits of paper and unspeakable odious fragments lace humans, railings, draping deck chairs and on the grandson's prize cowboy hat. As my painful eyes look further I see another young man's pride, his clean and shiny chrome motorcycle, its gleam completely lost! They strain to detect where the waste matter is coming from. With their fingers and hands dripping, they point to the offending party.

The Delta Queen has assaulted and bombarded The Delta Roamer.

"My God!" I screech. "Ed, stop it! Turn it off!"

Unaware of the chaotic mess Ed replies, "I can't. It won't stop. Why? What's wrong?"

The waste inundates and splashes everything and everyone as it continues its endless journey. I fall prone to the deck, to hide and cover my mortification. The Garcia's boat cannot back out fast enough. We never see them again.

Although we are friendless, our 'head' is again sweet smelling. We pray for amnesia. Within a few days it will be the end of our week on the Sacramento River Delta with 'over a thousand miles of gentle inland waterways at your beck and call!'

But today is fishing day, not that I have any desire to consume any catch from this river. We desperately need rest and even our daughters agree they would just like to stay in their bunks and read. Leona and I wistfully look forward to Los Angeles traffic and busy streets. They seem tame by comparison to river traffic.

Skipper Ed gives the new orders of the day. "We're going to the middle of the river to fish! Isn't that a good idea? That way it will be safer."

Great! We won't have to dock or tie to a tree. But I'm losing confidence in this mate's ability to lead.

We depart from the marina and quietly float to a new spot, passing many of our fellow warriors and their battered boats. There before us, is a wide portion of the river, serene, non-imposing and with few boats in our way. What could be better? This is good, right in the middle of the water. We will have lunch as soon as we position and secure the boat.

The Captain orders us to drop anchor. Right. The instructions read; 'Throw out rear anchor first. Proceed about 30 ft. and put your gear in neutral, tighten up rear anchor line and throw out forward anchor and tighten line.'

He commands Leona, the sickly Amazon, to stand at the back and I will be at the bow. Ed will steer. After a considerable delay we're ready to drop the heavy hooks.

Captain says, "When I say NOW, you drop it first Leona, and then I'll tell you, Vin, when to let go of yours."

Right. At this point Leona and I know not to upset him. The wise daughters are nowhere to be found.

"O.K. Leona, drop yours," he commands.

The deed is done. She's a pro. Ed barely moves forward his allotted 30 feet, and then my orders come. All is going well.

He once more orders, in a well-modulated voice, "O.K., Vin, drop yours."

I let the rope and anchor plunge down with a brilliance only Errol the Flynn could applaud. As it hits the water, we hear sounds of metal to metal. Clashing metal. The Queen suddenly begins to pirouette and rotate - and continues to turn, turn, turn. We look to Captain Ed for guidance.

"What the hell is wrong now, Ed?" I ask, as my mutinous voice reaches a frenzied tone.

"I don't know. We can't go forwards or backwards! We're locked in position. Can't get the anchors out either."

I notice Ed has a new manner; one of resignation. A strange calm has replaced his typically frantic demeanor.

Number 253 moves in a constant, slow, circular, movement. She is in distress and in need of assistance once more. Leona and I flag down the required three passing houseboats and request they send for help.

Fearless Ed understanding we are not leaving this spot for a while; has evolved a sense of 'what the hell'. He decides to fish and take advantage of the natural trolling qualities the Queen has established by her newly acquired revolving techniques.

But, God answers in mysterious ways. Rescue comes in three hours. He is only twelve years old, four feet high, and part fish. A man and his young son traveling in their speedboat stop to help us. The boat continues to twirl. We sheepishly tell them of our problem. The father, non-concerned, sends the lad to check it out. If we could only get Leona out of the pantry she might be able to perform one of her superhuman, Amazonian undersea feats.

The boy surfaces within minutes. He has unraveled both anchors that were wrapped around the motor and themselves. Fifty feet of water and only twenty-five feet of rope on the anchors just don't match up to a working duo.

Our last day finally arrives.

We sanitize our floating asylum and get it ready for its return to home dock; scrub and wash the dishes; clean our messes; pack our linens and clothing. We have lightened our load considerably for our drive home. Our food supply is gone.

We return the Delta Queen, number 253, to her owners. They salute us for surviving and hope to see us next year. (Oh yeah!) The Queen is checked over and lined up in the marina, waiting for another unsuspecting family to fill their memory banks.

Next year we're going to rent a housekeeping cabin, again, at Yosemite National Park...on *terra firma*.

#25 Captain Eddie Barles (1980's)

#26 Captain Eddie's adoring daughters

Venera Di Bella Barles

The BUSINESS WOMAN

I wonder who the couple is in Mr. Hazelton's office? They look pretty straight-laced to me. Holy mackerel! Oh, my gosh, they're coming towards my desk. Don't tell me these are my first clients? Oh God, they're not smiling. Why aren't they smiling? Let's see, where is that shoe? And my calculator, yikes where is my calculator? I hope my hairs aren't sticking out from under the wig. Here they come!

"This is, Vinny. I'm sure you'll find her very helpful. This is, Mr. and Mrs. Schnitzer, Vinny. They're looking for property in the neighborhood. I told them you would be happy to help them find something."

"So pleased to meet you, Mr. and Mrs. Chinzer...Oh, Schnitzer. I beg your pardon, so sorry...Please, won't you have a seat...Here's my card...Yes, you may call me, Vinny...Yes, I know it sounds like a man's name, but I assure you, this is a lot easier than my real name...Oh, I'm sorry you don't like nick-names."

Great. I'm in trouble already. They must be seven feet tall. Why won't they sit down? This gal is checking me over pretty carefully. Keeps looking at my high heels. I have a feeling she doesn't like me.

"Mrs. Schnitzer, that's a lovely jacket you're wearing...Oh, I'm sorry, you don't like it...Well, do you mind if I ask you what you will need in a home?...I'm sure you have some ideas of what you want?...What?...Oh, you've owned thirteen homes and you'll know exactly what you want when you see it?"

I better write this name down, or I'll screw it up again! After thirteen homes they should be real experienced with real estate. A couple of sharp cookies. Just my luck. Why couldn't I get a young, dumb twosome. I don't think she's taken that purse out from under her armpit for years.

"Are you familiar with this area? Oh, you are. Where did you say you've looked at houses? Oh, just about everywhere?"

Swell. 'Lookie-loos'. I can't get them to tell me what they want. Maybe I'll just stick them in the car; show them a couple of pieces of property and get a feel for something. I wonder if he speaks. Maybe there's a wind-up key in his back. I better be careful and not get too close to him or she'll eat me for lunch.

"Well, I have a couple of new properties on the market that I'd like to show you. My car is in the back of the building. Would you care for a cup of coffee before we leave? Oh, it gives you an acid stomach, I'm terribly sorry...How about you Mr. Schnitzer? Ah, yes, I understand Mrs. Schnitzer. I'll drive around and pick you up by the front door. Would that be all right? What's that you said, Mrs. Schnitzer? You have a dental appointment in an hour and half? We should be back in plenty of time...I'll make sure of it."

I'll bet they could drill her without Novocain. Why are they so stiff? At the rate I'm going, this may be my first and last client. They said there would be days like this in Real Estate School. Is this the day I die? Where is that damn street map? Just stay cool, Vin. Don't get rattled. You've been waiting for this day. Make it look good. Where's my briefcase? O.K., O.K. Bladder, hang tight!! Damn it's so hot!

"Who would like to sit in the front seat?...Oh, ha ha. You both want to sit in the back? How darling...Afraid of my driving?...Just kidding, just kidding."

Oh smart. This is not the audience to try out your comedy routine on. Naturally, all the crazies are out driving today. Hey, watch out, I'm driving here! Boy they aren't saying a word. Maybe they took a vow of silence with their oatmeal. Hmm, could be they don't know each other. Better try some more small talk.

"How about this smog? Pretty yukky isn't it?

Bad, bad move.

"Oh, the air conditioner gives you hay fever? Well, I can just turn it off. How's that? Oh, don't want the windows open either? Oh, ha ha."

Well, finally here's the blasted house. Oh great, the neighbor decided to open a car repair shop on his front lawn and that other guy across the street must be running for local dog catcher with all the political signs posted all over his property.

"Well, here we are at our first house...I'll just be a moment...I need to get the key from the lock-box and then I'll be right with you."

"Yes, the house is empty...Oh, you don't like a house facing south?...You say you hate detached garages?...Funny color for a roof?...Well, maybe we could rip those shutters right off...Shag rug...Yes, shag...Oh, you want wood floors?...I see, you don't want that many bedrooms?...Well maybe this one could be turned into a library...Oh, you don't like to read?...Don't like that big yard?...Yes, you're right, mowing has to be done often...Looks like gophers to me, but easy to get rid of...Oh, they're not?...Well you should get my husband the 'gopher trapper' to help you. Ha ha."

Cute. Real cute. So far they don't like a damn thing!

"Don't like facing other houses?...You're not going to find many tract houses, sitting by themselves."

Careful. Careful. You're getting close there. Not too mouthy.

"There's one and half baths...You want two full baths?"

Why didn't you tell me what you wanted, when I asked you? Where is that guy? Oh, great, I've lost control, they've disappeared. They hate this house. Wish I could read them a little better. Maybe I'll just go ahead and show them the next house; don't want to get them back late. God, I have a migraine. Maybe this is what death feels like, maybe it really starts in the head. I always thought it started in the toes.

"Hi you two...I couldn't find you...I'm sorry this doesn't fit your needs, but don't despair we'll find a little home for you...Shall we get into the car and we'll go see the next house...Anyone game for the front seat yet?...Ha ha."

How about one of your miracles, Bernadette?

"Let me see, I believe it's over here in the Flower Tract...You've never been in the Flower Tract?...Let's see Orchid, Poppy, Pansy...Should be right around the corner...Yes it does look as if we passed this a few minutes ago...Oh, did I?...Twice?"

Gimme a break. Is this the pits? Now I'm lost. Where the heck is Petunia? What else can go wrong? To top it off, it's damn hot in here and this wig is itchy. If she says one more word about being lost, I'm going to have a tongue sandwich for lunch.

"Can you believe it?...We found Petunia?...I'll bet you thought I'd never find it?...Whoa, you have to have more confidence in me than that...Ha ha...Watch your step getting out of the car...I'll get the key...What was that?...How long have I been in real estate?...Hold on a minute, the lock-box is down here on the garden faucet."

Boy who's bright idea was it to put this contraption down here. Between my girdle and my wig, I don't know which one is tighter. I think my brains are about to explode. Damn this thing. Practically have to stand on my head to get to this idiot box, especially with these heels and a dress. I can feel their eyes on my back, waiting for me to fail. Finally, I've got it. Now if I can get back up. Oh, oh. No, no, no, no. Now my damn slip is caught on my stupid heels? It's down around my ankles! God, what are you doing to me? Where are you death when I need you? Start thinking of something clever to say. Not that the Gothic Couple will answer, and where's their damn pitchfork! Step out of that thing fast, maybe they won't notice. Yeah right. Old eagle eyes.

"Well, what do you think?...Great house isn't it, Mr. and Mrs. Schnitzer?...What?...You've already seen this one?"

Don't say anything. Take them back to the office, and let the dentist take revenge.

"Do hope your mouth gets' better...Sorry I couldn't show you what you needed, but keep my card if there is anything I can do for you."

Whoooeeee. What an experience. Like having twins, breech-birth. Well, I guess I can kiss them off. I'll probably never see them again.

"Vinny, I'd like to see you in my office. Remember, Mr. and Mrs. Schnitzer?"

Here it comes. He's going to give me the what for. I knew I blew it the other day. My big career is over. I guess I can always sell brushes.

"Yes, Mr. Hazelton, they were here last Friday...You're right...They were my very first clients."

"Do you remember that house you showed them the other day? Good news, Vinny, they want to make an offer on it...Yes, the first house...I know you thought they didn't like it...And oh, Vinny, they only want to work with you...Also, they asked about getting your husband to do something...I'm not quite sure what they were referring to...Something about gophers?"

Venera Di Bella Barles

BOXING in a KANGAROO COURT

"She has lost her torturer, her tormenter, the daily poison,
the lack of which, may well kill her"
Colette (1873-1954)

My other friends warn me...

"You're making a mistake, Vinny. You're going to have big troubles. You know how weird and clingy she can be."

But, I state with confidence. "Hey, I've got my eyes wide open. With all the therapy I've had, I can smell upsets before they're cooking. Besides, we've talked and promised each other that we'll get together if there are any problems!"

With this promise, I make plans to go on the distant, lengthy vacation, with my older friend and neighbor of fifteen years.

She lives on the opposite corner from our house with three sons and her fairly dull husband, Iowa born, Walker. While stationed in Australia in the submarine service he meets and marries Jessica, an only child and a native of Perth.

I know her constricted joys are self-inflicted, and I know some of her quirks manifest themselves with money and an impossible case of penny pinching.

Nine times out of ten, she promptly returns purchases. Sadly, she agonizes over any small changes.

Jessica is quick to remind me, that my life is easier because I have daughters instead of sons. She doesn't spend much time asking about my woes, and she remains stone silent; offering little support or understanding, when I lose a son in infancy.

Unfortunately, as I look back at my sick relationship with her, it is based solely on my attendance to her needs and whims—a kind of, be my friend, at any price. I overlook many signals of her stilted and under-developed personality. Even my family racks up some pretty intense data of annoying situations. But do I listen to these blatant insights? Not on your life. I pave my own highway, no matter what kind of boulders I use. How often do we move into a neighborhood and feel compelled to make lifelong friends with our neighbors? If we met the same people living elsewhere we wouldn't even consider them for anything but passing acquaintanceships.

I'm convinced I am ready to take on the world. After all, I've just finished years of psychotherapy and psychoanalysis; searching to understand a mauled childhood. I reveal many answers in my therapy, but I don't learn a thing on how to apply them to everyday living experiences. This trip reminds me how inadequate I still was. It will teach me.

Through the years, Jessica often asks if I would join her for an adventurous sightseeing journey back to Australia. I covet the thought of travel, and it doesn't matter where or for what reason. For me to see Australia would be like walking through storybooks. I've never taken such an expensive and lengthy trip without my family, and feel undeserving of such a luxury, so I put her off when she asks.

"Vinny, I really want you to go," she pleads, "I've never seen any of Australia except for my hometown. Walker doesn't want to go back again. I'd love the company. Please come. I'll pay for your ticket."

She perseveres. Ed and I discuss the possibilities and problems. He, too, has misgivings but wants me to have the journey. We decide I should go, but I must pay my own way, even though it takes a chunk out of our budget.

Jessica is delighted. We are to be gone seven weeks: one week in New Zealand, a few days in Sydney, fly to Perth for a couple of days, to visit her friends and relatives, then small local trips in the western part of the country, eventually, we are to spend a short period in Sydney as our base for east coast travels. I am ecstatic with the plans, imagining a couple of old broads seeing the world.

After our long flight to Sydney, for a momentary stay, we fly to Auckland for a bus tour of New Zealand's North Island.

It's happening. I'm on my way. I'm finally taking this long dreamed of trip. I'll show Ed I can do this.

As planned, we spend two days in Auckland, getting acquainted with the city and it's shopping, visiting sheep stations, and meeting people who are as fascinated with me, as an American, as I am with them. I perceive all is well. But I do not see the gathering storm clouds.

While we are on the international flight, I widely discuss, with Jessica, plans I hope to accomplish.

"I'm going to buy sheepskin seat covers for Ed's, Ghia. He'll be so tickled. And I told him I would try and catch a trout in New Zealand."

She doesn't answer.

In New Zealand, I hunt down a shop selling the pelts, and immediately, I make an inquiry. I'm told, I am in luck. There is one set available. But out of the blue, Jessica decides that she also wants to buy covers, and with that, makes a fast move, before me, for the last set. I'm stunned by the deliberate offense. No explanation for her action, even though, she sees I am seriously irked. I don't say a word.

Our wonderful bus tour of New Zealand's North Island is filled with reserved Australian tourists not in the habit of making the first move in social encounters. As I make rounds to meet our fellow passengers, not an uncommon behavior for me, I immediately sense Jessica's disapproval. I know it is difficult for her to extend herself with strangers, so I don't press her to join me. By the second day, everyone chitchats, as if longtime friends, except for Jessica. I reason she is upset with me for not sitting quietly by her side.

She seems upset and resentful because I am enjoying these people. What is it about her? She reminds me of my mother.

There is a quiet, well groomed, foreign, gentleman, traveling by himself that the group appears to avoid. I acknowledge him, as I do the others, and continue my travels sitting next to Jessica. She falls noticeably silent since the beginning of our trip. I take the opportunity to talk to the man and ask about his travels. In retrospect, I recognize this sort of forwardness, is behavior older women of Australia do not openly engage in and may have established the groundwork for my future difficulties.

In my discussions with the man, I discover he is a well versed, educated and an extensive traveler from Lebanon; his business is throughout New Zealand. He tells me he has been cut-off from communicating with his family in war-ripped Beirut. He is able to add to our wisdom in most areas we visit. Soon the other travelers respond to his friendship. It is a fortuitous acquaintance from which I garner much knowledge. But Jessica is unhappy with the association. One evening, to show his appreciation of the friendship, he invites Jessica and me to join him in the lobby for a cocktail before our tour's dinner. Jessica does not refuse, but is noticeably stiff and cool. Again, I hope her silence will break.

Lake Taupo is our next stop. The bus driver asks if anyone wishes to fish? A charter boat is to leave the next morning at four-thirty. I jump at the opportunity and raise my hand along with three elderly men. I do another no-no. I am too forward. Women do not do that sort of thing. But I am determined I will catch a fish. My years of trout fishing with Ed, my mentor, pays off, and I catch a fine large one the next morning. I am convinced it is over the minimum size limit, but the men quickly measure the catch and decide promptly, before I can say yea or nay, to toss it back.

What kind of crap is this? Stupid chauvinistic old coots! They're ignoring me! Can you believe that?

That evening at dinner, everyone asks us about the fishing expedition. Not a word is mentioned that I caught the only fish. I am getting, a narrow-minded, Australian-style, hand slap.

The night before our tour ends, we are caught in a tremendous downpour and I get wet and chilled. The next morning I awake with my nemesis, a sore throat and fever. I am to be on the plane to Sydney in two days and my ears are messed up. The flight exacerbates my symptoms. During the entire trip, my ears stay out of commission, and I continually fight fevers and infections.

In Sydney, I hit bottom. I should have seen a doctor immediately, but foolishly, I choose to act as if I can handle it all without stressing my travel companion. I am so fearful I'll be an encumbrance; besides, I am determined not to miss a thing. Jessica knows I am having great difficulty. She is as unpleasant and as unhelpful as she can be.

What's with her? Why is she ignoring me? It's time to have a talk with her. I must stop parenting her. All it's doing is adding to my misery.

"Jessica, what's going on?" I plead. "Why are you so distant from me? And you've been leaving your belongings everywhere. Why are you having so much trouble? Is it because I'm not feeling well? Is there something we should discuss?"

Her stock answer is, "I don't know what you're talking about."

After a five-hour flight across Australia we arrive in Perth, Jessica's hometown. In 1980, Western Australia experiences a vicious drought; water is carefully monitored.

"You know Jessica, I really would like to stay in a local hotel rather than burden the rationings of your aunt and uncle. You can stay with them if you like and besides, it will only be for a few days."

But Jessica will not hear of this, she insists we will offend them if we do not stay.

The visit is gracious but problematic. I continue to suffer terrific throat and ear difficulties, not helped by a smoke-filled house, kept closed to keep the house cool. In my determination not to make waves, I do not seem to be able to get help for myself. Despite my illness and declining friendship with Jessica, I am delighted with her friends and relatives. If it had not been for the many colorful and cordial people I met daily, I would not have been able to overlook the problems I encountered with my traveling companion.

Perth is about twenty-five years behind Sydney in its political attitudes. World War II is talked about as if it has just ended and the people intensely discuss how it has affected their lives. Every battle is still fresh in their minds. They especially show a vast curiosity about the USA, asking me details about our people and most particularly about Hollywood. I am aware; I look and dress differently from most of their women. My makeup is more extensive

373

and pronounced, my clothing more cosmopolitan, I wear high heels and I am inclined to speak my political opinions. I am genuinely flattered at their interest and don't feel a hint of prejudice. The only problem was an ongoing awareness of Jessica's distancing.

"Jessica, we've been in Perth a week now. I think we should talk about our continuing to travel. Don't you agree?"

She dodges my inquiries.

"Why are you going out of your way to avoid me? If I'm doing something wrong, let me know! Are you upset because I spend time and talk with your aunt and uncle? They're so much fun and like the interplay."

Something has happened to her head. She is acting weird. I don't think she wants to move on. Well, maybe a couple of more days will do.

We're invited to her friend's home. Strangely Jessica does not want me to join them in the kitchen to share in dinner preparations or conversations. I am told to just sit in the living rooms, usually with their husbands and sons. At first I don't fret much about this arrangement, because I, at least, am able to learn about Australia through their eyes and I am treated respectfully. But soon my security is up-ended. Sarcastic comments, from Jessica, followed by mocking laughter, drift out of the kitchen.

"Watch out for your husbands. Vinny's alone in the parlor with them. She tends to pick up strange men. Ha, ha, ha."

I am embarrassed, but I choose a light-hearted response. Later, at the dinner table, she delivers another swift and unkind zinger.

"Ha ha, well, Vinny, picked up a foreign man on the bus tour and then she went fishing with three or four other men."

Oh, Momma, Momma! Stay out of my head! Why did you always make me feel dirty and wrong?

Normally, I humorously deal with these, but instead, I feel kicked in the brains. Again, I am afraid to respond to her pecks. The difficult part is that these folks have never met me before. I am humiliated and angry.

That night I am determined to corner Jessica to have our promised discussion.

"Why are you talking like this? You're saying stupid, embarrassing things without telling them the whole story!" She prepares for bed, ignoring me. "You're insulting me in front of your friends. They don't know who I am. Don't you care how I feel? Why? What the heck is happening, Jessica? Why are you trying to make me look bad? You're messing up this trip. I can't stand your petty jealousy. You must stop. I have feelings too! Why can't you answer me?"

"I don't know what you're talking about."

The words come, as from a stranger.

"What? You really don't know what it is you're doing? I've just told you."

I am lost with this response? I realize our friendship is breaking down. I can see Jessica drifting further away. I feel alone in a strange place and I can't admit to myself I am failing and not handling the situations well. I can't get her to travel any further. I finally decide to tell her, I plan to at least go on day trips and when she is done visiting, she can join me. But she does not want me to go without her. Foolishly I listen.

My poor health clouds my ability to make better decisions. Too many things are going wrong. It had been over three weeks since arriving in Perth and my vacation time is dwindling. Each night I lie in my bed not able to breathe, hear, or sleep.

Why don't I just pick up and leave? I feel so inadequate, so unable to take care of myself. I don't even have sense enough to get medical help. I'm turning into a child.

I agonize on how to proceed with the situation. Jessica is barely speaking to me now. I pursue her daily to move on with our trip. I fear the idea of leaving on my own.

After I spend a particularly foul, sleepless night, I awake the next morning to prepare to visit, yet another friend. I corner Jessica to get an answer. No response.

"Jessica why won't you discuss plans with me, and when are we moving on? Who are we visiting today? You are being childish in not answering. I'm very sick and I need some medical attention! Please be considerate." But, like a robot I follow.

As I stand numb and angry waiting in front of the house to be picked up, I ask her a question about the person we are about to meet. When she pays no heed to me again, I become completely unglued. I look directly into her eyes.

"You are without a doubt the most selfish person that has ever crossed my path and you will have to go without me. I intend to make other plans!"

"I don't care what you want to do."

"That's great, I don't care either, as a matter of fact go f—k yourself!!"

At last I feel free. I tell the truth of my feelings. Although anxious, my self-respect is restored.

Finally! Vinny! A decision!

I return to the house to pack my bags and phone for new airline arrangements. I make calls of farewell and appreciation to all the people who have befriended me. The next plane is to leave at midnight for the five-hour flight to Sydney. It is going to be a long day and night and a lonely wait at the airport.

While I sit in the waiting room, I think of what to do with my remaining sixteen days of vacation. My intention, when I reach Sydney, is to book tours and visit the rest of Australia by myself. In spite of my fears, I am convinced I can do it. I want it to happen. I feel brave and free from the idiocy.

Most of the day, I watch the few travelers that gather in the terminal. I am hungry, tired, and mentally exhausted. At 11:00 in the evening there are ten people waiting to board the plane. I look down the small room and see Jessica coming towards me. I can't believe my eyes.

I don't believe this! Is she coming to apologize and ask me to reconsider?

Without a glance, she walks past me, carrying a flight bag, and sits on the other side of the waiting area.

What is this all about? More games? Is she going to fly back at the same time? I can't stand the craziness. She's afraid I'll go back and tell Ed and Walker about what's happening.

I lose all perspective again.

On the plane she is seated across the aisle from me and for five solid hours she never speaks or looks at me.

She's nuts. I'm sick of this...I don't want to travel anymore. I want to go home. I must give thought as to how I am to proceed.

On top of everything I have to pay nearly a thousand dollars, a hefty penalty, in ticket changes to return sooner, money I would have loved to have used for the trip. I really think I can fix this farce, without involving Ed. I don't want to worry him, but worse, I don't want to feel like a child, unable to care for myself.

Damn! Nearly fifty years old and I still have so much to learn.

At Sydney airport, Jessica suddenly attempts to talk to me, but says nothing of the transpiring mess. She is aware I am serious at this point, and that I am making plans to leave Australia. But, again, being the forgiving wretch that I am, I feel it best not to make any more disruptions. In the terminal, she sits next to me as we wait for our tickets to get adjusted, and then follows me to the ticket-counter. At this point she is like flypaper. Now, she won't let me out her sight, mimicking my behaviors. At the counter, I remind Jessica she doesn't have her purse again.

"What is wrong with you, Jessica, that has all your money and travel papers? There it is on that bench!"

Annoyed with me for pointing out her mistake, she lips back at me, and like boxing kangaroos a verbal battle ensues.

"How does it feel to be a horse's ass? I can't believe I made such a disastrous decision to travel with such work of art! You have been jealous, petty, miserable and self-centered and unappreciative."

Idiot! I feel so damn cranky! I can't hear, my head hurts and I'm freezing with these chills. Now I have to sit for thirteen more hours on a plane in the smoking section with this half-wit of a woman I detest. I can't wait to get her out of my life.

I arrive in San Francisco, and telephone Ed and ask him to pick me up when I get to Orange County.

"I'm all right, and so is Jessica. I'll tell you all about everything when I get back. It's too long and complicated a story for now. I'll give you all the details soon enough."

We reach Southern California.

I'll bet when she gets home she'll fill her husband's head with her distorted views on this grim tale.

I tell Ed everything that has happened; fearful he will get twisted stories instead. He listens carefully and then he says he is going to cross the street and speak to Jessica.

"Good idea," I say. "I'd very much like to hear what she tells you happened, since she will not speak to me about anything."

When he knocks on their door, they are unfriendly, as if Ed has done something.

"Hey Jess, what happened between you two?"

"Oh, I don't know. I think it was something sexual with her."

"What are you saying? Vinny, got horny?"

"Well, no. I don't know."

"I don't understand why you don't know?"

Ed reports back to me.

"She never really gave me a good explanation. Something about she thought it was sexual."

"What? What a goddamn nerve!!"

I am shocked at her disturbing, distorted accusations.

If my husband had not heard my side of the story, he would have most certainly assumed the nastiest with such derogatory miserable comments. Jessica and I, never speak again.

This episode leaves a searing mark on my psyche for years. I failed to take care of myself. Whenever I see Jessica outside her home, I relive the awful experience and the hate. I am sure the pain stems from our unfinished business. I know I will never be able to make her hear my feelings. The coldness, distance, lack of caring and twisted explanations reminds me of the many unsettling interactions with my mother. How many unfinished, unloving mothers am I to gather in my life before I understand the part I play to promote this kind of sad relationship?

Jessica gave the impression of having regressed to an old style of living; she didn't dye her hair any longer, sold her car and began to walk everywhere, and she hung her clothes on a line instead of using the dryer.

Maybe, she experienced a bit of culture shock at seeing her friends in Australia. Maybe, I represented to her how much she had changed in America. Maybe, she too was embarrassed.

But, what the essence of this story is how easily I could fall into this mess.

When I move to the Northwest, eight years later, I feel free for the first time, free from the daily discomfort of seeing Jessica or her family out and about. But, a year after I settle, I am having lunch, alone, in a small obscure town in the mountains, when I recognize Jessica and Walker in the same restaurant. I cannot believe the coincidence. It rakes up all the old feelings, so much so, that I am shakily unable to eat my food. I know they have seen me, but opt to ignore me.

It takes many years before I am able to make peace with the misery this trip generates. It is one of the greatest lessons I am to learn about my own personality. I knew all the signs of disaster, but I chose to disregard them.

A further example of my insistence of having peace at any price.

TOBY'S ANGEL

"Like so many saviors, heavenly or earthly,
the angel tended to overdo her part."
Colette (1872-1954)

I recall the day the beat-up, aged, black pit bull, walked slowly into our house. Except for the tapping of her nails upon the kitchen tile, she never made a sound. She just looked around, bit by bit, at the rooms of her new surroundings. Her deeply scarred face and body showed a resigned weary expression, a look of melancholy, of maybe a hard and painful life. Her almond-shaped eyes, though clouded, revealed gentleness. At one time, she must have been a magnificent lady with her muscular body, short bow-curved legs and silky black hair. She still commanded a presence.

I saw that a piece of her ear appeared chewed. I could not help but think, as I looked at her with awe; Lord, what was her life and how many homes did she live in? How did she get all those scars? Was she loved and did she wear a spiked collar? Maybe she was kept for some human's egocentricity. Did someone use her for mindless dogfights, maybe forcing her to defend herself?

My daughter, Gina, rescued the dog they called, Earth. She had lived under a sound stage where its owner, a musician, performed. Gina, aware that her friend would not be able to care for the animal any longer, took Earth to live with her. The warmth and kindness must have restored the ugly old beast. My daughter, who was nursing wounds of her own, must have felt the protection she so desperately needed from Earthling, her newfound companion. But Gina, and her new dependent, fell on demanding times, and they moved into our home for a short stay.

We knew we would eventually lose our own dog, our much loved, friend, Toby, the eighteen-year-old, blind, wire-haired fox terrier. I wasn't sure how Earth, would fit into the family, or if Toby would even tolerate another dog in the house. But I was witnessing and meeting a dog angel.

This tough looking canine, bred to fight for her keep, was respectful of our pet. She spent her first few weeks just watching how Toby maneuvered through the house in his sightless state. She sensed his impairment.

Near the patio window, Earth, kept an eye on the family from her favorite safe-spot under the grand piano. She propped her chin upon her front legs, and the only movement you saw, were her eyes, observing everyone's progression, especially Toby's. She never barked.

When I would call Earth, she gradually picked up her arthritic body and slowly, but directly, would come. At dinner hour, I set out two dishes of food, for both dogs. Toby's declining state of health did not affect his appetite, and often, if allowed, would also polish off Earth's food. She let the elder dog do whatever he wanted and seemed to understand this was his territory. One felt the admission of respect. Often when Toby could not find his dish, Earth, gently nudged him over towards the food, and when she was sure he had finished, she cleaned the remaining morsels. At night Earth, would not settle down until we were all in our beds. She never, ever attempted to sleep in Toby's wicker-basket bed—even after his death.

There was something about her that I felt I knew. I found myself drawn to study my new friend. She reminded me of an old orphaned, crone Mother that had found shelter and love in the hearts of strangers. She was teaching me some of her skills of survival.

Our dog, used a pet door to go into the garden, and I noticed, Earth, usually followed right behind him. Again she observed as Toby wandered about his yard, marking spots, recalling his old favorite smells. And when Toby settled down for a afternoon rest, habitually, she took a siesta on the hot sunny pavement, near the garden, stretching her graying, black body on its side and letting out the only sound I would hear from her—a long, deep, guttural, basso sigh. Occasionally, she startled from her snoring sleep to look for Toby, lifting herself upon the stiff bowed legs to find him. When Earth came upon the sightless, old dog, she sniffed about his head as if to tell him she was still there like an aged mother, who checks and reassures her old bachelor son.

One day in my kitchen, I was cleaning up the breakfast dishes, and Earth came bounding into the house. I was surprised at her fast and agitated movement. She tried for my attention and let out only one woof. The only one I had ever heard her yelp.

"What's wrong, Earth?"

She circled me a few times. I sensed something was not right.

"Show me, ole girl!"

After a few nudges at my leg, I realized that she wanted me to follow her. She piloted me directly outdoors to Toby. He was choking. His choker chain was caught on a low metal fence surrounding a flowerbed.

"Oh, Earth, you sweetheart! Thank you," I said, as I patted the wonderful creature. Her black tail waved a reply to the service rendered.

When I unhooked Toby, she immediately went to him, cleaned his unseeing eyes, and rubbed his head with her chin.

I'm not sure why, Earth, came into our lives, but I choose to think she came as, Toby's, guardian angel, and maybe in his last requirements, fulfilled her own maternal shortages and mine. I grew to love the sweet elderly pooch.

I could tell how much Earth was affected, as it came close to Toby's last days. She knew he was very sick. From the safe spot, under the piano, she scrutinized our feeble attempts to prolong our dear little dog's existence. But the inevitable day came when we had to put him down. Toby came as a puppy, and saw our children reach adulthood. He lived nineteen, wonderful years with our family. He was an incredibly faithful, and handsome friend.

I saw how Earth, also mourned the loss of another respected anchor. Everyday, she smelled his wicker basket, but chose to never sleep in his place. She sat up straight when I talked to her, amidst my tears, about loses, and told her that she was a noble and good mother. As if we were old girlfriends on a park bench, she nudged my hand; verifying our lot as mothers.

She remained in my daughter's good nurturing hands to live out her life without further battles. I am glad she found some loving attendants in her waning days.

LIFE for SALE

"I'm telling you Ed, you're wearing out your side of this damn marriage contract."

This is how it typically starts. I find the plastic bags stuffed into a back closet, then I confront him with the goods. It's great interplay. So what am I talking about? Ed, my husband, loves to buy things. Lots of things. Truth is, I didn't recognize the malady until much later in our marital development.

I call it the *'chase'*. Once he buys the items his interest wanes. We have gone through many pur*chases;* books, shirts, sweaters, tropical fish, pants, shoes, fishing equipment, Don Quixote statues, hats, artifacts, stamps, the list goes on endlessly. It doesn't matter whether he needs or fits the bargain. At times, I do admit to being a co-dependent. Would a mistress have been easier?

Back in the 1970's, Ed's search for good deals often lead him to department stores in the Los Angeles garment district. The problem isn't one of fantastic quality, but quantity. Incredible quantities. Frequently, he buys the same items in all colors and sizes, and for an imagined body weight.

As his compulsiveness escalates out of control, I become more possessive of our closet space. In my fury to ascertain the truth, my beloved, becomes increasingly shy to 'show and tell'. But the 'closet' buyer, so to speak, slips up every once in a while, and I, inadvertently, discover the new buys. It is then that we have the predictable marital cat and mouse question and answer game. Ed fixates on cold and wet weather clothing, even though, it hardly ever rains in Southern California, and the temperature rarely falls below 80 degrees. He strikes a grand slam at a shop one day.

"Well what goodies do we have today, Eddie?"

"Oh just a couple of things I picked up."

"Here we go. Sometimes I think I've been as deprived as you when it comes to gray matter! For God's sake, what did you buy today?"

Proudly he shows me the great strike of the day. There they are before me. All lined up for admiration, in the finest of leathers, fifteen pair of fur-lined gloves. This bears repeating. I said, fifteen pair of fur-lined gloves in Southern California. I believe I am correct in saying that the lovely folks in Los Angeles continue to await the arrival of an epic blizzard snowstorm. You're asking, how can I be so unreasonable?

Ah, but wait. We are not through.

As any well-dressed man knows, a good quality raincoat is a fine finished addition to a groovy wardrobe. One might even invest in two or three in an adult's life. My spouse is not a slouch in this department; he knows exactly how to stay ahead of the game. Just in case there is a repeat of the biblical phenomenon, he is prepared for the eventual forty days and forty nights of rain. He manages to buy a raincoat in every color, style and size. I count nearly fifty. After all these years, most are still hanging in our closets with labels and tags still attached.

But there are times when things backfire.

When they are all the rage in the seventies, he is unable to pass up buying quite a few Leisure suits. One three-piece grabber is a white polyester beauty.

I am like a moth to a flame when it comes to Ed Barles and his ideas.

"Let's go, Vin. Let's try one of those new salad bars. Maybe we'll have a dance if we're up to it."

I am ready. I love it. I put on my finest and Edward, The Good, slips into his brand new white 'John Travolta' ensemble.

We arrive at the newest dining experience, a *salad bar*. As I approach the food bar, I am suddenly aware of people's interested glances. I can tell we have chosen our clothing well. I can hardly stand the gazes. I sense we are an absolute hit. The attention is seductive.

The stares and smiles continue throughout the evening, following us from the dining arena onto the disco dance floor. As we try the latest *Twist* steps, I again see we are still being checked out. I am beyond flattery. When our egos are thoroughly worn out and satisfied, we return home.

I walk to the kitchen to get a drink of water, while my date makes tracks to our bedroom. In a few minutes, I hear Eddie's distress call.

"Vin, where are you?"

Quickly I run to the back room.

"What's wrong? Are you all right? What's the matter with you?"

Disco Ed, is holding up the arm of his white jacket and pointing with his other hand.

From the jacket's armpit, running down the back of the arm to the cuff, are several sets of colorful store labels:

"Original Price"

"Wash & Wear Instructions"

"Sale Price" (in blue)

"Mark Down Price" (in black) and.

"Final Mark Down Sale Price" (in bright red felt tip pen).

Not a word is spoken, but tears of laughter run well into the night.

One can only imagine what our move to the Great Northwest in 1988 does for Ed's morale.

"Do you realize I'll be able to use all those heavy raincoats, fur-lined boots and gloves in Seattle?"

"And what about those colorful, twenty year-old, leisure suits, 'chicky pie'? You always say you'll get rid of this, not your size, outdated stuff', but it never happens! You know? I'm one large dumb."

He doesn't mention all the apple boxes and shelves upon shelves of woolen sweaters, shirts, pants, and several dozen of 'Don Loper' ties. And I am told, with all the wonderful rivers, the small tonnage of fishing gear will certainly get a workout. Right. And, I am also told, after retirement, he will read the classics he's collected since a young man. Right. And I will grow three inches.

I am then given, once again, the obligatory marital promise that he will seek a new level of abstention, and 'unload all this crap before we move'. But I am subject to wifely hearing impaction and I have a damaged promise receiver.

Ed wins. Most everything goes north. Moving this neurotic accumulation of goods practically takes an act of Congress. I spend months packing the unnerving commodities. A twenty-six foot U-Haul, packed to capacity, makes it to our new home, followed by a second vanload, equally as large. Ed has also stuffed his converted van with estate sale bronze statues and artifacts. A massive commercial moving truck takes the remainder of our trappings. After over a decade of living in the Northwest, many things are still boxed.

As of this writing, he has not given up any of these habits and I fear I have lost the battle. He has now discovered 'Garage Sales'. One might ask, what is wrong with a wife who lives with this 'mania'. Maybe I'm part of the collection, but I don't wish to discuss that!

His friends consider him intelligent, genteel and properly balanced, with an excellent sense of humor. He freely admits, to *some* quirks, but not many. My beloved consort quickly recognizes strange behaviors in others, but casts aside any hint that he is one can short of a six-pack.

Oh, did I mention, we moved from a fourteen square foot house, where we managed to raise two daughters, into a nearly six thousand square-foot trophy home? Two adults, in a very short time, have succeeded in filling the attic, the basement, walls and every closet.

I noticed, when Ed left California, the state's fiscal soundness slipped drastically downhill. Could it be that my husband, single-handedly, kept the economy afloat?

27 That cute, young Eddie (1940's)

EDWARD the GOOD, Are You Wearing Spats?

Women often tell me they feel comfortable with him.

"Oh, Venera, he's so cute and cuddly."

I know he feels the same about them, and I'm sure these same ingredients of courtesy and wittiness are what drew me to him. In most instances, he appears able to communicate in a fair but firm manner with strangers and friends, but as his wife, I have a tougher time getting a straight answer. Humor is essential to his ability to relate. He tells the same silly jokes to his audience, taking great joy with his own amusing tales, laughing the loudest, bringing tears to his eyes. But then, there are those times, without trying, that the curtain opens, and the stage lights shine upon him.

He takes great pleasure in playing pranks and teasing me in the early days of our marriage, just enough to keep me off center. It takes awhile, before I smarten up. Mistakenly, I think he is equally engrossed in our conversations as we drink our coffee, but I fail to recognize that he is taking the opportunity to practice his skills and is instead more dedicated to play. As he looks into my eyes, I attempt to sip, never do I see his finger calmly rising to the top of my cup and drawing it down. In my preoccupation, I think I have his undivided attention. I never notice my still full cup of coffee. But I am catching on. I easily get a good pay back, by grilling him about his past girlfriends. Then he has an infernal habit of walking two steps in back of me, like the Queen's consort. In all our years of marriage, I've yet to have him walk beside me. If I slow down, to have him join me, he deliberately cuts his pace. In those honeymoon years, he took time to do a little dance step, behind me. There is no way to win in these matters. He has seen too many comedy films of Charlie Chaplin, and Laurel and Hardy.

As Chief Psychologist and Administrator for the State's Correctional Clinic, my husband's long time career, brings him much respect and admiration amongst his colleagues. Every once in a while, Ed reminds me of how difficult life can be at work. He isn't just speaking of his hard core patients, but of some of the tedious interviews he must go through, searching for qualified secretaries from the cast of thousands in the civil service pool; typists who can't type, receptionists who can't speak English or answer phones, even file clerks who don't know the alphabet. Only after they are hired does he discover their hidden agendas or faked resumes. Occasionally they bring their own degree of paranoia or psychotic displays. Then, because of the State's idiotic rules, he can't replace them too easily. I'm sure it is hard enough to work with difficult and emotionally disturbed patients of the prison population without having to battle a lack of support from the system.

Part of his daily routine is to drive thirty miles to the Los Angeles clinic in 'up-to-the-eyeball' traffic, encased in his favorite old rusted, dirty, beat-up, blue 1965, convertible Karman Ghia. The one he says he can't fix, paint, or jazz up, because he is sure, if he does, he will not have it for very long. Ed reports, that guys drive along side of him on the freeway and yell out their window.

"Hey mister! Wanna sell your car?"

"Not interested!"

"Hey mister! If you don't sell it, we're gonna steal it!"

A few years ago he couldn't give the poor thing away. Suddenly it is in vogue again and every young stud is ready to own it.

It is another one of those miserably hot, Southern California, smoggy days, and Ed has an important meeting with several new psychiatrists, and since he will eventually be their superior, he wants to give a satisfactory impression and introduce them to office operations. This day, he dresses and grooms carefully, dons a sport jacket, tie, and light-colored slacks. His briefcase, bulging with case stories of the many fractured lives, is packed ready to go on the Santa Ana freeway. He survives the morning gridlock, and prepares to meet the hopeful, employable doctors. As the meeting advances, he senses he is gaining their trust as a serious boss, when he suddenly catches sight of the controlled laughing eyes of his onlookers. Ed follows their gaze to his crossed bare legs. His trousers are folded up to his calves, like pedal pushers. He has forgotten that he rolled them up in order not to soil the edges of his pants in his prize grubby car. It's at this moment his level of competency dissolves.

In addition to his administrative position, he holds group therapy for the sometimes-unwilling guests. Weekly his work takes him to different cities where he counsels parolees who travel from various parts of the state.

Edward ends a late Friday evening meeting in San Diego, and decides to ask about a local eatery before traveling back to Los Angeles. He is directed a couple of blocks away to an office building with a restaurant on the top floor. The building's lobby appears unoccupied, and he surmises most workers have already left for the weekend. Before Ed takes the elevator to the top floor, he determines to freshen up and use the restroom. A couple of janitors, working in the hall, have just walked into the men's room. He follows behind them and saunters into a private stall. After he finishes his ablutions, he neatens his three-piece suit and tie, picks up his briefcase and proceeds to leave.

The exit door is locked.

His heart jumps and pumps with fear at the prospect of being trapped in this distant office building's restroom for an entire weekend.

He rattles and shakes the door handle.

"You've locked me in! Hey, what the hell is the matter with you guys?"

But now, with more passion and vigor, "Unlock this door! Let me out! You've locked me in!"

No answer.

His weekend flashes before his eyes. His agitation and pallor worsen. No food or television for three long nights. No recliner. With that terrorizing, paralyzing thought, he takes off his shoe, and begins to beat the door violently.

"What the hell's the matter with you idiots? Get me out of here!"

He anxiously continues to pound the door with the shoe. Just then, a door behind him opens. In walk the two janitors, slack-jawed, staring apprehensively at the sight of my wild-eyed, close to foaming, husband. They move back from him cautiously.

"What's the matter, mister?"

"What's the matter? What's the matter? Can't you see you've locked me in here!"

"No sir, no sir, we didn't! This is the door going out over here. That's the utility closet you're banging on!"

And so it goes.

"Eddie, how is it these catastrophes follow you so much, especially with toilets? You're either locked in them, falling out of them, emptying the contents on unwary folks or swimming in the middle of the gunk! What's next Ed? What's next?"

After our retirement, I think all these traumatic antics will end, since Edward will not have as many opportunities to interact with the general public.

But I don't take into account his exposure to our family gatherings. One such occurs at my niece's wedding in Denver, Colorado.

There we are in our fineries, filing into the church for the wedding rehearsal. The new in-laws-to-be and relatives have all just met ours and everyone does their best to make a favorable impression on each side of the family. *They* are on *their* side and *we* are on *ours* passing smiles back and forth as if we are long-time friends with great history.

It has been quite some time since my husband and I attend such a distinguished formal gathering, and I am eager to save all our familial flaws, for a later event. After the rehearsal, a long, white limousine is to take us from the church to a grand dinner and party at one of the city's fashionable hotels.

We take our appointed positions in one of the church's pews. I am comfortably watching the repetitious interplay of all the lead actors, when I take note of how dapper my husband looks next to me in his coordinated beige silk sport jacket, cocoa slacks, and brand new brown shoes with matching socks. My eyes focus on his feet. I cannot believe what a great match he has made to the shoes. But something doesn't appear right. For vanity sake, I had removed my glasses, but I need a closer look. I lean over to my beloved and whisper, "Are you wearing spats, Eddie?"

With an uncertain face he glances down to check his footwear. "Naaa," he replies. "It's just a good match to my shoes and pants."

The rehearsal comes to an end, and we are nearly ready to leave the church.

"Are you sure? I ask. "It looks like a 'spat'."

To satisfy my inquiry he reaches down and pulls his pant leg up to show me the proof. I feel around his ankle and find the spat.

"Ah hah, my dear, chicky! What's this?"

Ed looks down at his shoe. "How about that?"

With that, Eddie, slips off his new shoe and removed the cardboard insert that has climbed up and wrapped itself about his ankle. He quickly removes it, and we leave for the waiting limo laughing hysterically.

As I near the automobile I ask, "That was only one piece of cardboard. Where is the other one?"

Again, he looks puzzled. My chic husband reaches down, takes off his other shoe, and with a sheepish grin removes the other paper insert jammed into the toe of the loafer.

"I'll bet this is going make dancing a lot more fun for you, Mr. Astair!"

The next day, is the marriage. My brother and sister-in-law, the bride's anesthetized mother and father, have done this wedding by the book, not a flower or bow has been spared or out of place. The bridal party is noble. Relatives come from across the nation, to check out what really happens when you spend next year's income on one event. They all agree this is a humdinger.

Since we are coming from the Pacific Northwest, and since this is to be a black-tie affair, we consent to let my helpful cousin from Colorado, rent a tuxedo for Ed. She says she can take care of all the details, given that her husband and son are also to rent their tuxedos.

The suits fit the men with *Armani* precision. *Bon vivant* Ed looks quite elegant in his black slacks, white jacket, and cummerbund, the first time, I might add, I have ever seen him in formal attire. Even though resistant to this sort of uniform, he feels better knowing that all the gentlemen will be similarly attired.

That afternoon, as he comes out of his bedroom, he spots my brother, Nick, dressed in a black rather than white jacket. Not thinking much about it, he justifies the difference because of his brother-in-law's important relationship to the matrimonial party.

It is time. The stretch drives us to the wedding and then on to the reception. As we enter the hall, Ed steps back stunned.

"For gods sake! Look at all those guys! They're all wearing BLACK tuxedos!"

Will this week of fun never end? The evening is long and hard. Poor Ed.

A finely coifed and distinguished gentleman approaches, Edward the Good.

"Hi. You must be, Ed, I understand you're Nick's, brother-in-law? Pretty nice gathering wouldn't you say? Everyone looks great."

Ed pitifully agrees.

"Yeah, I guess. But, I sure wish I had a black jacket like everyone else, instead."

"Hey, that's not a problem. You're not alone. Look over there, across the room at those two guys, they're wearing white jackets too."

My beloved Ed laments, "I know. They're my wife's cousins. They're the ones that rented mine for me!"

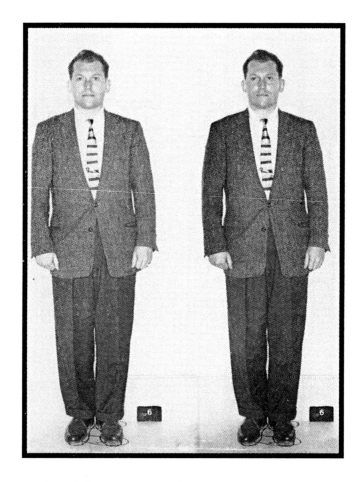

28 Edward the Good and the State of California (1950's)

The LAST STAND

I repeatedly agree to disquieting choices for vacations. This time, Ed's blue and white, coffee can size, weekend camper, is to house our frazzled memories of a forty-five day journey to the Northwest and Canada.

Let me clarify, that this vehicle is Ed's companion. I am very glad when he makes the purchase of the 1970 converted van, with its decal Peace sign, faux-wood contact paper and paneling. For a while, it gives him wonderful hours of fishing when he occasionally takes a two or three day trip, with his eight-track blaring his favorite 'Arlo and Willie' road songs. Housekeeping, typically, is steered in the direction of his comfort. He has perfected unkemptness to a higher art. The neat Marine is nowhere to be seen. His return to the city usually supplies enough delicious trout for family and friends.

But now, the thirteen year old 'love can' is quite in need of refurbishing. The fiberglass bubble top leaks, as does the rubber seals around the windows. Years ago, I made darling curtains but they have developed their own design with water stains and are a sickly, faded, sage green. The beautifully grained, contact paper paneling is now peeling. And there are enough molds in this mobile lab to bottle penicillin for a third world nation.

I am in desperate need of a vacation, maybe a little too frantic. Menopausal symptoms, hot flashes and mood swings, highlight my life. My spouse is jeopardizing his chances for a long life, by taking a trip with me.

The table converts to make-up into his bed, a little larger than a baby's crib, and I am, as usual, stuck having to take the slave unit above. Now in order to get to my mattress, a little larger than a bureau drawer, I must get up onto the sink, and once there, I have immediate decisions to make, such as, am I going to want to turn over? First order: restrict my salt intake, and pray not to bloat, since my face and body will have only eighteen inches of space. There will be no fluffing of pillows, or sitting up to read, or sipping of morning coffee.

The interior of this camper is the size of a small walk-in closet; complete with stove, refrigerator and port-a-potty. All you can do is cogitate your needs, as you sit on the inconvenient throne located in the clothes stall, amidst the parkas, Paul Bunyon shirts, and waders.

Since there isn't room for both of us to stand in the camper, one of us must step outside, usually in the rain. Love can be punishing.

Our plan is to travel into Canada; take the inside passage by ferry, get off in Prince Rupert, to see as much of the western provinces as time and attitude permits. On our journey from Southern California to the Northwest, we stop in San Francisco to pick up, for a short run, our youngest daughter, Carisa, who will do anything to travel, even go with her parents in the cramped van. Before she flies back from Seattle, she spends a couple of sleepless, rain drenching nights with us, as we drive to Vancouver, B.C.

Little do we know that this May 1983, is the wettest the Barles' ever experience.

As I've told you before, children of immigrants never go anywhere without unlimited food and supplies. We even include an electric fry pan to our typical overloading list of necessities. Of course, this leaves little space for the tenants of the canister.

The drive is uneventful, other than the cramped quarters, through California, Oregon, Washington and Vancouver, B.C. We are still fresh and untainted. A few rain showers, but at least our spirits are not dampened, and after our daughter departs, wisely I might add, we continue onto Vancouver Island.

And then it begins. The heavens open, with a vengeance, to torrential rains. Visibility is non-existent on these unfamiliar, two lane roads. Our one-speed windshield wipers have never worked this hard. We are driving fifteen miles an hour, top speed. We can't even pull over for fear of being hit by a new encounter, an unending parade of logging trucks. Once again, the New Yorkers are in the forest.

I only pray that this Jewish guy behind the wheel has been issued a guardian angel. Why? Why, am I here?

At Port Hardy, the northern point of Vancouver Island, an oversized ferry takes us to Prince Rupert, on the mainland of Canada, and I'd better say something positive about the trip at this point. These are, without a doubt, the most breathtaking scenic views we have ever seen—each out-doing the next; the rivers, streams and magnificent mountains, reward us well with their beauty. Daylight continues close to 11:00 in the evening. If I would have had more comfortable accommodations in a larger travel vehicle, I might have formed an appreciation. There I've said it.

Our ship is to leave the next morning, but this evening, we drive the, one block, small dismal town, looking for a suitable place to eat. A sign on a restaurant window selling salmon has me suggesting to Ed that since we're only about a hundred miles from Alaska, this would have to be the place to have the freshest and best tasting fish. I salivate at the thought of the dinner. His sensors agree. But, we are thoroughly disappointed at the pricey frozen, size of a fish stick, fare, and it was shipped from the East coast!

Now, by this time, the rain is getting on our nerves. Our tempers flare with great regularity. I'm sick of *Willie*, on the eight-track whining *On The Road Again,* and the tight quarters, are adding more stress then instant childbirth in an elevator. Most times, we drive all day until late afternoon, cook our evening meal, clean the small cubicle, and then spend the rest of the evening playing, mind numbing, Scrabble. Night after night, the same routine takes place. We are only into our second week, of our proposed month and a half trip, and all our unresolved problems of thirty years of marriage surface.

On the outskirts of a small town, we find a trailer park with superbly kept grounds; manicured lawns, flowers, running water, all managed by a tight lipped, cranky, thickly accented, foreign couple. We inquire for space for just one evening.

"Ve are full!" they affirm as they stand, crossed-armed, on their steps.

We plead, "Please, couldn't you just find an empty spot. We don't need to be hooked up to drains or anything. Maybe you have some room in the back somewhere. We'll just be here for the night. We'll pay you now because we want to leave early."

They offer us a patch of immaculate lawn towards the back of the property without a cement pad. We pay the unsmiling, robot couple their fee.

"Eddie, I can feel their eyes examining us. Let's hurry and get settled. Thank God, the rain has finally stopped." I say, optimism pushing its' way into my brain. "Maybe, we can have a decent dinner and restore our sanity."

The property is lovely and unsullied. Flowers do not dare droop.

We devour the fried pork chops and potatoes, clean up and Ed beats me at Scrabble. Since there is not much to occupy our senses, bedtime comes early each evening and as usual, I climb into my bed in the roof. At the break of dawn, we are ready to leave. But the van is not. Its back tires have sunk into the beautiful, but sodden turf. With each try forward, the rig goes deeper into the mud. The brilliant idea to move backwards finishes the lawn. Finally, we dislodge, leaving behind a mangled, grossly damaged, messed-up grass. Guilt sits besides me the whole day.

The rain starts again. The bleak and black skies let loose a continuous downpour. There is no way to see this marvelous and scenic country, since it takes both sets of eyes to watch the log jammed road. Ed gets wind of a good fishing stream's location. Our search leads us to an isolated and rustic public campground. We are absolutely alone, in this pitch black, saturated forest. My fears and imagination double up on me.

There is a certain madness that comes over me when I've had too much of a good thing. "Eddie, if this rain keeps up, the way it has, we will be washed away and join the river! No one will know we ever existed. That's it, Ed. I need a motel, tomorrow night. That is, if we make it out of here alive. I need a hot shower and a warm dry bed. This is not joyful, Eddie. You'd better stop or I will have to kill you!"

Lunacy is good. Even though, it is several notches down from Motel 4, it is still, the lap of luxury. My long snarled, scruffy, hair has not been washed since I left home. I look forward to the feel of clean.

I can stay in the bathroom alone. I can open and close the door. Mercy, look at those white things on the bed? Ah yes, sheets. I remember.

We are about twenty days, not quite half way, through this 'pleasure trip', and it is time to find another place to park baby blue. It seems as if most of the day is spent trying to figure out where our next camping stop will be. The bickering spears my aged hormones, and decisions come quickly.

The rain stops for a while. Our guidebook leads us to a campground, beside yet another raging and roaring river, but this one is located on an Indian reservation. The grounds are owned and run by the local tribe. It's arranged in an interesting shape, similar, to the tracks of the Roman Chariots.

Oval. As we drive around looking for a site, we approach several large identical camper vehicles parked along the outer ridge of the ovoid road.

"Oh, Eddie, this is going to be terrific. Finally, we won't be alone."

We discover, they are a traveling club from Germany, in rented RV's. We set-up 'bluebell', at the quieter end, near the washrooms.

O.K., now, I'm turning a new leaf. I am going to wash my hair and shower early. I'm going to be a new woman. I'll make us a good meal, and then, I can start my new crime story after dinner.

As I stand in the unpainted, cement shower, near a window, which has not been cleaned since it was installed, I am viciously attacked, by a swarm of pre-historic, giant B.C. mosquitoes. At first, I think their intentions are to carry me off, but they obviously enjoy the Herbal Essence shampoo, so instead, they decide to nest in my long tresses. I can't shake them out with the low trickle of water. I quickly rinse off, dry my overworked body, slip into my tired, wrinkled clothes, and wrap a towel around the bugs and my hair, thoroughly disgusted with the whole episode.

I've said this before that amnesia can be a wonderful thing. The weather permits us to cook and eat outside the van, and it is fantastic. The laughter from the German campers picks up volume and we can tell the brew, they are drinking, is taking affect. Dusk appears, and with it comes a bevy of tired, fifties cars filled with young native men and women, slowly driving around and around the track. Ed and I watch carefully. Their aboriginal eyes, set into the deadpan faces, stare at us. The tribe members are out for their evening of recreation. Circling the wagons. An ominous sensation fills our bodies as we finish our *Jello* pudding cup.

"Vin, hurry up and eat," nervous Ed commands. "Let's get this stuff back into the camper!"

I now know how Custer's people must have felt.

Dusk approaches. The cars make their last turn, leaving the park grounds, relieving my antiquated prejudices. We breathe deeply.

Evening arrives, and with it comes a view of massive, roaring, campfires at the Germanic camp, followed by full-bodied drinking songs that continue long into the night, triggering sweatbands on our upper lips. Ed's steadiness unravels. Here we are. The Germans, the Indians, the Jew, and the short-fused, bug-infested Italian. After they find us, I can see the article now, on the back page of the Sasquatch Gazette.

Chubby Couple, Found Scared To Death In Blue, Ford, Econoline Bubble-top moldy Camper. Scrabble tiles scattered about. Husband was found holding a Jello Pudding cup. Wife may have belonged to a cult. She was found with a wet turban wrapped about her mass of bug-infested hair.

We head for points East: Calgary, and eventually, Glacier National Park. We check the guides and choose Waterton Lakes to stay, a decidedly desolate place in off-season. The stately, wooden lodge reminds me of *Dragonwyck*. The mournful sound, from the constant high winds, is unsettling. At the Ranger Station, we ask for information on accommodations, but instead, we are greeted by a snarky, French-Canadian Ranger, who is unwilling to help. She speaks only French and feigns not to understand English. In a national park?

Again we are the only humans around.

I need Italian soul food. This is too much anxiety.

I cook a pot of linguini and clams, and we stuff our faces out of frustration and boredom. That evening Ed announces he isn't feeling well.

Is he getting another one of his gallbladder attacks? Right here in the middle of nowhere? Where will I find help? Nowhere!

Poor Ed is frightened that he is going to have a bad one, but luck is on his side, the pain lets up.

Most likely, too much linguini. Maybe three pounds of pasta was too much.

After forty days and forty nights in our ark, we are finally out of Canada and on our way to California. I pray for no more fun. I can't wait to get home. I'm sick to death, of Scrabble. I'm sick to death, of vacations. I am sick to death, of marriage and this traveling companion. How do people do this sort of journey without killing one another? I've known folks to sell all their household goods, live in their RVs, and stay on the road, moving from one place to another. I don't ever want to do this again! I have no desire to be packed in a blue and white can like an anchovy.

As we pull up in front of our home, my spouse who is usually careful and restrained, freely states his mind to me, declaring.

"You know, Vin, I think I hate you."

RAILROADED

One of the first perks in my new position, as a travel agent, is an opportunity to cruise on the Mississippi Queen, so to add another dimension to our memoirs of travel and adventure, Ed and I decide to return to Los Angeles by train. I've always felt, there is something intangible, romantic and exhilarating about rumbling across the wide-open spaces of America by rail.

The bi-level Superliner, called the "Sunset Limited", travels from New Orleans to Los Angeles. In 1983, we are booked for two sleeping nights.

The brochure reads:

First class service which includes complimentary meals, bedtime sweet, morning wake-up service with a newspaper, coffee, tea and orange juice. Smoking is allowed only in Sleeping Cars, and designated Coach or Lounge Cars.

According to the write-up, our train is to make its way across the Mississippi on the Huey P. Long Bridge, then out of the bayous of Louisiana, the bays and swamps once prowled by the pirate Jean Lafitte, past oil fields and tall riggings, and then to approach Texas on towards El Paso, across the Pecos River Canyon on the Pecos River High Bridge, on through Langtry, legendary country of Judge Roy Bean, across the Rio Grande into New Mexico and Arizona, and the splendor of the Sonora Desert with its Saguaro cacti and colorful arroyos, and, as Phoenix fades in the distance, we will continue across the desert to California.

At the end of our cruise, on the Mississippi Queen, we head for the rail station in New Orleans. I am overjoyed at the sight of the long, silver-gray locomotive that brings back childhood memories of the New York Central trains, near Grandpa's grocery store. We load the luggage into our compartment and wait for our return trip to Los Angeles, to start. Ed is deep in thought, as he stares out of the window at the bustling depot.

"Eddie, let's eat early," I eagerly say, "so we can check-out the views from the windows, as we have our dinner."

"Good idea." He moves to the upholstered swivel chair.

"This is so great! Isn't it?" I chatter. "I've dreamed of doing this for some time."

"Very nice."

"I just love trains." I say, aware this is a one sided love affair. "I know this is going to be fun. Don't you think?"

"Yeah, it should be good. Do you mind taking the upper bunk, Vin?"

Here we go. I always agree to the least comfortable spot!

"I guess not. Do I have a choice? "My hands move to my hips, in resignation. "I'm so glad we decided to get the deluxe bedroom, though. It's nice having a sitting area with sofa and chair during the day. But the best is having our own sink, toilet and private shower."

We spend the afternoon relaxing in the lounge car. The views of the passing panorama trigger thoughts of the many spectacular historical events that have been played on this land. I vow, that when I get back, I will read every history book. We listen to the conversations of couples adapting phrases to their new environment.

"Wouldn't you love to live out here in the peace and quiet of the desert, honey?" Said one young woman to her mate.

"You gotta be kidding," replied the man, as he preened himself in the reflection of the window. "I'll bet the TV reception is lousy. I'd have to go miles and miles to get to a lousy baseball stadium!"

At night, the desert sky makes the stars seem especially close and bright, because except for the area outside of the major towns most of the terrain is desolate, sparsely populated and pitch black. It is so.

We return to our compartment to change and freshen up for dinner. I fill my head with flights of possible encounters with famous sleuths finishing final details of their latest mysterious murder aboard the *Sunset Limited.*

We finally weave our way to the dining room, select a booth, then we wait for our server. I am prepared for our gourmand evening.

"Oh Ed, here comes the waiter. Gee, I thought there were going to be tablecloths!"

"Whataya gonna have?" He blurts in his surly voice.

"We don't know what you're serving." I ask politely. "May we see the menu?"

"I guess. I'll see if I can find one." He turns and leaves. I see that my husband has picked up a decided attitude in the pre-retirement man.

"Now Eddie, don't get negative on me. Have patience."

But I speak too soon. Another, tightly bound chap, promptly replaces our ill-mannered waiter.

"Are you ready yet?" he says, with pencil primed, but his head is turned to another overjoyed server. "What'll you have?"

I can tell, there will not be small talk or honeyed words exchanged with our soup jugglers. I'd love to meet the person, who put a gun to their heads and forced them to work with the public. My romantic feast and exhilarating train ride begins to lose its luster.

As my unrealistic eyes clear, I become aware that our dining experience is not in any fashion resembling the Orient Express. I am convinced that our ill-natured attendants are probably trained at the Motor Vehicle School of Dining.

We watch the waiters who seemed to be busily playing a shill game with one of the diners' money, adding a disgusting thrill to our tiresome, ground-level, airline food. We finish our evening meal, and he brings our check, and because this is a classy place to eat, we leave our plastic trays on the table, and head for our room.

All the while I think. Do I really want to repeat this same nonsense in the dining car for breakfast? Maybe they'll pick up a new crew in El Paso. Dream on, oh great short woman.

We are exhausted, but the last day in New Orleans plays out splendidly, and we look forward to a soothing and restful night in our Deluxe Bedroom, anticipating that the sway of the train will rock us to sleep. I can't wait to snuggle in bed with my new, juicy, true-crime paperback. Ed has brought a volume of his classic works to read; the one he takes on all his trips and never cracks. I remove the sixteen hours of make-up, then wash and cream my face and make plans to shower in the morning.

"This window is like a giant TV screen. Eddie I'm going to pull this shade while I get my P.J.'s on."

As Ed pulls the blankets up, he turns on his nightlight. I pull the window cover up again, relaxed with the thought that only prairie dogs will be interested in peering into our rented room. I climb up onto the, least favorite place of mine to sleep, the claustrophobic top bunk. I seem to have a knack of getting stuck on top shelves. A momentary flash enters my brain of a disastrous vacation with Ed in his van. I am not a fast learner.

"Goodnight, sweet prince."

"Goodnight, Vin. Are you going to be all right up there?"

"We'll see. I'll be O.K., I'm sure."

The 'who-done-it' book is just boring enough and the repetitious movement of the train is soothing enough, that I start to doze, and besides, my propped arm died about ten minutes before. I am almost into my twilight sleep, when I smell smoke. Cigarette smoke. Big time, cigarette smoke. Gagging, cigarette smoke is pouring through the ventilation grate next to my head. The obnoxious odor fills our cabin, stinging my eyes and nasal passages. My husband, whose snout has been dead since the day I met him, doesn't seem to be bothered by the offensive pollution. After all, not that I mind, his honor is sleeping on a lower shelf. My summation of the situation is, that every one decides to light up when they return to their cabins, and the waves of smoke flow through the ventilation system.

I wonder if it ever occurred to the gentlemen planners of this rolling city, to have a separate sleeping car for non-smokers? How silly I am. They're the ones that run the dining room!

I wash my face and eyes in the tiny washbowl and give the night another try.

"O.K. Eddie, I think I'm going to try to sleep again, even though my head is raw! Goodnight."

"All right honey. Hope you'll do O.K., goodnight. See you in the morning."

This time I succeed, despite the biting, rancid air. I can feel myself approach a deep sleep, when suddenly I am jolted awake.

I hear Ed's frantic voice from behind the closed bathroom door.

"Ohhhhh no, Goddammit!! How do you stop this thing? Holy Shhhhiit!"

Immediately I awake, but I am disoriented. I look at my watch and see it is 2:15 in the morning. The nightlight reflects in the large viewing window. My vision clears; I can see through the glass, that we are entering a station. A couple of cowboys are waiting to board, and one has a girlfriend that comes to his belt buckle with clothing barely covering her vitals. I have a sense of seeing a stage play. For a fleeting moment, I am distracted from the sounds emanating from the water closet.

"Eddie, what's the matter? Are you sick? Answer me, are you all right?"

I jump down from the bunk, and run to the small cubicle door, leaving the room light off so the colorful local spectators can't see in. The door is locked.

"Ed, for God's sake, what is it? Unlock the door! Are you sick?"

There is no answer, but soon the door opens slowly. *Edward the Good,* is drenched, sitting on the prime seat, the throne, and in full view of the train depot and its travelers. Ed's pajama bottoms are in a pile around his feet, and the leather bound edition is on his lap. On his face is the 'mother of miseries,' the look of poverty. He is dripping wet from head to toe.

"Good Lord, Ed, what happened?" I try hard to stifle an uncontrollable laugh. "It's almost three in the morning! What's wrong? Why are you all wet? I better close the door or the cowboys will see you from the window!"

"Can you believe this?" he sputters. "They've got two damn buttons here on the wall, both alike, and I couldn't see that well. One is for FLUSHING, and the other is for a SHOWER! Naturally, I pushed the wrong damn one." He points with his sopping hand. "I've managed to get several things done with this visit: go to the john, read a book, take a shower and wash my P.J.'s! Ridiculous!!"

I choose my words, carefully, "How and why, did your life become this painful, Ed?"

"Good morning, Mr. Barles. Here's your newspaper and orange juice. I trust you had a restful night?"

The DELIVERANCE

"l'ultima sera...'The farthest gloom'; death"
Dante

Antonietta is gravely ill.

As I sit staring out of the plane's window on my way to Denver, somehow I know she is going to leave me again. It's been done so often in the past. I'm not ready. We're just getting to know each other as women. Even though, I know in my heart I've made peace with her, and I believe I hold no remorse for my losses. But I still need more time to catch up.

No, no, no, I can't let you go now that you've come back into my heart! Please Momma!

It's been only two years. Two years since she buries Salvatore, her groom, in Italy. My cousin, who is very close to her Aunt Ann, greets Ed and I at the airport. She is to escort us to my mother's hospital bed. Gina, Carisa and our grandchild, Alexia, who is to turn three in a couple of days, are to arrive on a later flight. How good it feels that my children respect me enough to come to their grandma's bedside. Certainly their connection to my mother bares little resemblance of the typical grandmother and grandchild scenario. Through the many years, Antonietta, neglected her duties to these children. Why would they have to care?

I have only seen my mother a few times since her return from the seventeen-year stay in Italy. Nick and Ellen shoulder most of the physical and emotional brunt of my parents' last few years.

And now, Momma is dying.

Since my father's death, the last two years probably gives my mother the most peace and freedom she has had for a long time, if ever.

It must be stingingly difficult for Nick, a physician, to oversee the care that she receives in her last moments. He has tried so hard to fulfill his duties as a loving son. And now to know, everything has been done, that could be done, for Antonietta.

Within the hour she will be dead.

My knees turn gelatinous as I walk into the Intensive Care Unit, not knowing what I will face. The hospital bed looks so large in comparison to her small frame.

Do you remember, Momma when I put the cold washcloth on your bruised face? And I told you, "You'll be all right, Momma, don't worry, I'll take care of you." Did I fail?

She is surrounded with machines, as if they are her private angels, reporting to us how she is doing, sending us messages through beeps and lights, determining how long it will be until she is ready to go into her stillness.

The Colorado family, eight in all, is at her bedside. I can see on their faces the personal search for connection, as they realized her end is near. Each one of them has made an investment of love and caring and now they are finishing their thoughts.

I can feel myself going into a familiar pattern. Numbness. Hold on. Keep a deliberate controlled exterior. Don't reveal too much pain. If I do this well, I can survive this final loss.

We have kept the vigil since yesterday. At one point, it even looks as though she will rally and pull through this last struggle.

You don't know how much I wanted to save you, Momma. Save you from the terrors of your life. I often weep and think of you. Especially when I hear Willie Nelson sing.

Angeles flying too close to the ground
I patched up your broken wing and hung around awhile
Trying to keep your spirits up and your fever down
I knew someday that you'd fly away.
But loves the greatest healer to be found
So leave me if you need to.
I will still remember,
Fly on, Fly on past the speed of sound.
I'd rather see you up then see you down.
Angels flying too close to the ground.

Oh God, why are all these people around this bed? Why can't I be alone with her? Don't they know, I need to talk to her about our lost years? My cousin behaves like she is her daughter. Where is my place? She hovers too close. I know she has been helpful and near at hand for Momma, but why do I feel resentment and anger towards her? I hate being so needy. I need to be with her alone for just a few minutes.

"Please, Camille, would you and Jack wait outside for a little while. I need to be alone with her."

When oh when, are my daughters going to get here? They can't be cheated out of these last precious moments. Will this make up for all the times of indifference? Hurry up Gina! Hurry up Carisa! Hurry up girls! Momma, don't leave me, I haven't told you all my tales! I need your opinions. Tell me I will make it as a woman. Just tell me you love me pure and simple!

Why am I so self-absorbed? She never had it to give. I know her story. I know that she did the best she could. She needs me this one last time. Reach out. Touch her. Oh God! She's slipped into a coma. Momma, it's too soon. Momma, don't go yet. My girls are not here. Can you hear me? I love you, God I love you. The machines are telling me you're waiting. You care! Here, let me hold your head in my arms. I want to tell you how beautiful you have always looked to me. Your skin is still like a young woman's. I know how much you loved fixing yourself to look pretty. I'm sorry your life was sad. I wanted so, to make it better for you.

They're here! Everyone has arrived, Momma. We're all here—Nick, Ellen and their daughters, Camille, and her family Ed and your granddaughters—your great grandchild, Alexia. Everyone who cares! It is easier for me to tell you I love you, because, at last, I believe you have some love for me.

As I hold her hand, I whisper into her ear.

"I love you Momma...you did the best you could...you can go now and get some rest."

The machines release their final chant, and we are left with her silence.

#29 My young Momma with sparkling eyes. 1920's)

An OVERNIGHT CASE

Antonietta, my mother, is dead.

We lay her to rest in Denver, far from her own mother and father. She has on her new, blue, polka-dot dress and pearls. The one she chooses and buys. How strange, I married in a blue, polka-dot dress.

I feel starved for not having known her better. Everything I touch of hers brings intense sadness. The last time I spent with Mom, is a short week in July, and here it is only October, her breath is still warm in the ground. Our miserable, seventeen-year separation leaves a vacuous hole.

I watch as our families, Nick and mine, including Camille, our cousin, go over the few remaining personal effects, in her small apartment. I feel a possessive hunger about sharing her things.

I must be fair. I must be fair. Oh! Everyone is into everything. I must hurry. My God, what a terribly quick three days. Why did she die just when we were getting to know each other? There is no time. All I want is a few hours alone here to look at her meager possessions.

There is very little to give or share for keepsakes. Most items they reach for, are simple things; her Ponds Cold Cream, the pale ivory, Cody face powder, worn out cheap tubes of lipstick, the bits and pieces of inexpensive, broken jewelry. The lace head scarves she wore to church: a broken rosary, a few bent and scarred pots and pans, worn out underclothes and some ragged, badly formed shoes that encased her deformed toes, used before her son gave her the much needed medical attention.

One of my daughters wants the beat-up, fox, fur coat; Mom thought she looked special when she wore it with its' matching hat. I sense the influence of father's choices in the room. I take a small, cracked, heart-shaped, plastic box, into my hands. It contains an old, white gold, link watch, broken chains and the faded, pale, yellow-cream, faux, pearl earrings.

She's finished the housework. Yes, there she goes! Now she's heating the water to pour into the bathroom sink. Soon she'll sponge bathe herself with a washcloth lathered with Ivory Soap. I will remember her clean smell forever. She is careful never to let me see her unclothed. I see her only if she wears a full slip over her bra. Safety pins hold the threadbare garments together. When she is through, she will walk into the bedroom. I watch from a distance. There is no talking. She sits at the vanity to cold cream her face, wipes it off, and then dabs a little rouge, powder and the Ponds lipstick. Then, one by one, she removes the metal curlers from her pre-matured, silver-streaked hair. Now, her trademark, Bette Davis style hairdo is combed into place. A clean, starched, faded dress waits. And high heels, always, high heels. After that, the final application; yes, there they are, the fake pearl earrings.

This is part of her daily routine, despite abuse and sadness. Always tidy, always making believe.

I take the digital clock radio I purchased for her last July; the one I taught her how to work. And here is her Teflon, lined red lasagna pan; the scratches remind me of the many meals I missed. Next to it is the large badly worn, silver, serving ladle. I see the picture well. She stands at the stove stirring her

Venera Di Bella Barles

Sunday sauce. The spoon's one side is uneven from years of scraping against the aluminum pot.

I feel so needy. I can't breathe with this lump in my throat. I thought you would live forever, Momma! I thought I would have time.

A small pair of etched, glass, silver salt and pepper shakers—these are the remains of a household. Fifty-three years of trying to get it right and waiting for her turn while attending Salvatore. And before their marriage, she served her parents.

This place is strange; there is no history here. Has she been lonely living by herself since she buried my dad in Italy? The apartment has been her home for almost two years. She has never lived alone since she was born. What did she think about? She was always told what to do and what to say. Was she afraid? Did she think much of her family? Of her children and grandchildren? I hunger for her answers; questions that will never be answered.

When she returns from Italy, she carries only two personal suitcases; a hard-sided, scratched and patched ivory-colored valise, which holds most of her clothing, and a small dark-brown overnight case.

I sit with her, on the edge of the bed, when she opens the case. It contains the last bits and pieces, past and present, in photographs of the family, and of her recorded life.

I look into her sad and distant, washed out blue eyes. "This suitcase is very important, Venera," she says soberly. "Your father always wants me to watch where I keep it. So I have to be very careful."

She's nervous. She's afraid of doing something wrong. I'll be damned! Still taking orders from Salvatore, but now, it's from the grave. It's all in her lap, now. I don't want to appear too curious, but truth is, I want to examine every scrap of paper, scrutinize each photo, smell every relic of her past life, hoping I can recapture some moments I recognize of our lives together. A strange sensation is coming over me, remembering the day I left my home to elope. I carried a small suitcase with pieces of my own life jammed into its sides. I didn't know if I would ever see my family again. I wanted to take the photos. But I left them all. I could not stand to think I must forever forget my past. Now my mother has returned with this small satchel of albums and photos. My brain and heart will surely explode.

The plaid paper-lined case has a cutout picture pasted into the lid of her patron saint, St. Anthony. A ten-inch gold crucifix sits in the bottom, along with two keys. There are letters and cards, two tiny address books containing bits of information. In these she keeps note of Italian sizes, recipes, addresses of all their relatives and friends, vital statistics of those in Italy and U.S., of when they were born and when they died. Addresses scratched out; her grandchildren's names. My father insisted she be the keeper of the important documents of their married life; bank statements, real estate, and legal papers. Salvatore put everything in her name thinking to avoid litigious hassles. How frightened she was in those days.

And now, I am the adoptive parent of this vault.

The leather bound photo album is worn and falling apart. The pictures have been glued to the black blotter pages. We are all in there. This is all I have to tell me that we had a life, a life as brief as an overnight trip. I see the separate studio photos of Mother and Father when they were young and vital. Her teeth are straight and strong enclosed in a loving smile. Her beautiful chestnut-colored, waved hair is vibrant and full; her make-up is like a budding starlet. Father's clear eyes with a twinkle, exudes virility, secure with the assurance of a successful future. His mental instability is not yet registered. Her painful countenance begins to appear as the years are documented in photographs. Pictures that mark every occasion: weddings, births, holidays, visits to ancestors' homes, all tell the stories clearly.

I look at the fading prints and see that most of the faces are no more. My memory is also vanishing. I need the photos to answer my questions. I use a large magnifying glass to capture details I may have overlooked, trying hard to find a connection in our eyes.

 # 30 Momma and me, after Dad's death (1985)

WATERSHED

"La verita` e` figlia del tempo"
"Truth is the daughter of time"

Zowie, what a couple of wild years these are; deaths left and right of me, menopause, a stolen car, surgery, what else? Just tell me what else?

As my three-year old granddaughter succinctly states on my behalf, "It's too much for a little woman!"

How remarkable it is that she understands.

I am a physical wreck. Running to the doctor for this and that ache. I should rent a room there. Every orifice, joint and organ in my body decides to revolt. There is nothing too life threatening, except if I cut my throat. I can't tolerate my own intolerance.

To some women, menopause is like standing on railroad tracks, watching a locomotive bear down on you, and suddenly, you can't remember if it's worthwhile to jump away. Your life flashes before you, and leaves you with questions. What's this all about? Have I done it all? Why am I this dissatisfied? Why did it go so fast? What am I to do with the rest of my life?

Everything that crosses my path takes its toll. I sell a one-way airline ticket, as a travel agent, to a friend visiting her family in England. I can't figure out why she doesn't purchase a round-trip fare. I know she is dreadfully afraid of flying. She is private with her reasons. I receive a contented and cheerful postcard from her. I believed Rene was safe. Unfortunately, she doesn't tell anyone she has terminal cancer and has gone home to die. Her death shocks me.

Before I take a breath to recover from this sad notice, I am confronted with the death of Chauncey, my eccentric, elderly next-door neighbor. This odd, old duck, a lifelong bible student, spent most of his time with translations of Greek books and saved barrels upon barrels of bottles of every shape, size and color. Chauncey, even salvaged his rust colored, bat winged, old Cadillac.

He says, "These are all going to be very valuable some day."

That day is here. Where is the value?

Ed and I drive our twelve-year old, Ford LTD to a busy, flower market in downtown Los Angeles to purchase a funeral bouquet for Chauncey. We deposit our coins into the parking meter, and go into a shop. When we return, the parking spot is empty. We stand on the street in utter disbelief; feeling like a family member has been abducted.

"She's been stolen!" I cry.

I try to recall what I had in the trunk: a little zippered coin purse, the shape of a Scottish plaid cap, a faded green umbrella, my mother sent from Italy, a black sweater, an extra pair of walking shoes, a red box with maps, samples of wall paper, and ideas for decorating and miscellaneous necessities. Another friend is gone. Another piece of my life has just vanished.

But this year, 1984, is not through with me yet. My much loved, mother-in-law and friend, Minnie, has reached the end of her story. She is ninety-three and there is no more to write. I only know we exchanged hearts. Even though her body is tired and worn, we do not bury Minnie's legacy of life. I feel selfish and find it hard to let her go. I need her mothering during this trying time. I am thankful for my one-year-old granddaughter, Alexia, who helps to fill the vacancy.

A month later, as if on cue, my father, Salvatore, suddenly dies in Italy. After the seventeen-year, turmoil-ridden absence, Dad and Mom are about to come back into our lives. My plan is to make peace with him finally. But I have waited too long. I feel deeply tested.

I finally reach some physical relief the next year. I capitulate to a much-needed hysterectomy. But my body reacts to the stress. A few weeks after my surgery, every joint decides to freeze up with monstrous pain. I dread I'll be permanently disabled. For more than a week I am unable to move my arms, legs, or feet.

After, Father dies, my mother returns from Italy to live near my brother, Nick. I attempt to make-up, for all the lost years, with long distance phone calls to her. I begin to feel better, but still I experience the typical ups and downs of menopause; night sweats, lack of sleep and a myriad of small complaints. But now, another blow pierces my armor, again the rumble of death. Mother is dying in Colorado. I fly to her bedside. Life is too quick, and death too near at hand. I am not prepared for all this loss. A close friend and writer said it pretty clear for me the other day.

"I do know the difference between a tragedy and an inconvenience."

With the deaths and losses I had to learn to go on with my life. The two years are good teachers. I now understand what my lessons are. I discovered that I had put my life on hold, by waiting for people to fulfill their promises. I waited for someone to change things for me or give me permission. I waited for the right moment to make a difference. I neglected to appreciate the essence of what I had or who I was. I had not danced to my own drummer; as a child or as an adult. I had waited for my husband and children to change, instead of accepting them for who they were.

426

I cannot afford to waste precious time, and certainly I should not deny my own identity.

I too, am dying.

Venera Di Bella Barles

EDDIE, I HAVE a FEELING
WE'RE NOT in KANSAS

"Really Ed, are we going to spend the rest of our lives staring at these telephone poles, and watching ambulances go by? Why can't we pick a place from one of those damn real estate books of yours, and just do it!"

I spend the better part of my energy trying to get my husband motivated to look beyond his dream catalogs of the United Farm Agency; to discuss with me the possibility of finding a suitable retirement home, away from the rotting Southern California area. Every quarter, for years, a new book of available, nationally advertised property arrives in the mail. Ed sits in his recliner with a freshly poured cup of coffee, and commences the mind game; deciding which plot of land by a stream or river he'd like to buy when he retires. Somehow, I wonder if he sees himself as a land baron/gentleman fisherman, with tweeds, cap, cane and dog, standing at a creek's edge, sparring with the elusive trout. But as I see it, he really doesn't want to change anything about his life. He seems content to idle away time only dreaming about these places.

"Look at this farm in Arkansas, Vin, forty acres! It has stables, thirteen bedrooms, *one* bathroom, original kitchen, a stream, and a pond. It was built in 1819—needs some updating. Only seventy-nine thousand dollars."

"You can't be serious, Ed. You don't even enjoy hanging a picture, let alone restore an 1819 relic with forty acres. Are you sure the bathroom is even indoors?"

428

It doesn't take much of this conversation to usually open the floodgates of my dissatisfaction, and I launch into my soliloquy.

"Ed, I think we need to really consider some places soon. Your retirement is almost here and I'll be damned if I'm spending the rest of my years in this concrete jungle. Our only form of recreation is visiting malls on weekends, watching hordes of dull people, who like us, are avoiding the infernal heat. I can't stand another moment of this eternal sunshine, and this smoggy air is killing me." I go on. "Not to mention, the fact that the entire nation of malcontents has decided to live in California. We're back to the Old West again, except that we're not on horses anymore, just dodging bullets from passing cars. You must admit I'm not wrong. We've put in this wonderful bay window in the library and we can't even open it for air, because of the sirens delivering patients to the nursing home, down the block, and cars with boomboom speakers so loud it's like a heavy metal or Woodstock concert on wheels."

"Uh, oh! Here we go again! I don't want to hear it. When I'm ready to talk about this, I'll let you know!"

"Give me a break, Ed. You won't ever bring it up. I've been trying to leave this area for twenty years. I don't know if you've noticed, but it's my life too! I think it's time I consider a separation. I can't really talk to you. Whatever I say seems to fall on deaf ears. I'd like to relocate and get an apartment in Seattle. I've been thinking about this for a long time. I can't stop you from staying here. You refuse to discuss anything or make plans with me of any substance. I'm tired of trying to reason with someone who needs to have the final word without discussion. Maybe it's better we go our separate ways."

"That's a good idea. You go up there to Seattle and find *us* a little house."

"What? Are you listening to yourself? Are you nuts? What's this, *us* stuff? Have you been waiting for me to make the first move?"

And this is how our plans to live in the Pacific Northwest began to formulate. Ed decides to travel with me to look at property. And, as usual, I break my promise to myself.

First, we visit our birth home state of, New York; check out various parts of the country to see what area would be more suitable. Now Ed, is into it, and at one point, he says we should live in Arkansas because it's less expensive. I can just see Ed Barles searching, in that setting, for a deli to buy a pastrami sandwich. I can't even imagine ex-New Yorker Ed, being able to adjust to the different culture and politics. Talk about being out of your element. What's he thinking? But, I'm not settling for his choices so readily.

Finally, we opt for the Seattle area. My plans to leave Ed are temporarily set aside. After all, he sounds as if he's turned over a new leaf, but after nearly forty years of promises not taken seriously, I decide I am not going to be led by my heart, as I have been so often in the past. If I'm not going to get an apartment, it definitely will be a small house, low maintenance, and a small garden. It must be manageable. I want something else to do with my life besides being a housekeeper, gardener and handyman. By God, this time I'll be in charge! Right! And I will grow two inches!

This is to be the third purchased home, and very likely our last. Our first home, a new tract house in Garden Grove, California, was bought for twelve thousand dollars with Ed's G. I. loan. We stayed there for ten years after our two daughters were born. Then we procured our 'dream' home, a sprawling California, corner, ranch style with Bougainvillea vines on a split-rail fence surrounding the outer rim of the property. For twenty-five years we lived there; worked so hard to make it quite an eye-catcher, but now, it needed modernizing. If it weren't for its location, the miserable traffic noise, drive-bys and decay around us, we could have remodeled the fourteen hundred square foot house to live more comfortably. But, the choking atmosphere was doing me in.

We make several air trips to western Washington to find a suitable location. Our search for a new cave leads us to believe that we can live on an island across from Seattle and commute to the city by ferry when needed. I feared being isolated from humanity, with nothing to occupy my thoughts. But by living farther away from Seattle the price was right to buy waterfront property.

It is January 1988, and it is dismal, wet, and cold and we've seen every piece of property on the mainland and on the island. We are to fly back in a couple of days, but I am discouraged and know we are plumb out of luck in finding a house. But then, the Realtor announces he has one more to show us.

"You know, Mr. and Mrs. Barles, I'm thinking of this house that has been empty for a long time. I'm not even sure if it's even available."

"I really would like to see it." I say.

The minute we drive down the muddy dirt and gravel drive and look at the big white, empty house with its many-peaked roof, I know I'm in trouble.

Good God, I've found it! My dream cottage!

I can feel all my knowledge of real estate and any levelheaded thinking rush out of my ears. Not only is it *not* a small piece of property, it is twice the size of our last house. It has a multi-gabled, moss covered shake roof with conifers over-hanging its peaks, spreading needles and cones into all of its gutters. Painting this baby will be like the Brooklyn Bridge; start at one end and by the time you reach the other, it is time to start over. On either side of the main structure, are two foundations, poured and ready for framing. No garage.

Venera Di Bella Barles

For some reason the previous owners didn't finish this honey. The price is right, but of course that means we need to make a decision. If we opt to buy this place will we complete it? We need a garage.

When we go inside my heart stops beating.

Get me out of here! All this and it's facing this beautiful water and I can see Seattle!

I look at the view of Seattle and the large rolling lawn leading down to the blackberries and I feel I've been here before. I'm immediately transported to the banks and rolling lawns of the upper Hudson River in New York. Ed looks at me, and I return the glance in disbelief. He also is in trouble. Often, when we buy anything, there is a knowing look we reveal and each of us understands we probably are going to buy the sucker product. With glazed eyes I rationalize we can manage. But there is much to think about with this fantasy. According to the plans that are left for the prospective new buyers, a sunroom is proposed for one side of the house and on the other, a garage and whole upper and lower wing is to be added. Yes, I tell myself, it will keep us busy to take care of this place, but it's bound to keep us healthy in our declining years, and besides what else do we have to do out here in the wilderness?

We want the big white thing. Even after learning the facts. Like childbirth, amnesia has taken over. Our blinders are well in place, and poor Ed and me are duped into thinking we will do fine. We are told that the previous owners lost their shirts and marriage on the remodeling of the, once old beach house, without ever beginning on the new sections. Our prospective new neighbors hungrily fill us in on all the grim details, ending with the young couple's divorce.

I call the white house, Casablanca. I click my ruby red slippers and move in for a year and half, before Ed retires. My furnishings consist of a blow-up mattress, sofa, a card table, chair and a room filled with packed boxes. We won't discuss the painful contents of the boxes. But the sizes marked on the outsize tell the story; size thirty-four pants, size thirty-six pants, size thirty-eight pants. Shall I go further? I am determined to get the, three thousand square foot house as prepared and polished as possible. Each day there are new demands to tackle; sand walls, Spackle beams, moldings, and paint, and before the end of my first year, we contract with a builder to have the sunroom built, adding another six hundred square feet.

But, my fairy tale starts to fade. During that first year and a half, our quiet home in the forest is hit with every collection of weather and challenges. The many gabled roof starts to leak and the basement has turned into a reservoir. I arise one morning to a drug-taking sight; rainwater is pouring in through my beautiful kitchen light fixtures, flooding the electric range. And, if that isn't enough, an old deck is leaking water in through my freshly painted ceilings. The rain, as if from a hose, comes in any place it can find. The skylight leaks on my face as I lie on my air mattress. And that winter an Arctic blast brings an unrecognized snowstorm, freezing some of the fifty-year old garden roses. Winds knock over giant cedars, and transformers blow, with great regularity, leaving me with only candlepower and mighty cold temperatures in nature's war zone. Then the island experiences its first major crime in many of year. Three teenagers are murdered execution style in the woods! Hello L.A.

The natives are left scratching their heads.

"Never seen anything like this. These Californians must be bringing bad stuff with them."

Next, I am told the house is haunted. Oh swell! As the story goes, Mr. Peterson, who built the original beach house in 1932, was painting the side of the house when he slipped and fell into the cellar stairwell. He never does recover from the fall. But, my imagination blooms with gusto.

I just know I hear him walking the floor. Someone keeps opening and closing doors.

After the piercing sound of Los Angeles sirens, it is hard to fall asleep, at night, in the deafening silence. It is so quiet you can hear a gnat sneeze, except when pinecones pelt the roof. Each night, I look out my bedroom window and see raccoons squabbling on my neighbor's roof. I start imagining Mr. Peterson watching me. A mixture of sounds set my nerves on edge. But he is a good landlord. I eventually come to terms with his presence.

I know. I know, Mr. Peterson, we'll get to the painting soon! Stop nagging!

I leave the madness of Los Angeles, and it is good, but now, I must acknowledge the neurotic behavior the island dwellers have about trees obscuring their views. I am scarcely settled when my neighbor begins to badger me to cut my trees and shrubs to open his vista. One morning, as I'm taking a breather in my new garden, adjusting to my traumatic move, I am cornered near the back garden fence.

"I say, good morning neighbor," came the cheery English voice.

"Oh, Mr. Darwin, how are you this beautiful day?"

"Fine, just fine, but Penelope and I, were lying in bed this morning and we are not able to see Seattle because of your pear tree. We were thinking maybe you should cut it down?"

Cut it down? Is he nuts?

434

"Well, I have an excellent idea, Mr. Darwin," I reply in my most officious manner. "How about you and Penelope SIT-UP in bed."

The conversation takes a decided change.

Ed finally retires, and gives me all manner of promises that he will unload all his excess accumulation of outdated and unwearable clothes, the result of years of compulsive buying. But sadly, he doesn't keep his word. With our other house sold, we say good-by to our friends and start our new life together in the North. I need not have to tell you how intensely busy we become, as if we were both working full time and still raising our family.

Our sunroom turns out spiffy, and within the next two years, we take on building the other addition. We follow the house plans pretty close and add a two car-garage, two small bedrooms, a gigantic recreation room, equal to the ballroom at Versailles, and Ed's master bath, the size of our old living room, plus several walk-in closets for *him*. When we are through, we have close to six thousand square feet of living space, and lots of bare walls and rooms to fill. We have completely lost our perspective.

The local antique dealers hail us and rub their hands warmly, as we make our weekly rounds. Weekends are spent at flea markets and garage sales, and Mondays are spent separating the fleas from the velvet pictures. In two years we have managed to fill every inch of the floors and walls.

Our new friends ask, "Well Ed, been fishing lately?"

"I never have any time. I'm busier now retired, then when I was working for a living. That property takes a lot of care, besides, we also have a new puppy now and a ton of wild cats."

Now, that we live in Casablanca, it seems we have given up dreaming about far away places. It takes a ton of vitamins to keep these retired bodies moving. This 'big white thing' is incredibly hungry for attention. No time for vacations or sitting in the garden with our ice tea, or for that matter going to malls.

Oh yes, by the way, Mr. Darwin got his wish. The pear tree came down last year.

KATZ and MORE KATZ

While Ed is finishing his long, mind-numbing history of employment in California and hungrily looking forward to his retirement, I am living in Casablanca, our new home. Each evening we end the day with a phone call filled with the details of our day. For the last few nights he has been telling me about a sweet tabby cat who is hanging around the outside of the house.

"Vin, do you know what this cat's doing? I'm sitting at the desk and he's standing outside scratching the glass with both paws. He follows me from room to room just looking into the windows. Even while I'm showering! But I'm not letting him in. First thing you know we'll have a cat on our hands..."

I encourage him to take care of her and let her into the house for companionship. This is where my years of therapy did not serve me well. Minnie adopts Ed before he moves to the Northwest. He is hooked. Clearly hooked. A pure mush bag when it comes to animals.

In spring of 1991, our plans to build the garage and north wing onto Casablanca are about to start. We have our work cut out for us. Every day we are up at the crack of dawn to greet the builder and his crew with coffee and bear claws, insuring all was going according to blueprints. Staying ahead of contractors is much like going to the dentist; no getting out of that chair once you get that numbing injection. Then it wears off and you're in pain.

Ed doesn't have any problems letting go of his past life. He is ready for his new career as a retired land baron. I enjoy watching him walk the rim of his property each day. I can almost see the wheels of fantasy encroaching on his usually staid thinking.

"Hey, Vin!" Eddie calls one day. "You know there's this rust colored cat that hangs around the underground drain holes. I think she's trying to catch mice or something—she looks kinda' wild. She won't let me get close to her."

I complacently answer, "Mmm, sounds good Ed, we could use help to get rid of the rodents around here." But I have no idea where this conversation will eventually lead.

One evening, as we're inspecting the days accomplishments, Ed calls to me, "Look over there, by the side of the foundation. Over there, near that stack of lumber."

By the small laugh lines about his eyes, I surmise it will be friendly news. I see, staring at us, tiny button eyes. It's a gray-black kitten with small white patches on its chest, nose, and paws.

Fear grips my heart, "Oh, oh, where did it come from?"

My question is soon answered. It is not long before Momma, the rust colored cat takes and hides her baby in the blackberry patch.

Eddie says, "Maybe I'll just give them a little milk."

"If you give them anything they are ours forever!"

"Nah, I'll just give them a little bit."

No, No, No, Ed Barles. Why, must I be tested daily? We've been here before with at least twenty-five aquariums of tropical fish.

In that instant I know it is over, and we will become foster parents to the feral mother cat and her kitten. Ed is quite pleased with the prospect of step-fatherhood.

"Vin, I'm naming the kitten Adam."

"A name huh?"

"Yeah, because he's first born and Momma-cat, is Eve. You know, Adam and Eve. Oops! I better call her Evelyn. The other sounds too incestuous."

For the moment I settle with the idea of our wild little family, but Evelyn, is one grouchy, anti-social feline, not too interested in establishing trust. Daily Ed feeds the obliging twosome, and daily our life becomes more complicated with all the construction. Our indoor cat Minnie, the rescued stray, from the Southland, sits by the French doors and watches Evelyn with her new off-spring. Momma-bares her fangs at Minnie every chance she gets. Minnie, who is the mistress of congeniality, for the most part, ignores the unfriendly behavior, but occasionally when she has had enough of the cranky display, sits up like a rabbit and boxes the window and hisses back at Evelyn.

Before very long, fertile Evelyn, presents two more babies on the back steps for kind Ed, to tend and wet nurse. He names the kittens Gray and Red. Why? Ed's logic, "Because they're gray and red."

Amidst all this birthing, we are being sucked dry of life by the contractor and his team.

I become mildly agitated and I launch into my typical wifely tirade.

"You know Ed, now that Evelyn has figured out the formula for having babies she may not slow down and besides you're a great welfare system. You had better get her and the kids fixed. Norplant or something. This is getting damn serious! This is how all your collections start!"

I can see Ed's eyes clouding over. This is one of those vacant discussions we sometimes have in our marriage where I do all the talking and he gets to listen without responding. But wait, he sometimes gives me the right answer; it's just that it doesn't go anywhere. It's at this point his procrastination and denial skills kick in, and we're in for fun times.

Something frightens Evelyn, one day, and she frantically hides Gray, Red and Adam. They all disappear. For hours, we have no idea where she has taken her family.

"Ed quick! I can see Evelyn from this upstairs window. Oh, my gosh! She's carried Gray and Red up to the valley of the high gabled roof peak!"

Ed moves fast and swift like a nineteen-year-old Marine.

"Look! See there on the metal flashing. You'll never be able to reach them. There's a storm coming and if it rains it'll flush the babies off the roof! Good gravy! How will you get them off?"

Ed swings into action. With the garden hoe taped onto a long bamboo pole, he climbs a ladder to one of Casablanca's peaks, squeezing his uncooperative body into the small area of the pitched roof. After blessing his performance with a few choice words, he manages to scrape his new kids off the roof to safer ground. Each day I watch as my mate's life, the retired psychologist, gets busier and more entangled.

Occasionally first-born Adam allows Ed to hold and pet him, and often mother Evelyn, leaves knowing that Adam will take excellent care of his little brothers Gray and Red. The two younger males watch him carefully as he boomerangs from the barbecue grill to the ground, up trees, in and out of bushes showing them all his new tricks.

The next summer my daughter, Gina, and granddaughter, Alexia, come for their yearly two-week vacation visit and while we are in the garden, we hear a loud meow. We follow the sound. Under the maple tree, amidst the Red Hot Pokers, our bountiful Evelyn has given us FOUR more kittens.

Anger towards my spouse mounts and my sympathies lessen as the old refrain "I told you so!" threatens to leave my brain. How is Edward the Good, going to deal with these new additions? He promptly names them, Peaches, Camille (whom we later find out is a male), Rosie and Fertility.

By this time our whole island has heard about Ed's cats.

"Hi Ed, how's your cats? How many do you have now? Eight? Oh, nine including Minnie, the house cat. I see. How does Venera feel about that? Oh, I'm sorry. Do you play with them? Oh, no? Oh, they're wild, I see. Oh, you're going to try and catch them and get them fixed. Wow, that should be spectacular! But, that's probably a good idea."

I can feel myself malfunctioning. I am having nightmares of closets filled with tiny kittens alongside Ed's infamous hat, glove, book, and raincoat collections. My hair is turning gray so fast I should have stock in hair-color products. Our marriage has taken a decided turn for the worse.

"Listen Eddie, you had better do something real fast about these cats! If not you'll have to find another mate for your sandbox!"

The cats close in on him.

The final blow comes. Evelyn's daughter, Fertility, the goddess of feline love, deposits all four of her new brood in a box, which, Ed, has carefully hidden from my dragon eyes. I am in total disbelief. I decide to detach myself from the insane happenings.

The word is out.

"Hi Ed. How are your cats? Oh, I'm sorry. How many? Did you say, FIFTEEN? Holy Mackerel! You have a problem, don't you Ed? How did this happen? Oh, you are? How are you going to catch them?"

The next few weeks are uncommonly busy for my husband as he attempts to find homes for the new kittens. He finally makes a pact with our veterinarian. If Ed can catch them, he will give him a bulk rate on getting all the pussycats neutered. With borrowed cages he proceeds to bait the smart little tigers to step into the enclosures. All are caught and repaired except two who escape the surgeon's knife, Camille and our favorite gal, Fertility. Once again, Edward the Demented has beat the divorce lawyers.

I did get quite attached to them and when tragedy strikes, it is no less easy. Feral cats live a tougher life than domestics and we had our sad losses. The first one to go, Peaches, is found dead in a flowerbed by our driveway. Handsome Camille, the loud meower, disappears. A neighbor down the road tells us, that a car may, have hit Gray. And Mother Evelyn, missing for a few weeks, dies unnecessarily. She inadvertently is trapped in our hardly, used carport. Usually when Momma was younger, she sat by herself and had very little to do with her children, but this year she had been staying closer and was friendlier to Ed and myself. In spite of her meanness she produced sweet babies. It is a major blow for us. Just recently, the dearest and friendliest of the cats, first born Adam, meets his end with a raccoon vying for the cat food. Sadly, I'm always reminded how much we are part of the wild, here in the Northwest. A few years back, in spite of our good care, our beloved Minnie also lost her valiant fight to stay alive.

Losing these additions to our family is a mighty rough go for Ed. Red, Rosie, and Fertility, all remain close; even Camille, the meower, came back after an absence of several years. He'd travel the world and decided there is no place like Papa Ed's home. Remind me to tell you about the time he bought home two Angelfish for my daughter.

FAHGEDABOUDIT, the NEW CAR

People don't love their cars the way they used to. You don't even see many folks rubbing a good coat of wax on them, after a sudsy wash and rinse. Or for that matter, do you see guys under the hoods, tinkering with the innards. The new ones have such complicated motors and computerized systems that one can only guess where a can of oil goes. Take a look under the bonnet of an old Mercedes and you can identify its distinctive parts, each one knowing its job to get this old gal moving down the highway.

My husband and I decide our 1978 two-door, Mark V, Lincoln Continental is getting close to its last days. As time goes by, it becomes larger and more cumbersome with age, much like myself. Our sleek, black, Mr. Lincoln serves us very well in his youth, with its comfortable leather seats, moon roof and sweet-sounding radio, but little by little he loses some of his capabilities. The clock died nine years earlier, the air conditioner a couple of years before that, and an assortment of parts and knobs drop off or are slowly flunking out. Even our local car wash is not big enough to accommodate the old man. I usually take him to the next county to get a bath and when I do, I wear rain gear for protection from leaks in the sunroof.

The fun starts when we have guests in the back seat. They're left stranded inside until someone opens the monstrous two doors. We work out various methods to extract the detainees. Some bright and resourceful souls turn themselves around and back out, but not without catching their heads on the safety belts blocking their exit, consequently knocking their coiffeurs or hairpieces askew. Most unfortunate souls need to be pulled.

Parking this tootsie, in most instances, is no picnic since many stalls are made for compact cars. Inasmuch, as I'm only five feet tall on good days, and shrinking daily with age, most of my friends tell me that when they see the recognizable black, land cruiser they are unable to find me and are not sure if Mr. Lincoln is out on his own without a driver. And since I can barely see over the tractor-size steering wheel I am really challenged when I approach a hill on our narrow country roads. The back end of the car swoops down, while the hood rises high in the air, like the end of the sinking *Titanic*, and I literally drive blind. I pray that children, chickens or for that matter anything shorter than the front bumper will not walk in front of the black behemoth.

My brother and I, each caught the car disease, I believe, from our father who loved his big new vehicles, especially Buicks. Many times these metal giants took my family to wondrous zones and when I became a married woman, I saw it as an exciting form of independence. I always knew I could run to my four-wheel friend for a change of pace. Together we discovered new adventures and ways to meet the rest of the world.

As a reverential wife, I rearrange my desires of antique autos, to look at a newer car, but my thoughts will not leave the idea of old classic beauties. While Ed and I look at new and used cars, I fall in love with a particular old model Mercedes, thinking, because my husband loves me and I am cute, surely he will consider buying the wonderful beast. But my practical, unromantic spouse comes up with all the reasons it is a foolish idea to own such a vehicle.

When I was a young girl, I was able to identify cars by their names and models. They were beautifully designed and constructed, with leather interiors, shining chrome, and wooden dashboards. A horn was a horn and you could find it. Nowadays, I have problems recognizing any of the new automobiles. There are so many models and names that don't even match the machine, and all appear without character, stability, or nobility.

After months of research, to find the car with the most good credits, we settle on a new, conservative, four-door, silver gray blue, Lincoln Continental, very serviceable, stable, and totally devoid of personality. I will need a sonar system to find it in the parking lots amidst all the other silver gray blue, efficient body-movers. Now our Mr. Lincoln is sold to a young man who has visions of turning our distinguished sleek giant into a rocking low rider. We forfeit spread-out room, in our new high-price machine, by replacing our immense leather bench seat with bucket shape ones, well named I might add. To further the challenge, we now have a built-up step at the door where you must bring your leg up high in order to extricate your body. I wonder if the test engineers ever tried to get out of this container pregnant, or with an arthritic knee, a woman's purse, high heels, or for that matter a belly full of Thai food.

But wait. Not all is bad. We now have computerized comfort surrounding us. Buttons. Buttons, for all our needs. A system check. Push a button. Inside and outside temperatures. Push a button. Settings for our seats; up, down, back, forward. Push a button and air is pumped into your bottom. And in case we Americans ever decide to try the metric system all we have to do is, push a button. The radio's settings are preset, handy but unstable, especially if the car is not facing the right direction. I just want to fine-tune my selections and I want the classic station back from Mr. Lincoln. This thing looks like the interior of a spacecraft and about as spacious.

But the prize of this land ship is a remote control on our key ring. Four little buttons: Lock - Unlock - Trunk - Panic. It is a marvel to watch my husband getting used to 'Mr. Hulot's' Button World. As he gets into the car and settles in, I can see this new personal taxi is going to bring complications to our lives. For weeks, I watch my beloved bend to the idiosyncrasies of modern technology. Several minutes before he leaves the garage, I watch the technological show as the windows and his seat move up and down several times, while the windows are intermittently washed, unintentionally, by the windshield wipers which have become activated along with the turn signals. The side mirrors take on a life of their own, up, down, left, right, constantly moving, moving.

As soon as we put the gearshift into drive everyone is permanently locked in and only the driver has controls of the main lock. This places another burden on passengers, if they need to get in or out of the car. There is a subtle frenzied dance that occurs to signal the holder of the 'unlock' button, which has become misplaced. The grimacing individual, stuck outdoors, raps on the windows, and silently mouths his commands to the driver. My husband soon discovers another inconvenience to his button drama. He must get out of the car to close the inadvertently popped hood, every time we need to drive somewhere. It is to be a while before he stops using the hood release for an emergency brake release.

We decide to take our new talented family addition to dinner. We find, at Ed's request, the farthest parking spot at our popular restaurant. We attempt to step out of the car by lifting our legs high, not a pretty sight with a dress on. Spouse points the dynamic remote at the car, as if he is searching for the television-wrestling channel, and commands it to lock the doors. The trunk flies open. Once more spouse hits the button. The horn resounds with an anxious beat of panic. Once more. This time the horn continues to blow and the trunk again soars open. Once more.

He's got it. It's finally locked. Good, very good. At the rate we are gaining wisdom about these gadgets, we could be learning the accordion.

The problem with a new car is where to park this expensive bit of tin. My husband's paranoia with my parking choices, become our continual bone of contention.

"Why did you park here?" he asks.

"Because it's an empty place?"

"I don't like this spot. There's a car next to it."

"How's this one, dear?"

"No. There's one over there."

"That's two blocks away."

Mercedes where are you when I need you?

About a year later, I get my wish for an old Mercedes. She's a 1958 220SE. A regal pewter gray with beautifully tufted red leather seats, and dashboard and window frames made of lush grain hardwood. When you close a door, the sounds of stability ring forth. She is easily recognized and teaming with personality. Oh yes, I named her Mutti, German for momma. But, because of her pristine beauty I once again have problems with spouse.

"What's wrong, now Ed? If it's not one thing it's another. I can't drive it in the rain. I can't go far with it. I can't park it close to where I want to be, or do with it as I please! There are too many damn restrictions on it. What's the use of it all? No damn fun in this!"

"Well you know this is a collector's car and you don't want anyone to scratch it."

As of this writing the car mostly sits unused in our garage with a big yellow cover on it. The battery died six months ago.

HIGH ROLLERS

The day after our marriage, nearly fifty years ago, we are driving down the hot highway of Las Vegas, in Ed's 1949 green Chevy, decked with a wolf whistle.

"I can't believe we made it!" Eddie says, as I mop his hot head with a damp washcloth.

"And we're still alive! Jeez, we nearly froze in that damn motel last night. Couldn't get that air conditioner lowered."

But I am one worried bride. I'm thinking of how I eloped right under the nose of my authoritarian father.

"God knows what I'll have to face when we get back." I hang the cloth out of the window to cool. "I guess it's not how you expected to spend your twenty-fifth birthday, right honey? It sure isn't how I expected to get married."

"Yeah, but so far, so good. Boy! It's been quite a wild adventure!"

"No lie there." The massive marquees and billboards grab my attention. "Look at those signs, Eddie."

"I can't look. I'm driving. What do they say?"

"Can you believe that? Out here in the middle of nowhere!"

"Vin, what do they say?"

"Acreage offered at a one million dollars a frontage foot! That's incredible! You'd think with this entire desert, land would be dirt-cheap. So to speak."

"Really? Huh, that sure is something."

Then a couple of years later we make yet another trip to Las Vegas. This time we stay at Wright's Motel at the end of the Strip, another low budget winner on the main highway from Los Angeles.

"So, Mr. Wright," Mr. Businessman Ed, says, "tell me how can you afford to build on this road?"

Mr. Wright launches into his salesman role of convincing city slicker Ed, that if he were interested he could help him acquire government land in the desert. The conversation continues and before I know it, without too much conferring with me, this appealing stranger I have married is purchasing five acres of dry, unimproved, heaven knows where (not on the Strip), sand dune for four hundred dollars. I might add scarce money. But he is thrilled.

"Who knows, Vin, it might be worth a few bucks in the future."

Secretly, I love the idea of making our fortune through real estate, thinking about my father's ability to turn property into profit. I know I need to establish better trust with my new mate, but I'm not sure of his capabilities as yet.

"Well, O.K.," I say, reserving my unsure attitude towards this sort of speculative buying.

So, through the years, we are content to pay the minimal tax on the land. Each time we take vacation trips to Las Vegas, we see how many more bright lights of new casinos are built along the famous boulevard. After a few years, Mr. Wright's Motel is long gone. We secretly wonder if we ever will see a significant return on our investment. But, we're also aware that, more than likely, we probably will just leave the pile of sand to our kids.

In the early years, Uncle Sam requires owners to improve their property. One can see, as you drive through the desert, small one-room shacks/houses, planted on each aspiring land baron's acquisition, built to comply with Federal rulings. But thankfully, before it affects our five acres, the law changes and we didn't need to make 'improvements'.

Then once again, a big surge comes to the land where the lights never go out, where a gal can wear her bridesmaid dress during the day, where the local social disease is digital nickel poisoning, and one suffers with right shoulder bursitis from pulling levers to bring up three cherries: The land where you are force-fed, Steak and Lobster for $5.99, breakfast $1.99 or All You Can Eat Buffets for $3.99, where every day is a circus in the sun. *A Cirque du Soleil.*

Hence now, it is 1996. Every year we've had realtors wanting to list Eddie and Vinny's dry land. A few months ago, land brokers contacted Ed, to sell the property with more vigor than usual. Developers buy everything in sight and much of the land is for tract housing.

"If the appraisal is good, maybe we ought to think of selling," states, Land Baron Eddie.

Soon, as fate will have it, we are suddenly faced with three serious buyers and realize we need to bring ourselves up to date with facts. We decide to once more visit Las Vegas to better understand the building boom. We had not been back to look at the acreage for at least twelve years, not that it would have changed in any way.

We leave Ollie, our nine month-old puppy, in his first kennel and take off the next morning by ferry, metro bus and onto Sardine Airlines for our fast three-day stay in Nevada. I am in shock when we arrive to see the metamorphosis the once small airport had undergone.

"Holy cats, Eddie, look at this terminal! It looks like a hotel casino with those slot machines lined up in rows. It just grabs everybody as they get off and on a plane!" I stop to change my luggage to my other hand. "They've even sectioned off that large glassed room for smoking players. My God, money sure doesn't burn holes in your pocket here!"

450

A veteran cab driver, now shuttling clients to the car rental office, suggests to us the best buffet in town. We have never hesitated in making a decision in regards to foodstuff. No delay, we move into action. We enter the immense food auditorium and after paying our $6.50, we join a long line for a table. A gal with headphones speaks to another with a similar contraption then she electronically relays the info to the final waitress, who takes our drink order. Then we are faced with the big choice of the moment, what to eat. The sideboards and stalls of food are the length of an entire city block. They are some of the best eating counters we've ever seen: pasta salads, pasta fruits salads, hot and cold pasta dishes, breads and a pastry carousel. Did I mention pasta? Anyway, there is enough food to kill a carbohydrate deficiency. The orgy is complete. We roll our bodies out to the compact car, which by this time has shrunk, and head for our hotel, a city unto itself.

We step into the world of make-believe: mechanical noises, smoke, drinks and busloads of Asians and retired, middle-America couples holding large paper cups filled with nickels, quarters and silver dollars. The sight of these robotic, unsmiling, smoke, encrusted bodies, depositing coins one after the other into the upgraded, computerized, money-eating devices, reveals a latent sub-culture. One does not even need to worry about having the correct coins. A bill of any denomination up to twenty dollars can be changed without leaving your mesmerizing, dynamic, rendering machine. I see folks keep several of these in action at a time; never focusing on the slots they are playing. Their eyes busily search for better ones to conquer. As we walk through the lobby, many are having their afternoon cocktails at a long see-through bar made with slot machines placed under their drinking glasses. An opportunity is never missed to have a fix.

We settle our luggage in the hotel room and head for the lobby. We are to meet the two prospective buyers there. They are to take us to see our sandy property. I look around for a seat where we can wait, but chairs, benches and any seating contraptions have cleverly been removed except in front of slot machines and game tables. The two land reps arrive and we drive to check the property. Within minutes, after our return to the hotel, while standing, the men hand us a written offer for our five acres, of three hundred thousand dollars.

As we steady ourselves, Eddie says, "Well, we can't accept the offer at this time because we are still to meet with another interested person tomorrow morning." The men leave after they comprehend the facts surrounding the opposing competition.

"Whoa Eddie," I say, "how about that?"

Now, high roller Ed, decides he is going to up the ante to the next party by a large leap, with the knowledge he already has a likely worthy buyer in his pocket. The next morning we meet the new buyer representative in our office, the hotel lobby. We sit our client, an Asian in Levis, at our desk, three flat-surfaced, slot machines and we conduct business by the light of the flashing lights and bells. We give Mr. Buyer the facts about our previous interested proposition.

Hot Eddie then declares. "We are interested in selling the property to you, but we will need three hundred and fifty thousand dollars, and we have some conditions that need to be met."

The two men do not flinch. But, in my brain, cells are doing a bump and grind dance.

"Well Mr. Barles, I will take back your signed offer to my partners. We'll discuss it this afternoon, and let you know at five this evening. Right here again?"

"Yes, that'll be fine. Right here."

Ed and I rattle around with the six-figure conversation as we load up on another buffet. Our discussion takes on a new aura.

There is still a long wait before the five o'clock hour; we decide to check out our vast hotel, The Stratosphere. An entire mall is situated on the third level where we purchase a Lithuanian mug for a friend, but I see a crowd has gathered in an open front photo studio.

"Heh! Eddie," I say, "look at those people posing for the camera. They're flashing it on the giant screen." I pull him closer. "See that guy? He has his head super-imposed on the body of a muscled hockey player."

A three hundred pound-plus beauty steps up to the plate and decides on Miss Illinois' frame. The curious gather as they clap and squeal at the surprising transformations.

I poked Ed in the *ponza.*

"Whataya think? You wanta do it?"

Despite the fact we are the only old coots considering this exhibition, I am able to talk my husband into picking our body doubles from an album. Ed selects an over-developed, oiled and tanned Hercules, a body builder with shoulder length, dark wavy hair. Next to him stands his bronzed, siliconed-Xena, Warrior Princess, wearing only the bottom part of a bikini. Her hands deftly cover her outrageous breasts. By this time we have drawn a sizeable crowd. I can hear the whispers and giggles as they stare in wonderment of what possibly could be done for sixty-five and seventy year-olds with overly fat-saturated, white bodies, and where the hourglass figures of yesteryear have shifted to one end?

The magical camera computer takes over.

Ed and I immediately acquire a great tan. His salt and pepper, gray mustache is darkened to match his curly dark tresses, setting off his oiled, rippling muscles; bulges he hasn't seen since post-marine days. Flowing dark brown, wavy hair, like a model's, replaces my severe chignon coiffure. With the instant conjuring, I manage to loose three chins and sixty pounds. We are gorgeous and the hit of the mall. We leave, hysterical with laughter. Our childish fantasy fills a needed diversion from the serious life we have created.

Finally, the time arrives to meet our returning potential buyer, but after a half hour of waiting overtime near the dollar slot machines, Ed and I soberly conclude that our last offer is probably a tinge too high for approval and they likely won't even consider it. We are resigned to accept yesterday's deal. But soon a courier comes.

"Are you Mr. and Mrs. Barles?" the young man asks, and with a few short words, hands us the signed offer. "Your escrow papers will be coming."

He quickly leaves for his other deliveries. Ed and I stand staring at each other in utter incredulity, amidst the ringing and banging machines.

"Can you believe what just happened, Eddie? They've accepted!"

"Yeah!" We give each other a hug.

"My God, after forty-five years, our sand dune has finally turned into a pile of gold! Who would have thought?"

"Yeah!"

"I can only say one thing, Eddie. Our whole damn life has been a gamble!"

"Yeah, no kidding!"

"After a certain age—and for some of us that can be very young—there are no new people, beasts, dreams, faces, events: it has all happened before...and everything is an echo and a repetition; and there is no grief even that it is not a recurrence of something long out of memory."

Doris Lessing (1919) Ch. 2, Particularly Cats

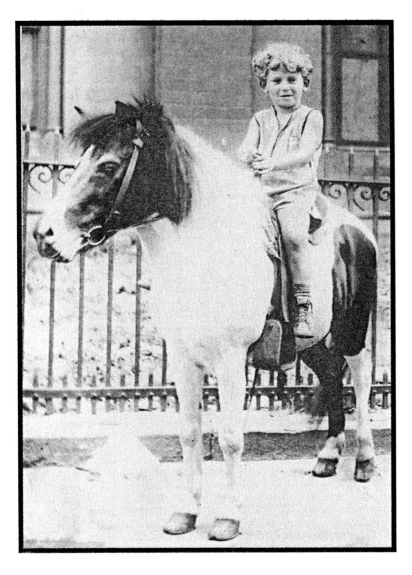

#31 Little Eddie, my knight on a white (and brown) horse. New York. (1920's)

Venera Di Bella Barles

COMES the DAWN

After a while you learn the subtle difference
Between holding a hand and chaining a soul,
And you learn that love doesn't mean security,
And you learn that kisses aren't contracts
And presents aren't promises,
And you begin to accept your defeats
With your head up and your eyes open,
With the grace of a woman, not the grief of a child,
And you learn to build all your roads on today,
Because tomorrow's ground is too uncertain for plans,
And futures have a way of falling down in midflight.
After awhile you learn that even sunshine
Burns if you get too much.
So you plant your own garden and decorate
Your own soul, instead of waiting
For someone else to bring you flowers.
And you learn that you really can endure...
That you really are strong
And you really do have worth.
And you learn and you learn...
With every goodbye you learn.

Attributed to: Veronica A. Schoffstall

ABOUT THE AUTHOR

Venera Di Bella Barles was born during the depression in upstate New York to Italian immigrant parents. She encounters a difficult pathway from the hot-blooded upbringing with her authoritarian father, who had one foot in Italy and one in America. The childhood tribulations chewed directly into her spirit. The residue was overpowering. *Marriage, Kidneys, and Other Dark Organs* reveals, with sadness and wit, her tricky path to maturity.

Di Bella Barles spent long years in search of answers to her fears, using humor to cover difficult circumstances; years to take responsibility for her own life; years to allay the anger in having to forfeit her childhood as the family referee; years before she understood her parents and replaced bitterness with forgiveness; years to find the love in all this disorder; years to recognize that the legacy that made her a peacemaker was not always a benefit. Peace at any price.

Woven amidst her long-term marriage and two children, were a number of diverse work experiences, which added much to her 'school of hard knocks' education.

Venera continues to write. She lives on Bainbridge Island in Washington with her husband, Edward, and a Wire-Hair Fox terrier, Oliver.

Printed in the United States
930500002B

9 780759 680609